MexAmerica

Other Books by Lester D. Langley

Central America: The Real Stakes (1985)

The Banana Wars: An Inner History of American Empire, 1900–1934 (1983)

The United States and the Caribbean in the Twentieth Century (1982)

The United States and the Caribbean, 1900–1970 (1980)

Struggle for the American Mediterranean: United States-European Rivalry in the Gulf-Caribbean, 1776–1904 (1976)

The United States and Latin America, with E. T. Glauert (1971)

The United States, Cuba, and the Cold War (1970)

The Cuban Policy of the United States: A Brief History (1968)

MexAmerica

TWO COUNTRIES, ONE FUTURE

LESTER D. LANGLEY

Crown Publishers, Inc.
New York

Excerpts from this book appeared in the
December 1987 issue of Georgia Review.

Published by Crown Publishers, Inc., 225 Park Avenue South, New York, New York 10003, and represented in Canada by the Canadian MANDA Group.

CROWN is a trademark of Crown Publishers, Inc.

Manufactured in the United States of America

Library of Congress Cataloging in Publication Data

Langley, Lester D.
   Mexamerica.

   Bibliography: p.
   Includes index.
   1. United States—Relations—Mexico.   2. Mexico—Relations—United States.   3. Mexican Americans.
I. Title.
E183.8.M6L28   1928   303.4'8273'072   87-22145
ISBN 0-517-56732-6

Designed by Jake Victor Thomas

10   9   8   7   6   5   4   3   2   1

First Edition

Contents

Acknowledgments

My thanks, again, to my agent, Julian Bach, and to Jim Wade, who edited my *Central America: The Real Stakes,* and his colleagues at Crown Publishers, especially Jane von Mehren; and to the dozens of interviewees (some of whom requested anonymity), especially Louise Kerr, Catherine Rocha, Carlos Cortés, Gene Müller, Michael Coniff, Teresa Márquez, Susan Deese, Ternot MacRenato, Félix Ramírez, and various *mexicano* taxi drivers, bartenders, and officials, some of whom talked more than they should have but all of whom said something worthwhile.

My deepest appreciation and gratitude to Wanda Langley, my wife, and Jonathan Langley, my son, my companions in a traffic accident in March 1986 that almost took my life. Without their support and assistance this book could not have been written.

Finally, after a delay of almost forty years, an *abrazo* to my Mexican pal in the cotton field of the Texas Panhandle in summer 1950. I found you everywhere in my trek through MexAmerica.

A Personal Odyssey

I first met them in the summer of 1950. We had crossed Oklahoma from McCurtain County, the southeasternmost angle of the state, into the arid Llano Estacado, the Staked Plains, that escarpment forming what modern promoters call the Golden Spread. Four centuries ago, Coronado had wandered through this desolate terrain and, it is written, had come on the Palo Duro Canyon, a geologic niche in the otherwise level vastness. But our destination was one of those eminently forgettable Panhandle towns, New Deal, named, I have always presumed, for Franklin Roosevelt's grand design. Perhaps New Deal did benefit from the New Deal in the long run, but when I first came on it the town was nothing more than a collection of modest stucco houses that stood alongside cotton fields and a rail line. My grandfather, a sometime Methodist preacher and now grocery-story entrepreneur, had lured my parents, fiftyish, from a declining Oklahoma farm into what he described as God's frontier in the Texas Panhandle. I was ten years old. In that summer of 1950, the year of Truman in the White House and the Korean War, I got my first job, picking cotton with "Messcans."

Since my folks came from solid yeoman stock, "Messcan" was then considered an acceptable term, like "nigger." "Greaser" stood as equivalent for "coon," so my parents were not being intentionally derogatory. Other old-timers may have called the Mexicans greasers, but not my old man; he at least

1

accorded them a certain dignity—not equality—by referring to them as Messcans.

The Mexican field hands represented the hands-across-the-border labor supply provided by the bracero program, initiated in World War II to supplement an Anglo work force seriously depleted by war and continued for almost two decades afterward. I don't remember much about picking cotton that summer except for the heat and the constant stooping and the sharp pricking of the cotton stem when I pulled the bolls out. But I do remember the Mexican field hands, blood descendants of Spanish conquerors and Indian conquered, whole families, diminutive males with lined faces and rapidly aging women with five or six half-naked kids trotting behind the cotton sacks. I remember, most of all, their perseverance. Three days into cotton-pickin' season I was ready for petty theft as a morally acceptable alternative, but the Mexicans kept at their work. Even the kids, several of them younger than I, helped out. They ran alongside their parents and picked randomly at the fluffy offerings and stood proudly at the wagon where the sacks were hung for weighing. I remember the beefy foreman, belly hanging over a silver buckle, his inexpensive cowboy hat lined with perspiration, hoisting their day's work and tallying their earnings with a stub pencil.

A week or so into the harvesting the foreman with the potbelly took me aside and slipped me a few dollars. "Son," he said in an avuncular tone, "you can't outwork no Messcan."

That was his and the country's assessment of their worth in those days. Even now, after three and a half decades and a formal education in their language and culture, these diminutive figures, stooped between two long cotton rows, dragging long white sacks, their hands darting incessantly at the white tufts, remain alien creatures. Then I knew nothing of their origin, though my father reassured me they were better than "niggers." Still, he said knowingly, they had to be "worked like niggers." I knew nothing of their cultural duality—Indian and Hispanic, stoicism and docility blended with individuality and combativeness, creating, Mexican philosophers remind us, a person at war with himself. I remember only their staccato chatter and a grimy-faced kid my own age always pulling ahead of me, snatching at the cotton and occasionally glancing back with a cry of _"Ándale, ándale"_ ("Hurry, hurry").

I could never keep up with him—but we became friends. And once he lured me reassuringly to the two-room shack that served as home away from home for him and the six other members of his _familia,_ a word I readily translated correctly as "family" but unknowingly concluded meant only those seven persons. By now I know he was referring to his larger family, most of them back in Mexico. He and his parents and brother and sisters had ventured _al norte_ ("up north") from Aguascalientes in central Mexico to earn money picking cotton in order to keep the _familia_ back in central Mexico going. I remember sitting at the small kitchen table with its fading oilcloth cover and eating tortillas and refried beans and listening to jibberish punctuated occasionally by a word I knew. My friend's _papá,_ who may have known a dozen English words, tried to explain his people. He would point to the veins on the underside of an arm bronzed by the sun and repeat the word _raza_ and keep saying "You know" and presume I would know what he meant by "race." He was trying to tell me about the "cosmic race," not race in any scientific sense but that Indian-Spanish fusion that shaped the modern Mexican.

When I got back to my house my parents were disapproving. "You shouldn't play with that dirty Messcan kid, and how do you know that kid's mama washed the plate you ate them beans and whatever from?" I tried to explain something about their meal and how much they talked while eating and how happy they seemed. I returned to the cotton fields for a week or so. But I never went back to the Mexican kid's shack. I learned sometime later that his family had moved on west, maybe to California. But I have not forgotten them.

In this book, written from the perspective of a historian (my vocation) and traveler (my avocation), I try to find that Mexican kid with the infectious smile who inhabits MexAmerica.

There are, a famous historian of Mexico once wrote, "many Mexicos." By that he meant something more than the regional variations common to both Mexico and the United States (or, for that matter, several other Latin American countries). For the "many Mexicos" refer as much to a heritage of Indian and Hispanic cultures, to traditional societies coexisting with a vigorous but turbulent modern state, or to innumerable little handicraft shops in the shadow of industrial smokestacks.

MexAmerica defies precise geographical definition. I began my odyssey with the traditional impressions of a border culture and economy etched in the American *and* Mexican consciousness, a swath of territory that is rapidly changing. But I soon plunged deep into America and Mexico to understand its imprint. Significant pockets of Hispanic Americans flourish in the unlikeliest places of the American heartland. There, in the traditional cultural mixing bowl of old-stock and turn-of-the-century European immigrant, the Mexican American has become, along with his fellow Hispanics (the Cubans and the sprinkling of other Latinos and Asians) the advance guard of a culturally powerful force that has been penetrating the inner domain of North America for almost a generation. They are no longer simply berry pickers in Michigan or dishwashers in Kansas City but far more significant, and powerful, participants in American culture.

Unarguably, Los Angeles and Mexico City are the urban centers of what I term MexAmerica. L.A. has the second-largest concentration of people of Mexican descent outside Mexico City. In a very real sense, it is for the American southwest and Mexico's northern third what Mexico City is to the central and southern regions of Mexico proper: two sprawling metropolises where the dynamic of material progress is on collision course with a seemingly unalterable cultural tradition. If one considers the concentration of Mexican Americans as geographical indicator, then the northern boundary of Mexico is not the Rio Grande (or Río Bravo, as *los mexicanos* say) or the barbed-wire fence separating Arizona and the Mexican state of Sonora, but a swathlike brushstroke meandering across southern California through central Arizona and New Mexico, then plunging across the arid Texas west toward San Antonio and then on to the Gulf. The southern boundary is more precise—the populated regions of central Mexico. Southeast of the City of the Aztecs lies Indian Mexico, another world. Indian Mexico presses from the south to remind modern Mexico of the nation's cultural roots; the United States, from the north to remind it of economic realities and to exact political demands. The force of these colliding and contradictory pressures, long felt south of the border, has pushed northward.

What impact is MexAmerica having on this country? Its influence, I believe, is expressed in three related subjects of vital concern to every United States citizen.

The first is political. Ethnicity (and its meritable companion religion) has always played a determining role in American politics. With the addition of a significantly large Hispanic population to half a dozen states in the past generation, the political fabric of the United States is changing. Hispanics are rapidly acquiring the political savvy to profoundly influence the nation's political agenda. Beginning with the election of Lincoln in 1860, the Great Lakes states served as the fulcrum of American politics for a century. In our age, that crucial function of geographic balance in the political system is shifting once more, some pundits say, to the "sunbelt." But the modern political balance of power resides not so much on geographic as on other economic and social factors. Six states—Florida, New York, New Jersey, Illinois, Texas, and California—have become (for very different reasons) the political bellwethers of the country. Aside from electoral strength and economic clout, they have little in common, it would appear, save for one common experience. These states have received the largest numbers of Hispanic (and Asian) immigrants of the past twenty-five years. MexAmerica lies at the heart of this new political reality. The political agenda is changing because of it, and our thinking about politics must change with it.

The second impact of MexAmerica is economic. A generation

ago, the country's image of the Hispanic may have been an indefatigable stoop laborer in the Imperial Valley or an orange picker in south Texas, doing a job no American would do. All that has changed. For political reasons, the United States has absorbed Cuba's professional classes, who have dramatically altered the social landscape of south Florida. MexAmerica's economic impact has been different and profoundly more consequential: its intrusion into the trade and service sectors of the economy has spawned in our economic life a debate likely to continue into the next century. There can be no doubt of its reality. This book will explore the complex economic imprint MexAmerica has on this society, its origin, and its ultimate consequence.

Finally, MexAmerica is altering our very conception of who or what an American is. There is an unspoken fear of a vanishing Americanness. It is a tacit element in the debates over immigration reform, bilingual education, and even the role of the school. Concerns about the cultural impact of thousands or even millions of newcomers speaking a veritable Babel of tongues is nothing new—after all, turn-of-the-century Americans watched apprehensively as the steamers from Europe disgorged their human cargoes. But Americans of that era never doubted but that these newcomers would somehow, sooner or later, be Americanized and that they would eventually forsake the old ways and most certainly acquire a new tongue. The urban political system might accommodate (even survive on) this cultural diversity, but ultimately, out of economic necessity or the rigors of public education or because they were cut off from their homeland, the immigrant would be Americanized.

For almost fifty years after the nakedly racist immigration bills of the 1920s, the United States received relatively few newcomers from Europe. It accommodated tragically small numbers of Jews fleeing Nazi Germany in the 1930s and, for political reasons, Hungarians who fled west during the revolution of 1956. By the mid-1960s, the numbers were rising once more. But this time they signaled the migration not from Europe but from Latin

America and (after Vietnam) Asia. With Latin American migration, legal and illegal, have come renewed fears about the mystical process of Americanization. Today there is a palpable concern that such traditional institutions as the school may no longer be able to transform the Hispanic kid the way the system molded the Italian or Irish or Polish youngster of an earlier age into an American.

This book speaks to these issues.

There are, certainly, numerous other works that speak to the impact of Hispanics on our cultural experience, fewer that address their impact on our politics, and lamentably too few that value Mexico's place in our culture, our economy, and, increasingly, in our politics. The reasons for this seem, at first glance, to be obvious. Our greatness as a nation, we believe, rests on internal, not external, forces. We have long recognized what the immigrant has brought to our shores, but once he is here, his influence on the shaping of American culture and politics is largely constrained by his desire to be as American as the native-born racist who vilifies him. There may be a recognition of external cultural influences—the Jewish lobby or the Polish American or Italo-American context of a particular issue—but there is rarely an admission that another country, either by its military strength or its geographic position or the numbers of its peoples deep within the United States, has somehow begun to exercise a determining force on what kind of society we are becoming and, more crucially, on the fundamental character of our politics.

I am _not_ suggesting that Mexico (and Mexican Americans) have become a central feature in either American culture or American politics. What I intend to show in this book is that Hispanic America and what it means for American culture and politics is heavily influenced by its Mexican American content and that MexAmerica from Chicago to Mexico City is shaping its values. We can measure the U.S. imprint on Mexico and on Mexican Americans. Until now we have been loath to recognize the effective reach of Mexico north of the Río Bravo. But the *mexicano* imprint is deeper than we want to admit. It goes beyond the numbers of Americans who identify with Mexico because their forebears were Mexican or of Mexicans who cross the border, legally or illegally, onto American soil. The Mexican connection reaches into the politics and economies of the southwest, obviously, and in subtler ways deep into American society across the country.

Our historical experience, our economy, our place in the western hemisphere—these and more are linked to our relationship with Mexico and the Mexicans. We speak of "our neighbor to the south," yet that neighbor remains a conundrum defying our efforts at understanding. We speak casually of our "bond with Mexico," yet cannot articulate what, precisely, the union means. Jimmy Carter perhaps unintentionally revealed the emotional predicament when he told President José López Portillo, "It's difficult being your neighbor." López Portillo did not reply directly but his facial contortion conveyed a universal Mexican view that if for the United States the relationship is "difficult," for Mexicans it can be exquisitely painful. The Mexican expression "So far from God and so close to the United States" is for many Mexicans the quintessential definition of their historical agony. For the Mexican the United States and especially American culture have been an inescapable presence. But too often we forget just how much the Mexican presence in the United States has shaped what we are and what we want to be.

We may have a distant neighbor about whom we refuse to know very much—but Mexico has a neighbor who is not only close but about whom too much is known and feared.

A Brief Comment on Demographics

This is an impressionistic and personal account, and I have spared the reader tables, charts, and the usual statistical and scholarly baggage that is ordinarily found in scholarly studies. But the reader deserves at the outset an advance warning about terminology. "Hispanic" denotes an ethnic, not a racial, category. Hispanics may belong to any race. But race is a variable when trying to decide who is an Hispanic. Another indicator is a Spanish surname. Thus, an Indian named García would technically qualify as an Hispanic. Language is another variable. A person named Smith whose native tongue is Spanish could be classified as Hispanic. In 1980, in a still controversial headcount, the Census Bureau depended on "self-identification of Hispanic origin or descent." (There are stories of people, mostly academics, who qualify under none of the designations but who add a Spanish surname, as "Professor Joe Jones de García," in order to gain more visibility and a chicano student following.) National origin is yet another indicator, but even here you have to remember that New Mexico's descendants of Spanish conquerors call themselves Hispanos and still resent being listed under "Mexican" in the census of 1930. As demographers point out, the size of the Hispanic population can vary according to which identifier you use.

I have used various terms in order to interject some literary variation and, more important, because Hispanic Americans rarely refer to themselves as Hispanic Americans. Mexican Americans can be the most infuriating: some will call themselves simply Americans or Mexican Americans or chicanos. There are variations as to place. In Chicago, the word is "Latino," which refers mostly to Mexicans and Puerto Ricans but can include, for example, Portuguese. In the midwest, "Mexican American" is a more commonly used term; in the southwest, "chicano." But in California, which now has a large Central American population, "Latino" and "Hispanic" are used increasingly because, technically, "chicano" refers specifically to a Mexican American. There are Mexican Americans who will give you a tongue-lashing if you call them chicanos and there are chicanos who insist on being called Mexicans.

I have followed another practice that may irritate or even offend. I have used "American" to refer to a citizen of the United States and "America" to refer to the United States. Linguists may object, arguing, correctly, that any resident of the western hemisphere is an American. In referring to U.S. citizens as "Americans" I am not excusing Kansans who circled "Central American" or Alabamans who identified themselves as "South Americans" for the 1980 census. But in twenty years of teaching about Latin America, throughout my travels in Latin America, and after a longer time in reading about and studying the peoples of the western hemisphere, I have rarely heard anybody but a citizen of the United States refer to himself as an American. As a matter of fact, most Latin Americans do *not* call themselves Latin Americans but Cubans, Mexicans, Guatemalans, and so on. There is, of course, a still latent resentment over our appropriation of the term. Interestingly, Latin Americans will often employ the scarcely more precise designation *norteamericano* to refer to a citizen of the United States and rarely use the word *estadounidense* (United Statesian). Also I have capitalized "Hispanic," "American," "Mexican," "Mexican American," "Black American," and "Anglo-American," but not capitalized "black," "white," or "*mexicano*," the last because in Spanish the capital letter is less prevalent in noting the nationality of a person (though, of course, the person's name and the name of the country would be capitalized).

How many Hispanics live in the United States? Nobody knows. In 1980 the Census Bureau, relying heavily on self-identification and statistics from the 1970 count, listed 14,603,683. It employed the equation Population (1980) = Population (1970) + Births (1970–1980) − Deaths (1970–1980) + Immigrants (1970–1980) − Emigrants (1970–1980). From the beginning there were charges of "overcount" followed by charges of "undercount." I side with the latter. Even the casual student knows that it would be virtually impossible to know precisely about the numbers of "immigrants" or "emigrants" because of so many undocumented entries and the number of people who go back and forth. But the other portions of the right side of the equation create problems because the data on Hispanics *legally* in this country are poor. The 1970 census was badly flawed by its imprecision in determining who is "Hispanic."

This question is not a matter of getting within "a few million" of a population count. The complexity of designating who is an Hispanic makes the use of records on vital statistics, social security files, or tax returns not all that helpful. Only five states employ "Spanish surname" as a means of identification. After the 1980 count, when several states and cities stood to lose out (or gain) in congressional seats or benefit from federal expenditures, there were challenges to the Census Bureau's enumeration of Hispanics. In one case, where the city of Detroit questioned the count, the judge decided that a demographic analysis of Hispanics could not employ methods used for whites and blacks and produce comparable accuracy. If there was an undercount in 1980, as demographers generally concede, then the political, social, and economic implications, in a country where statistical accuracy can mean so much in determining representation and monies allocated for social services, are more crucial than generally believed.

Part I

1

Dinner at Chihuahua Charlie's

≡≡≡

Growing up in the Texas Panhandle, in an era before the pill liberated males from the obligation of carrying a condom, I remember that the biggest stud in my high school was a ranch kid who drove a battered Chevy pickup with a plastic Jesus on the dashboard, a squirrel's tail as a banner on the radio aerial, and a bumper decal that read, "I'm from Dimmitt, Dammit." He never got dates with cheerleaders, but he carried *two* condoms in his wallet.

Once, sitting beside him in PE class, I watched as he took a "dry" from its foil cover and blew it into a balloon. Then he tied the end with a knot and tapped the bloated rubber so that it wafted over the gym where the girls were playing basketball. Spying the high-flying condom, some of them began to giggle or ask, incredulously, "What's that?" Their coach was not amused. She began complaining to *our* coach, a dim-witted character with a sloping forehead who also taught biology. We called him the missing link. He ordered us outside, lined us up like a drill instructor in *Battle Cry,* and strode in front, demanding that each of us produce a rubber. (It was commonly assumed in that innocent age that *every* able-bodied high school male carried one prophylactic. I sadly recall losing mine at an unpropitious moment, parked on the last row of a drive-in theater with a willing, gum-chewing ingenue. When I meekly asked if I could switch on the dome light to look for the wayward rubber, she fumed, "Don't you dare! I've never been so humiliated in all my life! I can't believe you've only got *one* rubber!") At least I had a replacement for the missing link's lineup. And on that day the stud had his spare to prove that he was guiltless, to quote the coach, of "dessikraten" the school's liberal experiment in combining boys and girls in gym class.

I've forgotten the unlucky character who didn't produce evidence of his innocence (and who suffered a beating, albeit a mild one, from the missing link), but the exploits of the cowboy with the Chevy pickup are etched in my mind. He was always showing up on Monday morning, when the "insies" gathered, to listen as they bragged about going to the hills and smoking a pack of Winstons with a cheerleader and cautioned, "Don't go to sleep with your motor running 'cause you'll wake up with twins." The cowboy always had a tantalizingly sordid tale for us "outsies." *His* Saturday nights were not spent necking in a DeSoto at the Plains Drive-In but always at some "establishment" on the way back from Nazareth, a small Catholic community on the High Plains (the "Golden Spread") where Protestant Panhandlers, who imposed prohibition elsewhere, bought their liquor.

In our minds, his most outstanding feat was his graduation present to himself. Instead of going on a trip to Pikes Peak (always a senior favorite), he went to Ciudad Juárez, Mexico, and got laid in a *casa de mujeres*. Not only did we get to hear the story ("I got to this place . . . we went upstairs . . . then she took off . . . and while we were making it she told me . . . then afterward she . . .") but he had *photos*. Rosa had not only performed "fantastically, man" but for an extra five bucks she had plopped naked into a chair, draped one leg over the arm, and smiled for the candid camera. I observed that she had crooked teeth. Envious but wanting to appear worldly and wary, I replied, "But what if she infected you?"

"No way, José," said the stud, "'cause when I was leavin' this fat woman unzipped my pants, pulled out my dick, and ran a tube right up that thing. Then she shot it full of somethin' that

16

burned like tequila and told me, _'Para su salud'_ ''—"For your health.''

His story was my first personal account of border culture. I thought of it and other adolescent images of the Border or, as El Pasoans say, the Frontier, when I was sitting in an El Paso motel bar on a Sunday afternoon sipping Tecate beer, Mexican-style with salt and lime. A chicana barmaid in a miniskirt was trying to keep the glasses filled and avoid involvement in a general conversation initiated by a drunken west Texan with everybody else at the bar—an Ohio kid assigned to Fort Bliss, an Italian from Massachusetts, a dapper Mexican American who had just returned from "over there," a ponderous black woman from Virginia who had never been "over there" and swore, in an intoxicated Virginia slur, that she "weren't never a'goin'," and me.

I tried to keep quiet, having discovered years ago that it is difficult to keep mental notes, sip beer (especially Mexican beer), and converse with a bullying Texan about "what you can do over there in Juárez on a Sunday afternoon." The Texan was trying to impress the rest of us with stories of his cross-river exploits, leaving out the squalid details so as not to offend (I presumed) the chicana barmaid and the fat black woman. The Mexican American male sipped on his _borbón y 7-Up_ and smiled knowingly.

The image of the border as a two-thousand-mile trek dotted with north Mexican towns whose solitary function is providing brothels, casinos, and Sunday-afternoon bullfights or dog racing for nominally proper Anglos from the other side, or, in modern times, serving as way stations for the narcotics trafficker, retains a powerful hold on most Americans. We still read lurid tales about a region the writer Ovid Demaris described as _Poso del Mundo,_ the Sink of the World, a racy description of the "sinful" north Mexican frontier, where during Prohibition you could get liquor and where libidinous American servicemen (the border has a large number of military bases) could find release from their daily frustrations in elegant brothels catering only to Anglos. A sense of fair play and national pride prompted the proprietors to

17

establish whorehouses that catered only to *mexicanos*. A generation ago Juárez earned a minor reputation as a divorce mill for frustrated New Yorkers with no easy legal solution for an unhappy marriage. Before the Empire State changed its divorce laws, a discontented married woman could take the "divorce flight" to El Paso, have a lawyer waiting for her at the airport, and within less than an hour get a decree from a compliant Mexican judge terminating her marriage. Mexican *puñeteros* ("cocksmen") still brag about their easy conquests of "gringo ladies" in those days.

A century ago El Paso was an isolated adobe village of eight hundred inhabitants. But four railroads came to town, and money followed. Across the river, Juárez remained a way station on the old "pass to the north," just one of the towns of *la frontera* that most Mexicans of the interior had long forgotten. The Mexican Revolution changed both places. The earliest battles were fought in Chihuahua state, at Casas Grandes and Juárez. One of them was a shoot-out between Mexican president Porfirio Díaz' demoralized local defense force and assaulting revolutionaries, among them American mercenaries. El Pasoans watched the battle for Juárez from rooftops on the American side. In later years, as northern Mexico plunged into a chaotic violence bequeathed by competing Revolutionary chieftains, El Paso served as supply station for contraband and, if you wanted to sell your services to the cause, a place where you could make the right connections. From here "Black Jack" Pershing launched his Punitive Expedition in 1916 in a year-long pursuit of Pancho Villa, whose Revolutionary band had raided Columbus, New Mexico, in a plan, Americans believed, to rouse abused *mexicanos* on the American side.

When Villa finally perished it was at the hands of other Mexican Revolutionaries, not Americans. The decade-long turbulence had left Juárez with a sordid reputation. In 1921 an otherwise forgettable American consul wrote, "Juárez is the most immoral, degenerate, and utterly wicked place I have ever seen or heard of in my travels. Murder and robbery are everyday occurrences and gambling, dope selling and using, drinking and sexual vices are continuous. It is a mecca for criminals and degenerates from both sides of the Border."[1]

Despite his obvious displeasure with the squalid world on the other side, the consul might have noted that El Paso and Juárez were already de facto urban partners with a mutual dependence and mutual resentments. From the early years of World War II both cities grew rapidly. Country people lured northward from the Mexican interior by the bracero program wound up in Juárez and built shantytowns that edged up to the boundary. El Paso built manufacturing plants (four hundred by 1985) and trade centers, and got more attention from the military and from tourists. But it always had to depend on Juárez for nocturnal diversions and for an abundant supply of cheap labor. El Paso industrialized, and so, eventually, did Juárez, in part to retain its own cheap labor *in Mexico* and, undeniably, to change border-town images as pestholes to more accurate representations of Mexican culture.

Towns on the American side expanded in population but not as fast as their Mexican urban counterparts. They grew much richer than their bloated Mexican twins, but they never matched the economic growth or acquired the wealth of interior American cities. Mexican border cities like Juárez, embarrassingly poor when matched with American border cities, were prosperous when compared with the impoverished Mexican interior. The benefits and resentments of mutual dependence inevitably followed—El Paso prospered because of Juárez and Juárez prospered because of El Paso, it was often said, but neither really wanted nor could escape their mutual dependence. El Paso could never catch up with, let us say, San Antonio on the economic charts because of its lower standard of living and isolation. And Juárez could never claim the accolade as true representation of Mexican culture because it had sold its heart and soul to the dispenser of gringo dollars.

The comic Rodney Dangerfield's career-making lament "I

don't get no respect" is a common El Paso refrain, and, I believe, a justifiable one. Here, political and economic decisions on both sides of the border must reflect decrees issued in faraway Washington or Mexico City, yet the realities often dictate contrary courses. If one excludes San Diego, which lies twelve miles from Tijuana, El Paso is the only large city in the United States lying on the Mexican border. Its experience in the history of MexAmerica is unique, they will tell you thereabouts, and provides a more accurate indicator to border politics and culture than San Antonio. Even El Pasoans with largely negative views of their city will voice the Dangerfield complaint.

On an already unpleasantly warm May morning, I breakfasted with a city official who gave me, "off the record," a personal assessment of border politics and economics. He didn't want to be quoted, because, as he told me between sips of coffee and audible munches on over-browned toast, "there are people *over there* I don't want to offend." The business and political leaders on both sides got along well enough, but neither could afford to say no. Juárez' *progressive* (my italics) elements could not risk letting the bosses down in Mexico City know they actually cooperated with (i.e., depended too much on) the Anglos in El Paso.

And, of course, the bureaucrats in Washington would never understand nor could they officially approve of two cities in different countries engaging in informal political cooperation. He spoke in a tone indicating he knew from experience about what the sociologists call "intercultural interface," only the political instincts he had acquired told him that in dealing with Mexicans the Anglo had to be careful so as to extend assistance not as charity but as a token of respect for the stature of the receiver. El Paso, he told me, dispatched trucks to Juárez to spray insecticide, and Juárez supplied the fuel—just one of numerous acts of informal diplomacy between the Twin Cities of the Rio.

Experience and necessity have fashioned two cultures, each vocal in its national pride, which have no alternative but to coexist as if the Rio Grande were no more an obstacle to

20

Juárez/El Paso than the Mississippi is to Minneapolis/St. Paul. To survive in business in downtown El Paso you have to employ bilingual workers. When the INS cracks down by holding up cars and pedestrians to search for drugs or delays the crossing of Mexicans who shop in El Paso the city suffers economically. Here a restrictive immigration bill would probably be meaningless because neither El Paso nor Juárez could tolerate the restrictions. People who cross downriver are another matter. They are truly "illegals," say the locals, because they're not going back and forth every day. They move into the interior of America—and more and more of them are staying.

Besides, the El Paso city official reminded me, you have to remember that the traffic is *two-way*. People back in Kansas City or Washington read about the clusters forming in the night or early morning to make a run for the other side, about "no-man's-land" in the Chula Vista hills south of San Diego, about "tidal waves of impoverished humanity," or about how "we can't control our borders." Such stories upset little old ladies in Dubuque about a real problem but say little about the normal, tolerable day-to-day crossings that are vital to the Juárez/El Paso economies. Everybody knows about the Anglo "missy lady and her Messcan maid" but few outsiders are really knowledgeable about the *skilled* labor from Mexico that crosses over into El Paso or about managerial types who go south every business day to run a plant or office. There is a plant over there, he said, that is almost completely robotic.

In textbook-correct Spanish, spoken with a noticeable midwestern accent, he politely asks the *mesera* for a refill on his coffee. Assessing Juárez' city government and Mexican politics generally—a not infrequent El Paso pastime—he is not uncritical but, unlike most Americans, understands the realities of border politics. American cities are continually asking for more, and while some get more than others, there is at least some assurance of a cushion. Mexico's urban politicians, especially those on the border, don't have the tax base to run their cities on local property valuations. And until the decentralization program,

21

Mexico City siphoned off more than its fair share southward. So the Juárez officials survive by tolerating—even encouraging—*la mordida,* the bite. In urban politics in the United States, if 10 or 20 percent of public officials are on the take, a scandal can be in the making, with demotions, fines, and a mayoralty campaign in which the challenger demands "honesty down at city hall." In Mexico, perhaps 80 or 90 percent of the governmental bureaucracy, from top to bottom, survives on the principle of *la mordida,* and the lowly mayors of the border cities are at the end of the line.

A few years back, a reform-minded Juárez mayor of the opposition National Action Party (PAN), Francisco Barrera (robbed of the Chihuahua governorship in the 1986 elections, *norteños* are saying), began dealing with police graft by paying higher salaries and ending the policy whereby cops had to purchase their *patrol cars.* PAN, essentially oriented toward middle-class business and the church in the old days, has stronger appeals nowadays to Mexican border towns trying to serve an overcrowded electorate with a municipal government addicted to the *mordida.* But my breakfast companion conceded, as do most political analysts, that a few victories here and there are not going to change the "system."[2]

Americans pride themselves on honest, efficient local government as an ideal to strive for even when they know it cannot be easily achieved. An election may not rid a town of its political corruption but it can make the graftees warier about taking too much or provide for a more equitable sharing of the loot. The great American cities of the late nineteenth century, losing their middle-class citizenry to the suburbs and bursting with ethnics demanding their fair share, survived on graft. City-boss machines exacted payoffs and ran their operations on the principle that you make sure that city government is more attentive to the needs of those who vote for you and so you employ public servants on the basis of political loyalty. With the exception of an occasional urban political cancer, we like to believe, the United States is largely rid of this system. Mexicans still have it.

For the time being, I was more interested in conditions over here. El Paso provides, undeniably, a more efficient and certainly more honest local government than Juárez, but how well does it serve the needs of the Spanish-speaking? Public officials must be alert to individual rights and social realities. In El Paso, as in other border cities, the social reality is an Anglo system penetrated by Hispanics. At the top, whether in government or business, comments about "cooperation" and "good relations" with "our neighbors across the border" are not uncommon, nor, I would argue, dissembling. Those who run El Paso confront, after all, problems not dissimilar in kind, if greatly diminished in quantity, to those encountered by the Juárez urban elite. But as you penetrate El Paso's still noticeably layered social structure, cultural antagonisms survive issues forgotten long ago by the establishment. As one explained to me, "We used to get a lot of rednecks here who treated Mexicans the way they did blacks back home in Alabama, but most of our Anglo immigrants now come from the midwest, and that makes a difference." I could not discern from the observation whether he believed the resentment was cultural or economic, a measure of the working-class antagonism to the lower pay scales and antiunion sentiment ascribed to El Paso employers who want cheap labor from "over there."

Yet the most troublesome assessments of El Paso come from those most responsible for molding the citizen of the future. They point to the ominous signs of a "two-world" El Paso, ruled by an Anglo/Hispanic coalition unable or unwilling to devise a public policy committed to dealing with a chicano underclass that remains persistently uneducated and poor. South El Paso, a squatter barrio known as Little Chihuahua, grew up between Santa Fe and Cotton streets on the border, a reminder of the squalor on the American side. As in Los Angeles, chicanos were able to move out to more attractive areas to the north, and Mexicans from across the river took their place. In this way, the chicanos could befriend their down-and-out brethren from the old country.

But the cultural price was high. El Paso's Hispanic elite had considerable influence and even political clout a generation ago, and benefited from the system. They could speak both proper English and Spanish, as they preferred. But the chicano underclass of the past generation found itself torn between two worlds. The economic system in their own country provided more jobs, but its managers obviously preferred the more compliant laborer from Juárez. The political structure adjusted to accommodate "Hispanic issues," but these were mostly the priorities of the Hispanic elite. In the schools, the chicanos believed, a new chicano, educated to survive in modern America yet retaining Mexican cultural pride, would arise. The result has been, here and elsewhere in MexAmerica Norte, a chicano culture of limited hope and considerable despair. As in MexAmerica Sur across the river, the familial tradition Anglos have long believed was intrinsic to Hispanics—a male authority symbol, a dutiful wife, and properly reared children—has disintegrated in the harsh realities of El Paso's chicano subculture. Those who break out must learn not only proper English but proper Spanish. In other words, they have to be "Anglicized," to go through a cultural transformation, to become "Muppies."

El Paso does have an image problem, an instructor from El Paso Community College casually informed me, because its ruling Anglos and Hispanics *believe* the city is a more underrated representation of bicultural America than San Antonio. In his mind, a more accurate comparison would be El Paso and South Africa. One-third of the city dominates the economic, political, and even social life of the community. He did not seem persuaded by my response that in El Paso's case Hispanics had been able to cross social, economic, and even political lines that made up obstacles elsewhere. But whatever the measure of its validity, his point struck at the center of the debate over such matters as immigration reform, bilingual education, and our fundamental civic values.

El Paso is like South Africa, he believes, because an upper-income group constituting one-third of the population, brown and white working *together,* controls the other two-thirds, brown, white, and black. Among Texas' ranking ten cities in population, El Paso is first in the average size of families and first in the percentage of youth under eighteen, and has one of the lowest per capita incomes of any major city in America. It is plagued with more cases of tuberculosis than seventeen states, and general health is poorer than in the rest of the country. None of these social debilitations makes El Paso an American variation of South Africa, of course. The symbolism derives from the economic and social pact Anglo and Hispanic elites have forged here. Apprehensive about the explosive forces lurking below, on both sides of the river, they have crafted a gentlemen's agreement to keep the lid on things. The gap between haves and have-nots is wider here. Those who govern El Paso's economy would, I think, like to narrow it, but like the South Africans they do not believe they have a realistic choice. Theirs is an economic substructure dependent on lower-cost labor and less-sophisticated technology in a world in which surface cordiality between Anglo and Hispanic masks class antagonisms. If poor white and poor brown crafted a political alliance, they would overwhelm their rulers by the sheer weight of their numbers. But they will probably not be able to do this in the foreseeable future.

I went from the college instructor's harsh assessment in the morning to an afternoon meeting with three of his colleagues—two Anglos and a chicano from Chicago. They were less severe but no less frank. They taught chicanos who had managed to get through high school—in El Paso the Hispanic dropout rate parallels the national high rate of 50 percent—but ones who had survived *without* going beyond a rudimentary knowledge of English. Enrollment in the public high schools, which is the basis for state funding, is maintained by admitting Mexicans from Juárez who give an El Paso address. There is no problem in finding plenty of people named García or Rodríguez in the phone book.

The University of Texas, Austin, is shifting to a curriculum aimed at the more qualified student who emerges from high school with what pedagogues call the "proper credentials" for university courses. At El Paso Community College the largest division, taught by 150 faculty, contains *eight* levels of courses in English as a second language—everything from basic English for local chicanos who know little of proper Spanish to technical English for Spanish-speaking engineers from Mexico. For those who cannot attend class, the college runs an educational outreach program, aimed mostly at chicanas. A disturbing number of them have a drunken, wife-beating *cholo* (tough guy) at home, husbands who can't or won't get a job. She plunges into the Anglo business world with few marketable skills. The program provides basic English and sufficient training in a skill to enable her to land a job, but this may cause problems at home. She acquires self-esteem and reminds her loutish spouse that at age eighteen *she* could have married an Anglo and *he* couldn't. Throughout she demands greater independence because she is paying the rent.

The comparison of El Paso and South Africa disturbs me, though it does not make me more critical of the Anglo-Hispanic elite that still rules here. Just as liberal-minded South Africans and even a few of the unrelentingly rigid in that country can make a case for "understanding why we can't move any faster on dismantling apartheid or why we can't do here what the United States did in the sixties," it is possible for even the unyielding social reformer to pause before attempting to "explain" the MexAmerican character of the city. In El Paso, as in South Africa, there is a turbulence welling up from below, pressing against the old order, brown and white, and the outside world, even a few hundred miles away in Austin or San Antonio, doesn't understand. If the rest of Texas is becoming bicultural, then El Paso deserves much credit for advancing that cause. But the bicultural milieu it has formed over the years has not brought it the reassurance of community solidarity or the promise of a more harmonious political future.

The reasons for the depressing prognosis lie at the very heart of border culture. El Paso represents more than an intrusion of

26

American culture into a Mexican setting; the history of the city symbolizes the dynamics of an American frontier economy built on mining, transportation, and small factories—not a cowboy town but an outpost of American industrialism. To sustain this most vigorous example of southwestern capitalism, El Paso's ambitious developers eagerly sought and ultimately depended on Mexican labor. They came north to Juárez, moved across the river, and in subtle ways appeared to become more American, in their heightened commitments to education, social organizations, and churches, and in their noticeably imitative pursuit of the material things of life.

They may have crossed the river to work and to live, in some cases permanently, but they did not leave their "Mexicanness" on the other side. Over the years, dependent on an El Paso employer for their livelihood, as he depended on them for his economic survival, they found their emotional commitments to Mexico and Mexican culture weakening. Middle-class _mexicanos_ who fled the Revolutionary turmoil for the political and economic security they saw in the north readily tossed aside old traditions to accommodate the Anglos willing to accept them if only they would, as cynical Mexicans say, start acting like a "gringo son of a bitch." But the vast numbers of working-class _mexicanos_ who joined them knew why they were valued—for their labor. And the close presence of a homeland, however impoverished its economic landscape or unresponsive its political leaders, provided cultural reassurance. So those on the bottom felt no compelling urgency to talk like a gringo or act like a gringo nor good reason to naturalize. Enticed by economic opportunity or responsive to Anglo social values, they sometimes displayed a "go-getter" determination or modified their social habits to impress an Anglo employer or to ease their way in a bicultural ambience.

True, they were paid better—often receiving much higher wages than they could ever have dreamed of in Mexico—and they lived better in Little Chihuahua on the American side than in the squalid hillside huts over in Juárez. But, like the vast numbers

27

of Africans who push into South African factories and black townships, where they can earn more and live better than in any African country where blacks rule, the Mexican laborer in El Paso has always known he can advance only so far and no farther. To go beyond means betrayal of the culture on the other side of the river. There is a sometimes infuriating determination in the Mexican at the bottom to maintain the "Mexican" within him, to retain his ways, to always speak with an accent (when a Puerto Rican is told that he speaks without an accent he feels complimented, but a Mexican considers himself insulted), to prohibit his wife from learning English, even when it benefits family income, because it lessens his control over her. He does not easily change even when the golden door to the promised land of El Norte is open. An American cultural truism holds that "you can take the boy out of the country, but you can never take the country out of the boy." A Mexican can migrate north and never return, but as one descends in the economic and social order, the "Mexican" inside him retains its hold.[3]

Even at the top of the social and political order the bicultural ambience can be deceptive in its apparent harmony. El Paso's Anglo elites speak warmly of their Hispanic friends on both sides of the border. In numerous instances, undeniably, genuine amicability exists, but this may be less because of conviction than the willingness of Hispanic elites in both cities to accommodate Anglo cultural imperatives. In Juárez those who run things speak English without an accent and strive to speak Spanish without an accent, have attended American schools, "know what makes America work," and express their admiration for American political, social, and economic values. They may call themselves *mexicanos* but they do so a bit apologetically. Their Anglo friends across the way respond politely but do not absorb *Mexican* ideas or values simply because they believe Mexico has little to offer Anglo America except its laborers. Business leaders in both El Paso and Juárez may get together informally and even formally to talk about border economic problems. Government officials often cooperate on matters of public safety and public health. But on larger questions, such as housing, city development, budgeting, or labor, they have little to say to one another. Both cities may promote events such as "cultural understanding week" or the like, but in Juárez they know the Anglo doesn't really understand, much less appreciate, the cultural symbolism of the Mexican event but has shown the courtesy of making a gesture. The Mexican graciously acknowledges what he knows is yet another example of the American's need for self-deception.[4]

In El Paso, as in South Africa, there is a fire raging down below. It is not as menacing to the social and political order, but it has provoked public debate and guarded discussion. What is frustrating for those who hold political power in El Paso is a perceived inability to accommodate the pressures from below, in a city that is 60 percent Hispanic, through traditional American political and social trade-offs. Even liberal Anglos, who often look to San Antonio as a model worth imitating, are disturbed by the news of a report of the El Paso Hispanic Task Force, which righteously declared that Hispanics deserved to occupy 60 percent of the seats in the county's public offices, boards, and commissions, and were entitled to an Hispanic mayor and county judge in every decade. The sensitive editor of the _El Paso Times,_ Barbara Funkhouser, assessing the recommendations, found nothing objectionable about promoting more Hispanics for office. But she was horrified at suggestions that Hispanics pull out of local politics as a signal of their potential strength, then demand pledges from Anglo candidates as a condition of their political participation. A few outspoken Hispanic leaders lauded the report, others denied it existed. But a local Hispanic organization, El Concilio, while endorsing the spirit of greater Hispanic political activity, disdained the radical proposal of an Hispanic boycott. Ethnic lines in politics, its leader declared, are not realistic. The Hispanic president of the El Paso Central Labor Council, which has twelve thousand members, announced that his members were concentrating on "issues, not ethnicity."[5]

The threat of a boycott, even if quickly dismissed by most of El Paso's Hispanics, represents an ancient Hispanic practice of *retraimiento,* literally a retreat or seclusion, not for meditation but as a calculated gesture of defiance of the established order. It does not indicate, as does the person who never votes, an indifference to the political process. Like the minuscule but vocal *independistas* of Puerto Rico, who condemn the periodic plebiscites on statehood or commonwealth status as examples of "colonial manipulation," those Hispanics of El Paso who refuse to participate in the city's politics until *their* priorities and *their* notion of *real* democracy are satisfied are an unsettling omen for its promise of "togetherness." They are often unable to articulate what they want beyond more Hispanics in office, which the system can accommodate. But the system, no matter how wide it opens its doors to them, cannot adjust to their cultural defiance.

In the desert twilight my son and I join an El Paso family and a visiting Belgian commercial attaché for an evening meal on the "other side," at a place called Chihuahua Charlie's.

From the outside the restaurant looks depressingly similar to some deteriorating eating joint long ago bypassed by the turnpike. But inside is a decor that can be characterized as "antique MexAmerican"—a blend of Latin with American casual. The cashier's paneled station displays business cards as proudly as small-town diners back in Kansas. There is a mariachi band that alters with Muzak in providing entertainment *à la mexicana* or *à la* Lawrence Welk. Polite *mexicano* waiters provide liquid refreshments and a menu that contains, I am told, representative selections from every region in the country. Charlie began in Mexico City in 1952, has moved every two or three years, and has at last brought his cuisine to the northern pass. The Belgian begins with a margarita and by the time he plunges into a plate of chicken enchiladas smothered in sour cream is overwhelmed. "Is this what Mexicans eat?" he asks. "Sometimes," I reply, "but most of them don't eat this well. What you're eating is more Tex/Mex than authentic Mexican haute cuisine."

Still, he appeared persuaded that C.C.'s is the "real" Mexico. The evening before, I had talked with an Australian who had heard of Chihuahua Charlie's and looked forward to seeing the "real" Mexico, just as he had been absorbing the "real" America—in Miami, Death Valley, and Las Vegas. If he made it to Chihuahua Charlie's, he found not the "real" Mexico but Mexican cuisine in a MexAmerican ambience. It is the artful imitation of what middle-class Americans from Iowa or just across the river in the "frontier" want to believe is the "real" Mexico. Chihuahua Charlie is happy to oblige, probably because he learned long ago, as have millions of Mexicans whose business is dealing with Americans, that economic survival often depends on how well you accommodate the preconceptions of what your clients believe you ought to be. He has learned, if the ambience of his restaurant is any indication, a gringo cultural truth: style is more important than substance. If you're offering Mexican cuisine, which can range from hideous to modestly tasteful, that can be an important credo to remember. And he probably learned years ago that the city across the river applies the same principle to its politics.

2

The Maquila Man

Among Mexicans and sensitive Americans there is an image of the north Mexican border that remains a lingering embarrassment. It was the *zona rosa* or *zona de tolerancia,* what Texas high schoolers called Boys' Town, where you could get the traditional ten-minute workout or sixty-nine or forty-one or even something without a name in cathouses in the United States. There were stories of aging whores with pendulous breasts who accommodated customers with solely upper-torso fixations right at the bar. One accumulated a hefty retirement fund by charging $1 (per breast) to allow a client to douse her tits with brandy or tequila and lick them. With enough money and enough liquor you could get drunk and sexually satisfied at the same time. Or if you liked floor shows, you could see a woman and a man, two women and a man, two men and a woman, or a human (male or female) and a dog or a pig or burro. Even children were impressed into the act, often at an early age. For the writer Ovid Demaris, describing the prevailing wickedness of border culture (on the Mexican side) from Matamoras to Tijuana, those who headed south to partake were, basically, willing but morally innocent victims of every prostitute, smuggler, and con artist on the other side. When an American, particularly an American male, crossed over, he left his moral convictions on his own side. In Mexico, *he* was not responsible for the immorality, graft, and corruption that he believed constituted Mexican culture. "Good heavens," exclaimed one American who witnessed some young Mexicans practicing onstage bestiality, "these kids have got to be a million miles from home to fuck those pigs." Still another, a journalist who covered Juárez for thirty years for the *El Paso Times,* could never get over his wonderment at the air of innocence in the red-light districts across the river, where prostitutes at places like Irma's, the most famous, actually seemed to enjoy their business.

Lamentably, as the chicano historian Oscar Martínez has shown, Juárez and other border towns *might* have developed with less sordid reputations. In the late nineteenth century, in an age when aggressive *norteamericano* venture capitalists and industrialists were pushing against the isolated north Mexican towns, the *norteños* got the benefit of free zones. When Juárez (and the border towns to the west) joined the Mexican *zona libre* in 1885, the city went through a momentary boom. When the government terminated its free-zone status in 1905, the *juarenses* had to develop enterprises catering to the needs of Americans on the other side. Reformist movements north of the border, such as the closing down of bordellos and the final triumph of Prohibition, provided the north Mexican towns with a viable industry that possessed a continually expanding market—sin. Lacking a realistic alternative, Juárez and the other towns built their reputations on the most elementary economic laws of supply and demand. For the price of admission, they were willing to accommodate the gringo's sexual appetite and thirst. And they may have appeared to bear the sordid reputation that went along with such businesses, but they always felt, in their tormented inner selves, that the real sinners were the buyers and not the sellers.

In the twenties, Juárez prospered, but the money flowing in from American tourists demanding a drink flowed out when Mexicans crossed the river to buy American goods. Locals championed the revival of free trade, but in the nationalistic temper of post-Revolutionary Mexico, the new political order, locked in a bitter dispute with the U.S. government over American mining and petroleum companies in the country, were adamant against further penetration of the border economy. In the

Depression, Juárez suffered even more when the government began closing down its brothels and casinos and streams of repatriated *mexicanos* passed through on their way south. Conditions were bad on both sides of the border, but the Mexican *frontera,* punished as much by its own government, it was said, as by American deportation of its countrymen, suffered more.

Just as World War II regenerated the economic life of the towns on the American side, it revived their Mexican counterparts. Tourism returned, the brothels and casinos reappeared. But when the war ended and the soldiers left, some in Juárez wanted a different image for the city. One of them was Antonio Bermúdez, who as mayor began a campaign against the whorehouses and gambling joints, not so much to wipe them out, an impossible task for even the most dedicated social reformer, but to provide Juárez with an economic base other than catering to libidinous Anglos from the other side.

Mexico City took another decade to alter its essentially neglectful northern economic policy. But as the fifties ended, the government, surveying the expanding and ambitious northern elites, came to a prudent decision. For several years Bermúdez, now head of PEMEX, the state-owned petroleum company, had been vigorously pushing a plan to integrate the frontier into the Mexican national economy. Otherwise, he warned, the region would slip from national influence.

How to bind the frontier more closely to the nation, not only economically but politically, posed a quandary. Mexico clearly lacked the capital to industrialize the north, which meant the government would have to modify its traditional hostility to the intrusion of foreign investment and begin inviting American companies back into the country. Yet their return, it was widely feared, would result in American domination in a region of Mexico where people were inclined to measure life's rewards by the economic standard across the border.

So, with great publicity, as much on the American side as in Mexico, the government proudly announced PRONAF, the National Frontier Program. The professed objective was the transformation of the border—a large order, given the dependence of so many Mexican officials, high and low, on its sordid economic base, to say nothing of the long tradition of Mexicans crossing over to the U.S. side to do their shopping. Still, Bermúdez and his disciples persisted. Border industrialization and commercial lures to American companies offered the only sensible way for Mexico to reclaim its northern border. Places like Juárez and Tijuana became more competitive in legal enterprises. The stake was more than economic. Mexico was rapidly changing from a rural society, but its image in the United States remained a diptych of a stoop laborer and a *puta,* a whore.

Juárez got its facelift. Bulldozers leveled the odious brothels and gin mills hovering on the border. In their place rose craft shops and stores, where *Mexican* articles were marketed to tourists (lured over by peso devaluation) and Mexicans who could no longer afford the higher prices in El Paso. In the beginning old buildings were transformed into "bonded-in" plants, *maquiladoras,* where American companies established Mexican twin plants. In the *maquilas* they obtained a ready work force costing only a fraction of what union labor in the States demanded for electronics assembly or garment manufacturing. Taking advantage of U.S. tariff schedules 806.30 and 807, American companies were able to assemble parts in their Mexican subsidiaries, paying a duty only on the value added to the product. Mexican labor was more expensive than Oriental, but the companies realized early that the savings in shipping and the ability to pull out quickly if there was "political trouble" made the Mexican border towns an attractive place for investment.[1]

In time the *maquilas* moved out into industrial parks, much like those promoted by harassed smaller U.S. cities trying to lure more industry, where more investment produced ever bigger and more sophisticated operations. By 1985, less than twenty years after the program began, the El Paso Foreign Trade Association announced, Juárez had 180 plants—one-fourth of all *maquiladoras* in Mexico—employing eighty thousand workers, 25 percent of Juárez' male and more than 50 percent of its female labor force. More revealing of the economic interdependence of the two cities, perhaps, was the number of El Paso suppliers to these plants, 4,684 in 1984, up from 2,010 in 1980, employing ninety thousand, and the thousand El Pasoans who served in a managerial capacity in the *maquilas*.[2]

The program has never really accomplished the initial goal of its early boosters, but the *maquilas* have come to occupy a critical segment of the Mexican economy. And their numbers (662 plants with 260,000 workers) are a reminder of the transformation of the border from a rural economy to an industrial workplace, exporting only $7 million in products in 1966 but more than $5 billion annually twenty years later. Illicit trafficking in dope, booze, or people may still generate huge profits, and the *maquilas* make only a dent in Mexico's unemployment statistics, but they *do* show that the border is a more sophisticated economy than it used to be.

One who knows about this diversity is an energetic *mexicano*, Enrique Esparzo, who operates out of National City, a San Diego suburb. His clients are American companies which want to establish a Mexican twin plant. Esparza, the head of Assemble in Mexico, Inc., will locate a building, move in the necessary equipment, and identify a reliable Mexican to hire workers at $5 or $6 a day. What this means is that smaller operators who manufacture furniture or eyeglass frames or sprinklers can escape the labor costs of the United States and join the "biggies" like General Motors or General Electric, which already have seventeen and eleven plants, respectively, in Mexico.

Esparza and the other promoters of the program argue that the *maquilas* allow the giants to compete more effectively with their unrelentingly aggressive competitors abroad. The electronic or textile or shoe manufacturers generally complain about "dumping practices" by their rivals in the Orient. The *maquilas,* they believe, give them a chance to survive. Zenith, for example, closed a huge plant in Sioux City, Iowa, in 1978, shifting almost nineteen thousand jobs to its *maquilas* in Mexico, where laborers work for considerably less but permit the company to retain twelve thousand employees in the United States.[3]

When AFL-CIO critics assess the *maquilas* they predictably arrive at strikingly different conclusions. To the harassed union officer back in the States, the "bonded-in" program on the north Mexican frontier constitutes a dual threat: American jobs are exported from the country, and the *maquilas* lure too many Mexicans northward. Unable to survive in Juárez or Nogales or Tijuana, they enter the more promising U.S. workplace and take a job rightfully belonging to an American.[4]

There is a parallel—and potentially more ominous—interpretation of the impact of the *maquilas*. Its proponents charge that whatever the economic balance sheet—as American businessmen say, "the bottom line"—or the contributing influence the *maquilas* have on illegal migration, these plants represent yet another example of labor's exploitation. On the Mexican side, the *maquilas* are, for the left, another reminder of the nation's dependence on the United States. And for social conservatives, the large employment of women in the *maquilas* threatens the supply of domestics, to say nothing of the disruptive effects on traditional familial roles. As one disgruntled male in Monterrey complained to me over coffee at Sanborn's, "I can't keep a chica maid anymore. They all run off to the north to work in a *maquila* or cross over to mop the floor of some damn gringa."

I responded with a joke about a Mexican variation of "Rosa the Riveter." He was not amused.

His irritation revealed much about the success of the *maquila* program and the inevitable frustrations it has produced. The border's image has changed with the economic transformation the *maquilas* symbolize. But the character of the Mexican-American relationship in its political and especially in its cultural context has not miraculously blossomed in good will and understanding. The presence of the *maquilas* may explain why there are two hundred registered prostitutes in Juárez today where twenty-five years ago there were seven thousand. But the plants have not done that much, one feminist writer (who passed herself as a *mexicana* worker and got a job in a Juárez *maquila*) has written, to change social realities. In the early years of operation, the *maquila* managers welcomed visitors, courted publicists, and generally expected favorable reports. After all, they were providing everything from higher wages for the largely female labor force to social betterment by keeping them off the streets.

The American intruder discovered a different Mexican woman, to be sure, but not necessarily one whose social situation had dramatically improved. Too many of them had given birth at fifteen or sixteen, then after another child had been deserted or left with supporting an unemployed male. Absorbed into one of Juárez' textile or electronic *maquilas,* they have to live in an adobe pesthole in one of the city's dirt-street *colonias.* There idle men with even less education than they have harass them. As the women age they may shift from electronics to textiles, which require more developed skills, but they become more vulnerable to the competition from younger women. And their skills do not develop well enough to break the bonds of economic servitude and, more critically, of the continued social and political manipulation of the Mexican state.[5]

Among Mexican economists there has been a spreading pessimism about the utility of the *maquilas* in the country's development schemes. A quarter-century ago, when the government's plans for the border were just getting underway, the *maquilas* promised, it seemed, a rapid way to expand employment among unskilled Mexican workers. After half a dozen years, when it became clear that the *maquilas* were becoming a permanent feature of the northern economies, the economic wizards to the south expected the United States to repay Mexico for providing cheap labor with more sophisticated technology and training for its inexpensive workforce. The ultimate dream was "Mexico—the next Japan," with the *maquilas* integrated into the national economy by moving some into the interior and opening the "nationalized" *maquilas* to the Mexican market. Mexico would still export, but, in time, Mexicans would be buying more and more of their own products. Even some of the American-dominated *maquilas* foresaw the day when their plants would be buying *and* selling in Mexico.

Instead, northern Mexico, some Mexicans cynically remark, has become not another Japan but a "new Taiwan," providing a huge semiskilled work force to American companies with no intention of changing their plans (nor, say the American investors, is there any enthusiastic Mexican support for such change). The Border Industrialization Program is effectively undercut by *maquila* entrepreneurs who prefer docile women laborers. Such companies begrudgingly train too few of them in more advanced skills, and even deny Mexico the patent rights on technical innovations these plants develop. American capital demands, and gets, special privileges in a country desperate for its economic presence. Labor unions, politically subservient to Mexico City, are compliant; taxes are low; and the complaints of a *maquila* operator get advance (and usually sympathetic) consideration by the bureaucracy, at every level.

Resentful of American domination, Mexico's economic nationalists indict their countrymen as well. When Tijuana and Juárez and the other border cities had more sordid reputations, based on what their puritanical neighbors to the north regarded as "innate sexual perversion," embittered Mexicans in the interior retaliated with sardonic comments about Anglo tourists less interested in trinkets than in sexual diversion. The *maquila* program, admittedly, has reduced the number of whores in town by making them honest women on an assembly line. But in the process a new "sinner" has emerged to thwart not only Mexican economic development but social betterment in the north. Local, state, and federal officials readily facilitate the transfer to developers of public land on which they create industrial parks to house the *maquilas*. Their friends quickly get wind of what is happening, buy up land around the parks, and reap huge profits. Juárez has less than twenty-five acres of public land because of the frantic real estate speculation. So the migrants streaming in from the interior must survive in hillside dwellings almost unreachable by municipal services.

The transnational *maquilas* and their Mexican border-town beneficiaries are technically blameless. They profit because the rules on both sides of the border were drafted to their advantage. Periodically, a social cooperative, using *Mexican* capital, tries to break into the border economy. But the outcome is usually years of frustration in dealing with the national bureaucracy in Mexico City, wrangles about exchange rates or getting dollars to use in border exchanges. And their efforts are impeded by yet another Mexican legal peculiarity and bureaucratic whim: because there are so few Mexican-owned border industries, the Mexican Finance Ministry subjects them to a tax on products sold *inside* the country. The national government professes to encourage Mexican border industry but treats its own with less favor than the outsider.

A century ago, the Mexican dictator Porfirio Díaz, committed to building an industrial economy, extended such generous benefits to American companies that cynics were saying the Mexican government was the "father of foreigners and the stepfather of Mexicans." For the official at every level the choice lies between the immediate gains wrought by the *maquilas* and the uncertain financial return of Mexican-owned border enterprise. A century ago, the Mexican government did not concern itself with the social costs of modernization. Its Revolutionary inheritors must. They have to calculate the damage inflicted by a distorted border economy on the expanding Mexican subclasses in border cities like Juárez and Tijuana, where Mexican workers have a larger income, to be sure, but not enough to offset the higher living costs of *la frontera*.

Rural people, accustomed to large families, a bane to Mexico's economic calculations, are following their ancestral traditions when they migrate to these places. In the *maquila* world, a family needs more daughters because the males are unemployed or underemployed. In their desperation, the rootless males of the congested *colonias* of the border cities have adopted the *pachuco* style of the chicanos on the U.S. side. They organize gangs of *cholos* (tough guys) who divide territories to dominate and defend, to the death. Arrest, punishment, and even imprisonment in the notorious Mexican jails mean little save enhanced stature among their *cholo* comrades.

In time the stern-minded *maquila* operators began hiring women gang members (*cholas*), only to find out they could be as disruptive inside the plants as in their own neighborhoods.[6] Trying to rid themselves of these laboring gangs by the expedient of mass firing, the companies discovered, only provoked their destructive wrath. Ten years ago, passing through El Paso, I spent several hours with an old high school classmate who had gotten into the clothing business, using Mexican labor in Juárez to produce stylish men's clothing. For a while things had gone well, but he had decided to get out of the business because of "labor problems" in the plant, which had led not only to economic reverses but to personal threats. He had learned through personal experience that the putatively docile Mexican laborer possessed an aggressive temperament. My friend spoke disparagingly about these unforeseen problems and talked of leaving the border for good, "heading for Nebraska and getting into farming."

He had discovered what critics on both sides are calling the "negative effects" of the *maquila* program. Had he lasted into this decade the economic calamities visited on Mexico, which brought a resurgence of the *maquilas* and the old debate about integrating the border economy, might have changed things for him. In the last year of José López Portillo's presidential term, 1982, the frustrated Mexican president announced a series of draconian economic measures—the severest was the nationalization of the banks—that plunged the border into uncertainty. Dollars grew scarce and the peso commenced a downward plunge. Middle-class *juarenses* who preferred American-made to Mexican-made and who had depended on cheap dollars found they needed a lot more pesos at the banks, and El Paso businesses accustomed to selling to *maquila* workers grimly watched their sales dwindle even as they accepted a devalued peso.[7]

But the *maquila* promoters made profits even in the face of these depressing statistics. Minimum wages for Mexican workers had to go up, of course, but the annually devaluating peso signaled a real *decline* in the cost of doing business. In its desperate search for hard currency to satisfy its increasingly aggressive creditors, the Mexican government found in the *maquilas,* which must pay their workers in pesos, a ready source of dollars. Mexican officials presented American corporate giants with elaborate charts showing how they could save up to $20,000 a year in costs per worker and reminded them that in Mexico there is no OSHA, no EPA, no EEOC. Mexico "understood" their problems.

By 2000, the Banco de México estimated in 1985, one million Mexicans will be working in the *maquilas.* But to meet the country's labor needs at the end of the century, when its population will be more than 100 million, the *maquilas* will have to employ *ten* million if Mexico hopes to satisfy its employment demands in the north. Already there are ominous portents of social and economic calamity. The lure of *la frontera norte* has brought, the famed Mexican writer Carlos Fuentes has noted, the third world to America's doorstep. Across the river from a towering downtown El Paso business or the plush Spanish-style home of an Anglo, the cardboard-and-tin shanties creep up the Chihuahua hillside. The only thing the two have in common, it is said, is that with altitude you can avoid the pollution that afflicts both sides of the river.

And on the American front the growth of twin plants has not diminished union complaints about job losses because of the "cheap labor on the other side." Itinerant Democrats scurrying the country looking for political issues have begun to listen more politely to their charges about "unfair trade." But they are drowned out by the ceaseless praise coming from the *maquila* men in the El Paso Industrial Development Corporation and Grupo Bermúdez about the "boom towns" on the border. An Ohioan representing Grupo Bermúdez spoke confidently in 1985 about plans for a 25,000-acre industrial park that would be a "diminutive Juárez" with schools, churches, and housing. Francisco Barrera, then mayor, reinforced his enthusiastic remarks with a reminder that the *maquilas* "have created better conditions than the local economy could ever have done."

Government officials talk more and more about shifting the *maquilas* deeper into the country, putting them physically closer to the interior market and, in effect, expanding Mexico City's control over the frontier, integrating the northern cities into the national economy. It is *un plan grande*, a great plan. In Spanish the word "plan" takes on spiritual powers, a dream from which one often awakes to, as Americans like to say, the "real world." And the economic reality the *maquila* men boast about is the dollars (and jobs) saved in El Paso by the expansion of the American economy into Mexico, what for them is the "real" frontier south of Juárez. They have powerful Mexican allies in Juárez who respond to critics by pointing to the polite young *maquila* women enjoying lunch or shopping instead of parading in gaudy miniskirts outside taverns and greeting Texas school-boys with "You want go fokee?" Mexican lawyers who once made a living wage on quickie divorces now direct *maquila* investors through the maze of Mexican law. Mexican entrepreneurs have learned that setting up a *maquila* for an Anglo client offers less risk than pushing a Mexican company, and it is much more profitable. One promoter who constructed five *maquilas* in Juárez boasted: "The reward has been seven digits, and I'm not talking pesos."[8]

His boastful self-assessment is a reminder that the Anglo is not the only one, to quote "Corky" Gonzales of Denver, "who can make money off anything."

For the Mexican government, the *maquilas* pose a seemingly insurmountable problem. Like the fleshpots and saloons of a half-century ago, they represent the sale of Mexican labor at a cheaper rate than it commands north of the border but at a higher price than it would receive in the interior. Mexico desperately wants to get control of its national economy, but an indebted Mexican government has, in the *maquilas,* a precious source of foreign exchange. The whore, the *narcotraficante,* the sa-loonkeeper, and the assemblers of televisions, toys, textiles, office machines, electronic instruments, and automobile engines have a common economic function—they bring in dollars. For the nationalistic *mexicano* who deplores the crassness of *norteño* culture, the *maquila* laborers, though engaged in morally acceptable work, do not represent the true *mexicano* of the interior cities. What they do, he contends, is the equivalent of taking in the gringo's dirty laundry. Mexicans tolerate the *maquilas* for reasons not dissimilar to their earlier acceptance of a sordid border culture. They believe they have no realistic choice, but they are not proud of the choices they have had to make to keep the border economies going.

Just as the migratory worker headed north represents the internationalization of labor, so, too, do the *maquilas* symbolize the international migration of capital. If the dollars that are sunk into the *maquilas* in Juárez, Tijuana, Tecate, or Nogales were withdrawn, they would reappear in Taiwan or Korea. Deprived of the dollar, the Mexicans *perhaps* could acquire the technology and make the tough economic (read *political*) decisions to place the emphasis on national economic development elsewhere. An astute observer of the program, Joseph Grunwald, noted some years ago that where the *maquilas* are concerned, the Mexicans want the best of all worlds. They rail against the foreign domination of the plants yet in the same breath argue that national capital should go into other enterprises. If the operations are crucial for the national economy, Mexico should strive to break down the barriers that prevent their full integration into the Mexican development scheme. Even if the industrial giants like the United States and Japan automate their assembly plants, there will remain numerous functions requiring the abundant labor Mexico can provide.[9]

So, as the American is always saying, "the bottom line is money." In the vigorous border cities the Mexican laborer in the *maquila* knows his worth, to the culture north of the border and to his own. He will always have less than the Anglo laborer on the other side; he will have more material possessions than he had back in Michoacán or Jalisco or even in Monterrey—but he somehow feels less Mexican. He reaffirms his nationalism in countless ways, fiestas and celebrations, yet his daily life is a reminder of the economic and political modernity just across the fence or on the other side of the Rio. His *compañeros* come from every section of Mexico and they bring the poverty, the despair, and the dream of a better world into Juárez and Tijuana and Nogales. And they camp on the threshold of the golden door and live in wretched housing and drink putrid water and send their diseased children into the streets to beg and to work and to fuck pigs if the gringo ''sanvabitches'' will pay to watch them. If the border were an endless stream of *maquiladoras* it would not change things all that much. Their countrymen would swell their ranks by even greater numbers, and the world on the other side, where everything from politics to education to religion is a business, operated by the dictates of ''sound business practices,'' and the cultural credo that ''you are what you do'' is a personal faith, would swallow their labor and ensure their economic survival but contribute little to their cultural sense of self-worth.

They wait and they dream of a world that will never be unless the golden door is opened.

3
Chicago Latino

Pilsen, a deteriorating neighborhood in southwest Chicago, was once a more prosperous community of eastern Europeans, mostly Czechs and Polish children of nineteenth-century immigrants who had flocked into the industrial midwest. Nowadays it is 80 percent Latino. Most of the residents are Mexican, and Pilsen has taken on the look of a barrio where Spanish has long since displaced Polish or Czech.

Waiting on Blue Island Avenue for a bus to take me back downtown, I struck up a conversation with an aging Pilsen woman whose forebears came from eastern Europe. She had lived her life here and remembered the old days when Cermak Avenue, Pilsen's main drag, had reverberated every Saturday night from the noise of the ethnic taverns. Most were gone. In their place were diminutive bars or hole-in-the-wall restaurants catering to Pilsen's newcomers. Everywhere, it seemed to me, they had left their distinctive mark, from the advertisements in Spanish on the market across the way and the sleazy bars with their *cerveza fría* (cold beer) signs to the murals adorning the wall of Benito Juárez High School and the sprayed-on "Avenida México" underneath "Blue Island" on the street signs.

Yet she did not resent the cultural pummeling the Latinos had given Pilsen. "They're probably illegals," she said, pointing to a brown-skinned man and woman waiting near the corner, "but they treat me okay. Besides, they want to work."

In a few remarks she had summed up the economic case for what students of immigration are calling the "fourth wave." Whatever cultural or political cost their presence meant for Pilsen was, to her, worth the price. (In her case, I surmised, there was a reassurance that the Mexican invasion of the past generation would keep Pilsen's color line from shifting too far into the black. She spoke bitterly of a terrifying incident on a bus coming from downtown—a gang of black thugs had forced the driver to pull off on a side street and robbed the working-class passengers. "These people," she said, referring to the Mexicans, "treat their elders with respect.")

Chicago prides itself as a city of ethnic neighborhoods, but the Polish spinster's accommodating spirit does not reflect what Mexicans (and other Latinos) have suffered there. The Mexicans were the first Spanish-speaking peoples to settle in Chicago, and their roots go back to World War I. They came to South Chicago, Back of the Yards, and the near west side. In 1916, they numbered a mere thousand; in 1930, lured up from the fields of south Texas to the stockyards of Kansas City and finally to the South Chicago steel mills or the Back of the Yard packing houses or the near west side railroad stations, they grew to twenty thousand. In these European enclaves they scattered, never dominating but managing to survive until, for some, the Depression brought deportation back to Mexico. In the 1960s a flurry of urban renewal shoved the last wave of them into the eastern European enclave of Pilsen.

Having lived in Texas or other midwestern cities before moving to Chicago, the Mexicans, it would seem, should have been able to adjust more readily than their countrymen who had just crossed over the border. Like their Polish and Irish neighbors they had encountered ethnic slurs and the inevitable discrimination in housing and public schools. Even the Catholic church, its leaders hostile to the anticlerical program of post-Revolutionary Mexico, shunned the Mexican newcomer.

In two respects, they encountered obstacles the European ethnics had been able to surmount. Their employment was less permanent and their legal status less certain. Lured to Chicago by the meatpackers and railroad magnates, the migrants were thrown into the perennial struggle between management and labor; they were employed as strikebreakers. The issues between employer and union resolved, the Mexicans found themselves jobless or relegated to menial tasks. The transition from permanent to temporary employee in the industrial heartland proved a swift and sobering experience. In an era when minimally skilled industrial laborers in the city could expect $200 a month, two-thirds of the Mexican workers received less than $100, a subsistence salary that in almost half the cases included the paltry income of their spouses.

What killed their dream was the economic collapse of the 1930s. Confronting municipal bankruptcy and public anger over expenditures, Chicago's city government and Illinois welfare agencies, with the collusion of U.S. immigration authorities, initiated a program of repatriation of Mexicans, aliens and citizens alike. Throughout MexAmerica, from Chicago and Detroit to Houston and Los Angeles, local officials, arguing that Mexicans were unnecessary charges on already burdened welfare rolls, overcrowded schools, and even the town jail, rounded them up and sent them south on special trains. Occasionally, a local Mexican consular officer interjected a mild protest, which might delay a few cases but rarely reversed a decision. Some, realizing their chances of survival on rapidly dwindling public relief rolls were slim, packed their meager belongings and departed voluntarily. In too many instances, sadly, American-born children of Mexican aliens, as entitled as any citizen to public relief, accompanied the dispossessed.[1]

World War II, even more than World War I, brought demands for Mexican labor to fill the ranks vacated by Americans dispatched to war. In the brief span of two years, fifteen thousand braceros, legal migrants from south of the border, joined by a lesser number of illegals, moved to Chicago. By the end of the forties their numbers had swelled beyond those of the twenties, bringing the Windy City's Mexican population to 24,000 in

1950. Yet the prosperity of the era largely bypassed them. Lagging behind the city's other ethnics in income though often surpassing their educational level, Chicago's Mexican Americans, according to a *Sun-Times* survey in 1953, boasted only seven nurses, five teachers, one lawyer, one dentist, and one cop. Already their school attendance was declining, a lamentable statistic that has prevailed amid an expanding Mexican American population in Chicago (and elsewhere) to the present.

With the Puerto Ricans, who began to migrate to Chicago in the postwar era, the Mexican Americans found themselves, as Chicago's economy became more sophisticated, dumped into an expanding pool of unskilled laborers. A small percentage were lucky enough to land jobs in the city's declining manufacturing plants, but most wound up as janitors, kitchen workers, or waiters, forced by circumstances into menial work that even the blacks were shunning.

The Puerto Ricans, because they came to the mainland as citizens and were thus more determined to defend their rights in a city dominated by non-Spanish ethnics, proved more aggressive in local politics than the Mexican Americans. They formed social organizations with the intention of helping newcomers to adjust to the strange milieu of Chicago. Thus, the *riqueños* and not the Mexican Americans were first to galvanize their splintered wards into a larger movement for political action. Their first significant group, the Caballeros, organized baseball teams and sponsored fiestas, the most spectacular of which was St. John's Day. By the mid-1960s St. John's Day had become the Puerto Rican Parade, an occasion for not only festive social celebration but speeches from political leaders from the island.

When in 1965 several of Mayor Richard Daley's finest took out their frustrations with nightsticks on two Puerto Ricans (whose only offense, it was alleged, was standing on a street-corner watching the police chase some children away from an open fire hydrant), the Puerto Rican organization publicly complained of general police insensitivity to all Spanish-speaking Chicagoans. The following year the cumulative anger of the *riqueños* (who, if thoroughly Americanized, are called "Co-colars") burst into the country's first major Puerto Rican riot, touched off when a policeman shot a twenty-one-year-old in West Town. For two days uncontrollable mobs of Puerto Ricans repelled police onslaughts and torched Anglo-owned businesses.

Despite their numbers—250,000 in 1970—the Latinos did not have much clout in Chicago politics. Undercounted in the metropolitan census, they had yet to penetrate in any significant way the technical and professional fields or do much better in the sales and clerical areas. Forty percent, classified as "operatives," formed a vast low-skilled work force. In the labyrinthine urban political bureaucracy the Latinos possessed in mid-decade exactly four slots out of the several hundred elected offices and less then 2 percent of the city's sizable work force.

Astute analysts have attributed this condition to several factors, which reveal a great deal about the peculiarities of Chicago politics and tell us something about the obstacles Hispanics face when they are a minority among other minorities. In the Chicago of the seventies they lived in wards at the beck and call of Chicago's powerful machine, which had expended most if its energies in accommodating European ethnics. What worried the moguls at city hall was Chicago's increasingly influential black middle class and its demands on an already bloated urban bureaucracy.[2]

Largely shut out of the city's political system, the Latino leaders joined the crusade for a union of the Spanish-speaking. Among a people who may be more conscious of being, let us say, Cuban or Puerto Rican or Mexican than Hispanic or Latin (which are generic terms), a movement aimed at mobilizing the dispossessed and alienated on linguistic ties can be risky. But Chicago's Latinos—the word has as much political as cultural connotation—have learned to exploit the Spanish language. They use it the way blacks extolled color as a unifying force in the 1960s. As one explained, "We are experiencing that we are not only Mexicans, Puerto Ricans, Cubans but also Latinos. I feel pity for those leaders [who say] we must fight and struggle for the rights of the

Puerto Ricans, the Mexicans, or the Cubans separately. . . . They do not understand Latinismo. They do not know that we have basically the same culture and needs. And the only way to alleviate those problems and gain political respect is to work as one group."[3]

The "cooperative spirit," of course, runs throughout the American creed, commonly expressed as "what makes this country great," "let's all pull together," or, as Lyndon Johnson, citing Scripture, often said, "Come, let us reason together." But in the political realm, the spiritual (or in this case, the cultural) bonds degenerate into such realities as "you vote for a dam in my district and I'll vote for one in yours." In traditional Chicago politics the voting turnout of ethnics means a great deal more than numbers of ethnics. The Latinos in Chicago and elsewhere in America are not going to get what they deserve from the system by promoting only cultural bonds—they have to get out the votes and they must make their votes count.

Here is where Chicago's Latinos have lost ground to blacks. In the early eighties, Latinos had half a million residents in Chicago, 75,000 of them registered voters, yet did not have even one alderman on the powerful city council. The Latinos were scattered among the ethnic communities in nineteen wards— Puerto Ricans in Uptown, Lakeview, Lincoln Park, the near north side, Logan Square, Humboldt Park, West Town; Mexicans in the near west side, South Lawndale, Pilsen, South Chicago, South Dearborn, and Back of the Yards. Still, their economic conditions might have provided a common cause with Chicago's rapidly expanding black population. Like the black migrants from the south, they wound up in the lowest-paying jobs, received few social services, and benefited only marginally from the public education systems. But, unlike Chicago's blacks, the Latinos scattered throughout the city, dominating in numbers in only a few of Chicago's seventy-six communities, areas which tend to be socially homogeneous and have neighborhood organizations.

But Chicago's social service districts and, especially, its fifty political divisions follow very different boundaries. In one hotly contested race for aldermen in the neighborhood around the steel mills, the Mexican community organizers so frightened the politicians downtown that they redistricted the area, effectively dividing the Mexican vote. In two other wards, where the Latino vote escalated rapidly in the 1970s, the well-entrenched Italian politicians expressed little concern because, reputedly, they had "connections" downtown and the Latinos remained a minority in the ward.

As much abused by the system as the Latinos, Chicago's blacks, because they are not as scattered, have begun to reap political rewards. Rigid segregation of housing in Chicago, which Martin Luther King, Jr., condemned in the late sixties, ironically benefited blacks politically in the following years. Unlike the Latinos, who might predominate in neighborhoods, the blacks could control entire wards, just a few but enough to provide a political base the power brokers downtown could not ignore.[4]

In 1983, when Harold Washington first ran for mayor, race became the predominant issue in the campaign, as crucial as old-line Democratic political loyalties to the machine. For the first time in the city's stormy political history, the Latino vote, generally taken for granted because it had historically voted the Democratic ticket, loomed more important in the calculations of the fierce combatants for the Democratic nomination. Jane Byrne, then rapidly undergoing her transformation from the "old Jane" political tigress to the "new Jane," assiduously cultivated Hispanics. She represented the machine, and they had always voted for it. Anticipating Washington's strategy of promoting a black/brown coalition on common economic issues, she began appearing at Hispanic rallies with *her* Hispanic appointees, a reminder of the "doors now opened to them down at city hall." Washington, she told them, would favor blacks on the city payroll, and her Spanish-speaking assistant reminded Chicago's Latinos about their troubles with the Department of Human Services. "We can go [there] . . . and we will see how dark that department is. Can you imagine how it would be with a mayor with a face of that color?''

In the primary, a three-way race between Washington, Byrne, and Richard Daley, Jr., Washington fared poorly among both Puerto Ricans and Mexicans. But again, as in previous political struggles, the Latino voter turnout was less than 25 percent. Even in the general election, where race was a dominating issue and Washington's skillful mobilizing of the black vote provoked a large number of ethnic Catholics, traditionally Democratic, to cast their ballots for a wealthy Lake Shore Jewish Republican, Bernard Upton, the Hispanic turnout was again only 25 percent. Up against someone who had little to offer Chicago's Spanish-speaking, of course, Washington won their approval. But for the architects of a black/brown coalition _against_ the machine his margin of victory in the Mexican wards was uncomfortably narrow. His victory was essentially a black triumph, with an unenthusiastic Latino support, over the machine.

Why not a black/brown, or, as the Rev. Jesse Jackson urges, a Rainbow Coalition of the urban dispossessed?

I posed this seemingly logical alliance to virtually everyone I spoke with, citing the dismal statistics in employment, housing, and education that afflict both. In response each pointed to barriers that have proved difficult to surmount. Asked about an alliance a decade ago, a California Hispanic leader conceded there existed an ''unannounced coalition'' but Hispanics retained their bitterness over favoritism to blacks in federal programs. Among others he blamed the Jews for helping blacks but not chicanos.[5]

But what suffered in the 1984 election campaign was Jesse Jackson's Rainbow Coalition and its publicized goal of uniting blacks with other minorities, including Hispanics. Early in the year the Senate Labor and Human Resources Committee, chaired by Republican senator Orrin Hatch of Utah, listened to a parade of Hispanic spokesmen complain of discrimination by the Equal Employment Opportunity Commission. For years, said Hatch, ''there has been a perception on behalf of some minority groups that the EEOC has primarily assisted the black community and done little if anything to serve other minorities.'' In the course of the hearings Hatch alluded frequently to a controversial study, based on EEOC records and 125 witnesses in hearings in six cities (Chicago, Los Angeles, New York, Miami, San Antonio, and Denver), which chastised the agency for its sometimes casual approach and occasional indifference to Hispanic complaints. Staff attorneys had developed the habit of dismissing too many Hispanic cases in order to concentrate on charges brought by blacks. The agency itself, several witnesses argued, violated its own credos by discriminating against Hispanics for high-level positions.

Publicly, of course, the Hispanics voicing their protest against EEOC reaffirmed their commitment to its purpose and denied any resentment about the benefits blacks had received. But the impact on Jackson's campaign for unity among minorities was noticeable. Old Hispanic anger about Democratic favoritism to blacks at the expense of other minorities resurfaced. Jackson's hortatory call for his Rainbow Coalition rang hollow among Hispanic activists. ''The blacks have always used us in these coalitions,'' said one Hispanic businessman in Detroit, ''then they get the jobs and screw us.''[6] It was not a universal sentiment, and Jackson's offices countered with their own broadsides about Republican tactics in trying to divide the colors of the Rainbow Coalition. But the report, and more important the publicity it received among Hispanics, revealed something more than Hispanic anger over the indifference of a federal agency or its alleged favoritism toward blacks. It showed the complexity of the Hispanic American political ambience and the difficulty even other minorities with similar complaints of social injustice have in penetrating it. The Mexican American in neighborhoods like Pilsen requires more of a leader than merely the dynamic presence of an orator who continually reminds him that he is ''somebody.''

If the California Hispanic visited the Chicago of today he would discover an emerging alliance, not of black and brown, but of Jew and Latin. In Pilsen the Mexican Americans who are packed into dilapidated housing take their chances on a local

"lottery" sponsored by the 18th Street Development Corporation. The lottery has a lengthy waiting list but winning it can
mean a move from a rat-infested tenement to a refurbished
apartment on the next block. The financier of the corporation is
the Jewish Council for Urban Affairs. From the early seventies it
has been subsidizing the rehabilitation of Pilsen, but only in
recent years has the link become publicized. It has ramifications
even in foreign affairs. Before Reagan headed out for Geneva to
meet with Gorbachev, the Hispanic Congressional Caucus urged
him to press the issue of Jewish emigration from the Soviet Union
and criticized his visit to a West German cemetery because it
contains the graves of former Nazi Waffen SS.

In Chicago the Hispanic-Jewish alliance is rapidly advancing
because Jewish enthusiasm for black causes has withered. There
are hardliners in both camps, the Jews who point to Jesse
Jackson's sympathetic comments on the PLO and the perceived
anti-Semitism of black leaders, and the black leaders who decry
Jewish paternalism and, more pointedly, blame Jewish landlords
and merchants for selling out their tenements and shops in the
ghetto to the Arabs. A disconcerting statistic of the black/Jewish
antagonism is that among blacks anti-Semitism _increases_ with
education.

Increasingly alienated from blacks—mostly from a sense of
betrayal after having supported black demands for social justice—
Jews quickly realized the potential of an Hispanic alliance. The
urban domain of most American Jews, a half-dozen cities,
became in the early 1980s the homeland of the country's rapidly
expanding Hispanic minority. Among the new arrivals Jewish
organizations found deserving recipients for local social programs, people who might speak a different language but who
exhibited little interest in Middle East politics and who, like the
Jews, understand the importance of alliances. Even on the touchy
issue of immigration reform, their instinctive belief in fairness
and the benefits of a more democratic society has swung Jewish
leaders away from an early advocacy of tough policies to more
lenient ones.

The Hispanic-Jewish union may be social politics but, so far, it has been beneficial for both groups. Since the Pilsen redevelopment project the Jewish Council for Urban Affairs has worked for Latino causes in other neighborhoods. In Humboldt Park it encouraged Latinos to demand more Spanish-speaking postal employees. Jewish organizers worked for an affirmative action program that opened slots for Latinos in the post offices in Humboldt Park and, at the same time, pacified blacks who sensed a threat to their employment. The momentary understanding eventually led to the creation of Blacks and Latinos in Action and the Black-Latino Alliance for Political Progress. In the process Chicago's Latinos, apprehensive over the naming of a black school superintendent for fear he might reduce remedial studies programs, came around to his support.

But the black/Latino bond in Chicago is at best tenuous and is not likely to displace the emerging Jewish/Latino alliance. In Pilsen the Latinos have witnessed what determined Jewish efforts can accomplish—protesting the expansion of the University of Illinois, Chicago, as well as the bulldozing of older buildings to make way for upper-middle-class housing, and relentlessly politicking against the 1992 World's Fair, which would have meant even further intrusion into Pilsen's fragile environment. There the Jews promote self-help programs and community pride, a reaffirmation of the Jewish commitment in the Mexican community. Among blacks there remains deep resentment of Jewish paternalism, which, to them, symbolizes white society's meager reparation for generations of oppression and neglect. Jewish leaders—even some who speak bitterly of the black-Jewish alienation—concede that the Jewish-Hispanic coalition may be working because there is a shared immigrant experience and no unpleasant history of neighborhood confrontation. There exists a commitment to family in private life and go-getter enthusiasm in business that Jews and Hispanics readily attribute to each other but only begrudgingly concede to blacks.

Above all, the Jews have discovered an opportunity to fulfill the Hebrew invocation *tikkun olam,* ''fix the world,'' from fixing up Pilsen's tenements to harboring Central American refugees. Two aging Jews who endured the Holocaust succinctly expressed the newfound sentiment after viewing the film *El Norte,* about two teenagers who flee the political terror of Guatemala and make their way into L.A.'s underground of dingy rooms and sweatshops. "It was just exactly what happened to us," one said after watching the movie. "After the hell they've gone through, these people are just like Jews."[7]

Pilsen is a community, but its Hispanic character has created in Chicago a variation on the city's traditional politics. Here, as in other Hispanic islands of MexAmerica, the Spanish-speaking have fused their cultural values and political expectations in such a manner as to confuse the outsider. Ruth Horowitz, a sociologist, lived among them and wrote of her experience in *Honor and the American Dream.* Outsiders, she discovered, portrayed Pilsen as a crime-ridden, decaying urban blight where tattooed young chicanos (and chicanas) freely roamed and menaced civilized society. Political leaders and private developers generally agreed that its closeness to a medical complex and the University of Illinois at Chicago campus warranted the razing of dilapidated buildings and the construction of attractive high rises to house the returning inner-city professionals. Only a vigorous protest movement prompted the developers to give serious consideration to the plight of those who would have been dislocated. But even this attention, wrote Horowitz, brought little change in the condition of life in the area and merely validated the sense of powerlessness that pervaded Pilsen.

Because it has become the domain of the uneducated (only twenty percent of its residents over twenty-five are high school graduates and the dropout rate is a staggering 70 percent) and, increasingly, the illegal migrant from Mexico, Pilsen has acquired the reputation as a dismal slum. But those who live there still retain their aspirations for a better life; they are simply unwilling to accept the verdict of the outside about what kind of life they deserve. In the past they became exasperated with the declining quality of the public schools and resentful of the school board's emphasis on special education, a euphemistic term for programs directed at the "educationally and mentally handicapped." Parents formed protest organizations or scraped up enough money to send their children to parochial schools. Their intent was not only to obtain a better education, providing an outlet into the professional world for their sons, but to do so in an environment where both sexes could acquire greater respect for traditional familial values. Yet those who achieve these expectations and acquire status in the outside world cannot readily adjust to an Anglo society because their cultural heritage is different, nor can they easily fit back into the old network of friends. Only the family, hallowed for its strength and perseverance, and for Hispanics more reliable as a supportive institution than corporation or even government, retains their deepest loyalty.[8]

The Jewish couple who were moved by El Norte and the plight of Central American refugees in the States may have learned what Hispanics call *simpático*, a feeling of empathy. But theirs is an old-world experience. At the Lake Shore campus of Loyola University, I encountered a different kind of *simpático*, this time from another historian, Luisa Año Nuevo de Kerr (who is known among the faculty at the University of Illinois, Chicago, where she received a doctorate in history with a dissertation on the chicano in Chicago, as Louise Kerr). A California native, she spoke bitterly about working in the fields as a young woman and suffering the harassment of INS (Immigration and Naturalization Service) officers who doubted her U.S. citizenship because of her Hispanic name and brown skin color.[9]

Like most Californians of Mexican heritage, she prefers the term "chicano" to "Mexican American," which some sensitive observers, remembering the pre–world war prejudice against hyphenates, insist should be written without the hyphen. But, given the political realities of Chicago's Hispanic cultural makeup, which includes representatives from *every* Spanish-speaking country, she employs "Latino." Like some other chicanas I encountered, she has passed into the American mainstream, living not in Pilsen but in the more sedate neighborhood of Evanston. Her choice is understandable, given her remarkable rise from the California orchards into academia.

On virtually every issue about MexAmerica she reveals in her responses the complexity of the Mexican American experience, an early illustration of the *diversity* of its values. One issue we touched on was bilingual education. It hasn't really been tried, she believes, and in Chicago there is a woeful lack of Spanish-speaking teachers. Besides, she said, the United States is ashamed of having a bilingual society. (We did not pursue this, though the subject of bilingual education, or bilingualism, has become a volatile issue not only in education but in immigration law and local government.) She is a blend of traditional Hispanic values and more radical notions, proudly displaying a family portrait on her desk and uttering standard (and trite) radical chicano comments about the Mexican-U.S. relationship as "all give [on Mexico's part] and all take by the Americans." The real fear among the Anglos is Hispanic *political* strength, the unarticulated apprehension of an emerging minority's power in half a dozen states.

"You've got to educate the Polish American in ethnic Chicago," she said, a bit hesitantly, "that the U.S. and Mexico have a special relationship." Later I regretted she was not with me to meet the *simpática* eastern European at the bus stop.

In Pilsen and the nearby Hispanic-dominated wards of Little Village and Humboldt Park the old ethnic politics of Italians, Poles, Croatians, and Irish has given way to a new political order. It has not yet achieved a base as formidable as that of Harold Washington, but its strategists are rapidly learning what must be done to survive in Chicago politics. In Pilsen, they gather at pool halls and talk about Richard Daley's rise to power on the foundation of the Hamburg Club. The Mexicans and Puerto Ricans, they believe, can transform their network of social relationships, in every respect as intricate as Daley's, into a political force. Manuel Velázquez, owner of Pilsen's best-known pool hall, migrated from Mexico and went to work at International Harvester. He established Manny's in 1956 as a gathering place for local Mexican laborers who were shut out of the ethnic watering holes of Pilsen. His son, Juan, who has political ambitions, remembers the old days when Manny's served as "social service agency" for Mexicans with problems no alderman could, or would, do anything to correct.

In early 1986, Velázquez and the other Hispanic political aspirants of the area, benefiting from a court-mandated restructuring of seven Chicago wards, sensed triumph for the Hispanic cause. In Little Village, where a generation ago the Mexican Americans began pushing for recognition against an intractable alliance of eastern and southern Europeans, the incumbent, Frank Stemberk, recognizing the political wind shift, dropped out of the race. In Pilsen, the newcomers believed they now had a chance to dismantle the craftily structured political machine of Vito Marzullo, who for years had locked out the Mexicans from the inner domain of ward politics.

But in these and other races in which Chicago's Hispanics aspired to rapid political victory, they discovered that the old order, when attacked, can effectively resist. In Little Village, the retiring alderman threw his support behind a shoe-store proprietor/grocer, and in a short time the Hispanic trio vying for his seat on the city council had turned into a Latin version of predictably combative Chicago politics. Before long the contending Hispanics in Little Village and Pilsen were hurling charges at each other of disloyalty to Latino values while Chicago's power brokers pursued a strategy of divide and conquer. One of the rising political stars of Pilsen, Juan Soliz, threw in with Edward Vrdolyak, the symbol of ethnic politics in Chicago and Harold Washington's archenemy on the city council.

The new Hispanic faces in the Chicago political arena have thus far proved themselves calculating but not firmly committed to either faction or, quite frankly, even to Hispanic unity. But the vision of an Hispanic bloc remains. Soliz, distrusted and probably envied by the other Hispanic aldermen, talks of a Chicago Hispanic coalition and a caucus on the city council that will be able to reap benefits for Chicago's Hispanics because they now hold the balance of power. The old urban political order, alert to the potentiality of a Latino balance of power, calculates not only the size of the vote—7 percent of the electorate—but what issues and, more crucially, what _style_ Chicago's Latinos demand in their politics. Symbolism, apparently, has become the key the old-timers have selected to decipher the Latino voter.[10] In the bitter mayoralty race of 1987, both Washington and Jane Byrne publicized their commitments to the Latinos in a manner that offered more style than substance. In the primary the Latinos preferred Washington, who was re-elected

But symbolic gestures may not be enough to satisfy the rising generation of Chicago's politically minded Latinos. In Pilsen, Little Village, and the other Latino wards there is a heightened sense of having moved beyond "brown power" rhetoric and slogans to demanding that city government and its functionaries, whatever their color, come through with some real, substantial benefits and concessions. With their numbers and their votes, Chicago's Latinos have at last gotten the attention of those who rule. And they have begun to pursue results with a determination and persistence that show they are prepared to join the political battles down at city hall.

4

"I'm Just as White as You"

That Hispanics have a problem about the image they want to project to Anglos is beyond serious debate. How to deal with it is another matter, especially for Mexican Americans, who recognize that language, even more than color and proximity to the country of their heritage, offers temptations to identify too closely with another country. Like the turn-of-the-century hyphenates whose loyalty to the United States was suspect, they have responded in different ways to the sometimes relentless scrutiny of the Anglo-Saxon (and the European ethnics). Some Anglicized their names, others drifted into the chicano equivalent of the black power movement, insisting not only on the glorification of chicano culture but in a few instances on the creation of separate diminutive but self-ruling societies. They sang and wrote about Aztlán, the mythical northern kingdom in the southwest centuries before the rapacious gringos absorbed the land. Still others became, more out of conviction than self-preservation, I would argue, thoroughly American. But just as the typical American will always argue there is no typical American, so the Spanish-speaking in this country dispute characterizations of a typical Hispanic. On this point they echo Representative Henry González of San Antonio, the Hispanic American Democratic patriarch, who insists on the diversity of Hispanic America.

I expected to encounter bitter Mexican Americans decrying the unfairness of everything from television images (Ricardo Montalban conducted a small crusade against the Frito Bandido, then, when he was successful, gloomily observed he had driven a _compañero_ off the screen) to occasionally intense debate over bilingual education and its merits. I did not expect to meet many Mexican Americans who disliked the word "chicano," could out-Reagan Reagan on everything from welfare to getting tough with the Sandinistas, or whose vision of the good life derived more from the wholesome images on _Leave It to Beaver_ than from the combative rhetoric of chicano radicals. By the time I got to Puerto Vallarta and a session with a couple of _mexicanos_ who believed Senator Jesse Helms spoke an unarguable truth in his condemnations of Mexican political corruption, I was a caricature of the proverbial ivory-tower academic who has fallen into the "real world."

If there exists a word to describe the Hispanic American in the midwest it is "permanency" or perhaps "determination." Iowa, a state with few Spanish-speaking a generation ago, proudly records the arrival of the first permanent Hispanic settler before the Civil War. A few counties memorialized the country's victories in the Mexican-American War by changing their names to Buena Vista or Cerro Gordo. In the 1890s Mexicans moved up from Texas to work on farms or for the Sante Fe Railroad and established the state's first Mexican community at Fort Madison.[1]

Even with their early successes in the 1920s the Mexicans in Iowa might have suffered the fate of most migrants in the Depression—massive deportation from Chicago, Detroit, Kansas City, and other cities, dumped into a Mexico scarcely able to care for them. Those who survived the economic downturn found an unexpected rehabilitation in World War II and its demands for manpower. A railroad laborer in Grinnell with seven children, fired in the early thirties, became a farmhand. His children might have followed him into the fields had the U.S. government not constructed an ordnance facility that absorbed six of them. None ever returned to farm labor.

Here, as elsewhere, the Hispanics talk about opportunity and complain of the nagging persistence of discrimination, more

63

subtle than in the old days but still pervasive in their lives. They occupy too few professional positions, say the leaders of LULAC, the League of United Latin American Citizens—four Hispanic lawyers in the state in 1975, only one more a decade later. Slowly the barriers to social mobility are crumbling. In Des Moines, where Hispanics were once confined to segregated housing, they are now moving into formerly restricted areas. "Money whitens," a Brazilian proverb, is a not uncommon cynical refrain among Iowa Hispanics. The civil rights legislation of the 1960s, which unarguably benefited blacks more than Hispanics, as they are constantly saying, did make a difference for them in the state.

Now they have community organizations, cable television (which transmits SIN, the Spanish network), the *mestizo* dancers of Des Moines, and heavy enrollments in Spanish language classes throughout the state's public school system. "Language is culture" has become a motto encompassing everything from ethnic pride to Hispanic efforts in promoting Iowa products in the Latin American market. The state trades with every mainland country in Latin America except Nicaragua, and two hundred of its companies deal with Mexico, yet only reluctantly are Iowa businesses providing translators for visiting entrepreneurs who speak only Spanish or Portuguese.

As their numbers grow here in the cornbelt—26,279, according to the 1980 census—Hispanics fret over the dilemma wrought by moving into the Anglo mainstream. No longer confined to segregated housing, moving out of the fields and into the factories and small businesses, the second- or third-generation Hispanic in the heartland glories in the opportunity to enter the middle class but is troubled that his children cannot speak Spanish and know little of their heritage.

In Kansas City I encountered yet another variation of the midwestern Hispanic American—antichicano and feminist. Catherine Rocha, as director of records in the Jackson County, Missouri, Courthouse, is the highest-ranking appointed Mexican American in Kansas City, which is geographically and culturally the center of the American heartland. We spoke above the chatter of daily business penetrating her office door. On the desk were piles of records, copies of real estate documents, and the like.[2]

Given her youthful vigor and attractiveness, I was incredulous when she told me of her three grown children, two away at college. There seemed little of the presumably typical matronly Hispanic woman, save for a few reminders about the centrality of the family in her life. Her husband is the first Hispanic judge in Kansas City, so the entire clan had obviously latched onto the American mainstream. With her traditional values coupled with a noticeable strain of feminism, Catherine Rocha struck me as a cross between Phyllis Schlafley and Gloria Steinem, an improbable and potentially explosive combination.

For one thing she cares little for the term "chicano," which becomes standard terminology once you hit the southwest, where more radical Mexican Americans launched the movement of *la raza*. "I prefer Mexican American," she said rather bluntly, not telling me if retaining the hyphen indicated ethnic insensitivity. César Chávez, the militant organizer of the Delano, California, grape boycott of the late sixties, had appeared in Kansas City a year or so before and had received (to her obvious satisfaction) a lukewarm reception.

Kansas City has a small Hispanic community—blacks are thought of as *the* minority—but hereabouts in the middle-class heartland they avidly pursue the American dream. "Equality of opportunity" is a phrase the upwardly bound Mexican American uses unhesitatingly. But, as in Chicago, cultural pride, which often stems as much from country of origin as language, has had to accommodate political reality. "We got here first," she said, referring to the Mexican migration into the midwest, but in the Hispanic Chamber of Commerce the Mexican Americans have brought in the Cubans and Puerto Ricans "because it gives us strength."

When I raised the issue of minority politics and equality of opportunity I obviously struck a raw nerve. Like most ambitious middle-class Mexican Americans, Catherine Rocha has some rueful memories of other days, especially the early 1960s, when the Hispanic vote went solidly for Democrats. In Texas it probably guaranteed Kennedy's victory. But when the big federal programs began rolling out from Democratic-controlled Washington, she reminded me, the blacks got most of the largess—not just civil rights, which they deserved, but here in Kansas City they pocketed most of the money filtering into small business and community redevelopment.

Very few of her views, it seemed to me, varied much from those of a staunchly Republican small-town Kansan. With her (and surprisingly large numbers of middle-class Hispanics) the Republican presidents after LBJ rate highly—even Nixon merits a few kind words—because they alertly responded to latent Hispanic resentment by channeling more federal money to the small but rapidly growing Hispanic business community. Black leaders argue, of course, that the Republicans gave the support to Hispanics because they wanted to punish an overwhelmingly Democratic black constituency. (Some readers may recall Dick Gregory's quip in the 1964 campaign: "I know the blacks for Goldwater, and they're both nice guys.")

Her chosen candidate is Henry Cisneros, the nationally known mayor of San Antonio. The reason lies only partly in their cultural bond. Language and skin color often provide strong links in the political world, but for her and other Hispanics Cisneros is an appealing candidate not so much because he is another Hispanic political hopeful but because he has managed to cultivate the all-American image and still retain his cultural identity. "He's educated and not an embarrassment for us," she said proudly. I sensed that she believes her own career in some respects paralleled Cisneros' and that Hispanics have been ignored because they didn't fit any stereotype of the "typical" Hispanic. "I grew up in a Mexican neighborhood. I come from the same background, but I have aspirations." Then with a reminder that education is vital for fulfilling the (Hispanic-and-all-other-ethnic-categories) American dream, she said, a bit haughtily, "I'm just as white as you."

She shares a conviction of "equality of opportunity" with another Kansas City Mexican American, Hector Barreto, a founder and former head of the U.S. Hispanic American Chamber of Commerce.[3] Over the years the chamber has quietly expanded across the country, promoting the interests of Hispanic-owned business. Barreto was not born American but represents that go-getter enthusiasm in business Americans are fond of attributing to themselves but persist in denying to the Mexican. Back in Guadalajara, he plunged into the cattle business at age sixteen. By twenty-one he was broke, but in the financial disaster had learned the proverbial economic lesson that keeping money is a great deal more difficult than making it. That persistent Hispanic trait of pride meant he couldn't stay in Mexico and embarrass his *familia,* so he headed north, believing, as many Mexicans still do, that the American economy generates endless wealth and unparalleled opportunity. His first job was grubbing for potatoes. No *campesino* (farm worker) accustomed to the backbreaking work of the fields (as were my fellow cotton pickers in the Panhandle), he stayed at it only to get enough money to go into something else—and because he could not return home a failure. Then, following the migratory trail deep into the heartland, the Mexican variation of the cattle drive of the nineteenth century, he hired on as a railroader, driving spikes, and from there moved to toting two-hundred-pound slabs of meat from packing houses into boxcars.

He wound up a restaurateur; he knew nothing of haute cuisine or, frankly, how to cook hamburgers. But the tacos he carried in his lunch pail fascinated the tough Yankees he worked with, so he opened a taco stand to satisfy the presumably endless demand of two thousand packing-house laborers for what must have been for them an exotic dish. When the packing house closed, his customers vanished. Barreto got a job as a janitor and, on the side, started another restaurant, turning it into a family affair. A few years later he had $5,000 in the bank and connections with another businessman who imported from Mexico. Barreto began selling the distinctive Mexican tile to shopping centers across the country. Kansas City newspapers began to print stories about "potato picker makes good."

But his success—and that of other Hispanics in business—did little to alter the American image of the Spanish-speaking. Though there already existed Hispanic chambers of commerce in San Antonio and Miami and elsewhere, they had done little more than promote local Hispanic causes or sponsor traditional Mexican celebrations like the Cinco de Mayo, which commemorates the famous Mexican victory over an invading French army in 1862. Media scenes of indolent *campesinos* propped up against a cactus sleeping away the afternoon so infuriated Barreto he was determined to change things.

In 1979 at a White House Conference on Small Business he discovered another barrier—blacks had twice the number of delegates as the Hispanics. Few wanted to join forces because, as Barreto learned, the Hispanics had too little to offer. More bluntly, the black delegates made it clear their goal was the promotion of *black* minority business. Through this experience Barreto realized the agenda Hispanic entrepreneurs had to chart if they were to enter the mainstream of American business. With a blistering denunciation of the unfairness of government toward Hispanic business, which he attributed mostly to Hispanics' failures to organize and use their economic clout, he transformed the U.S. Hispanic Chamber of Commerce into a truly national pressure group. After that he began meeting with hemispheric leaders. He had joined that proverbial American elite known as "movers and shakers." In a more meaningful way (at least for Barreto) he had fought his way into the American middle class.

In the past decade or so the social science literature dealing with Mexican Americans and other Hispanics has begun to address the question: what is a middle-class Hispanic and what does he stand for? It is not a simple question, because for Hispanics, more so than for blacks, crossing that economic line dividing the working from the middle class can often demand rejection of one's cultural heritage or ethnic identity.[4] Those academics continually befuddled by the twin forces playing on the Hispanic American conscience—the one a determination to "make it" in WASP society, the other a desire to preserve one's cultural heritage, which may mean staying in the barrio or taking a firmer stand for, or even against, bilingualism—are often guilt-ridden products of a privileged social class.

Mexican Americans like Catherine Rocha, who was born an American citizen, and Hector Barreto, who became one through naturalization, know about the pitfalls confronting the Hispanic middle class without, as blacks used to say, "wise white guidance." Middle-class Hispanics are greater believers in those vaunted American values of education, hard work, persistence, and, above all, equality of opportunity than the most devoted WASP. But the middle-class Mexican American often feels a suppressed need to show he is 110 percent American. Much like the southerner of an earlier era who boasted his loyalty to the country in one breath and his affection for "Dixie" in the second, the middle-class Hispanic American, especially those of Mexican heritage, often laud solid middle-class values yet speak fondly of *la cultura* or the barrio. These seemingly contradictory worlds pose less a dilemma for them than for their mainstream American observers who persist in believing that the middle class constitutes a culture.

Still, even those Mexican Americans who long ago were absorbed into the mainstream have a few lingering doubts about their acceptance by the Anglos. The successful government official speaks of being "just as white as you," the high-powered businessman of the need to organize Hispanic entrepreneurs. On the placid campus of the University of California, Riverside, I found the middle-class chicano academic Carlos Cortés, who reminded me that "chicano" was preferable to "Mexican American" (with or without the hyphen) and that his name carried an accent.[5] A scholar—among other works he has written of the chicano image in American film—he personifies that not insignificant chicano academic elite who are continually torn between the demands of scholarly discipline and chicano politics in the United States. It is an uncertain and sometimes frustrating route the chicano academic must follow: if you stray too far from the strictures of academia you betray the scholar's oath to the truth, but if you cannot satisfy the occasionally volatile demands of a politicized chicano student constituency then you have sold out to the establishment.

Cortés belongs in this assessment of the Mexican American heartland for at least two reasons. He was born the son of a Mexican father and a Jewish mother. And he grew up in the small but not insignificant *mexicano* world of Kansas City. His life has genealogical roots that go back to Mexican elitist *políticos* who served both the Emperor Maximilian, that well-intentioned but naive Austrian who ruled the country in the mid-1860s, and Maximilian's Mexican enemies, the Liberals, who ruled Mexico after he was executed.

Cortés is thoroughly American yet in no sense embarrassed by his Mexican cultural roots. He embodies the complexities and diversity of the chicano middle class, combining its belief in education and opportunity with a sometimes fervent reaffirmation of his Mexican heritage. Growing up in K.C. he experienced little prejudice because his father was Mexican but suffered taunts because he lived in a family that was half Catholic, half Jewish. Light-skinned, he never "looked Mexican," but the religious slurs persisted until he left the midwest for the more tolerant climate of Berkeley (where his parents had been educated).

The Hispanic familial links, a father insistent upon the child's remembering his Mexican background yet requiring English at the dinner table, and a well-educated mother have produced in Cortés that admirable and often misunderstood chicano middle-class American. After a few minutes I vaguely sensed his frustration when trying to explain to another academic why chicanos (and other Hispanic Americans) cannot get across to WASP America (or even Black America) certain truths about being brown in a white/black world. Bilingual education, for example, is especially an irritant. The Anglos are divided on its merits, some arguing immersion in English in grade one and beyond as fundamental to an English-speaking society; others, just as persuasive, say that, given the increasing numbers of Spanish-speaking children, the public schools must provide a transition by offering courses in Spanish, especially in the critical early grades.

For Cortés (and numerous other Hispanic Americans) bilingual education constitutes little threat to "Americanism" but is, put simply, a way station on the road to learning English. Just as universities discovered in the 1960s that few blacks enrolled in black history or black literature, so in the 1980s chicanos like Cortés are trying to explain that Mexican immigrants don't need bilingualism to express their "Mexicanness." Bilingual education, he reminded me, has much pedagogical value but does little (nor can do much) to reinforce the Spanish-speaking students' *cultural* pride. Schools go wrong, he continued, when they try to Americanize by denigrating minority culture. Early-twentieth-century Anglo-Saxon America, alarmed over the wave of southern and eastern European immigrants, employed matronly teachers who browbeat the Polish and Italian urchins at their mercy in the public schools. Throughout he emphasized what to him was the *real* America, a multicultural society.

Eventually our conversation drifted into a discussion of California, its kaleidoscopic culture and its infuriatingly complex politics. Toward the end he spoke of East Los Angeles as "another country" and about the rapidly escalating numbers of Central American and Mexican refugees in Los Angeles County. His hesitancy in evaluating what these changes meant revealed, I believe, an inner uncertainty about the future of California, and of America, that often unarticulated fear of the American mainstream—white, brown, or black—that the country may not be able to accommodate such rapid changes.

Like their *mexicano* counterparts in MexAmerica South, middle-class Mexican Americans have what talk-show psychologists call an identity crisis. They are quintessential Americans thrust into a battle not of their making but in which they are participants, willingly or unwillingly. Just as the middle-class American of a century ago felt compelled to identify with the values and mores of the prevailing social order because it assured stability even if it did not always exhibit the proper moral behavior, so, too, have middle-class Hispanics had to choose between the chicano assault on traditional America and its defenders. But for them the decision can mean more than pulling a Democratic or Republican lever in the election booth. It can involve everything from questioning one's self-worth and place in society to one's faith or even such casual matters as how one pronounces (or spells) his name. The number of Mexican Americans who have changed their names from Carlos to Charles and back to Carlos is sizable.

Blacks will argue that they went through a similar cultural deprogramming and that what middle-class Hispanic Americans have experienced is roughly akin to what middle-class Negroes confronted in the sixties. There is, admittedly, much validity in the comparison, Hispanics often respond, but at least blacks do not have to accommodate a culture next door that reaches northward and affects Hispanic America's self-estimation. Blacks may be defiant separatists or eager participants in American life and feel no sense of cultural betrayal. Mexican Americans did not come here as slaves (though some have labored at slave wages) and have not been ground under so harshly by the American political and economic system. They have confronted in the chicano movement a challenge to their Americanness. The chicanos forced the Mexican Americans to glorify the Mexican and not the American in them. For some middle-class Mexican Americans, who had grown up believing—and rightly so—they were 100 percent American though they happened to be of Mexican instead of, let us say, Polish or Italian ancestry, the challenge of sometimes abusive young brown berets demanding everything from ethnic studies to the restoration of lands illegally seized by the gringos in their war against the "bronze race" has been a psychic shock. Blacks who migrated into the middle class, it can be argued, may have had to accommodate white America's middle-class social codes but they have not had to reject their cultural origins, feel ashamed about knowing Spanish because to Anglo-America it is a foreign tongue, or disdain the festivity of barrio life that emanates from religious holidays because to middle-class Anglos these celebrations are associated with pagan rituals.

So powerful has been the inner drive of some Mexican Americans to break the shackles of the barrio and join the Anglo middle class that they have subjected themselves to a familial torture. Parents who make it instill their children with the ambitions for success and material reward they identify with the Anglos. But upon reaching the pinnacle they discover, as Manuel Machado, Jr., reminds us, that "all of these pretensions to reach the top of the social ladder usually have minimal results. . . . To many an Anglo they are still Mexicans aping the *mores* and actions of their betters . . . [who should] stay with their own kind and realize that money does not whiten."[6]

With this frustrating realization the Mexican American who identifies with middle America confronts a dilemma: if his fundamental values are those of his WASP neighbor who rejects him as an equal, what alternatives does he have? Should he throw in his lot with the chicano militants with their strident calls for brown power? Or concentrate more on transforming middle America's attitude, if necessary by much greater political involvement in *both* the Democratic and Republican parties? Or remind himself that the Anglo, for all his economic and political influence, has been drained of his spiritual essence in his endless quest for money and power and thus lacks the cultural reassurance the Hispanic American possesses? In other words, the choices seem to be to join the chicanos because they are your racial brothers even though deep down you think they're crazies; to demonstrate through political action that Hispanic Americans want essentially the same things that Anglo-Americans want and are just as capable of producing the leadership the country needs to obtain them; or, finally, to reconcile yourself with the belief that the Anglo may never accept you as an equal but he secretly envies your inner strength.

For the middle-class Mexican American the problem with the first is the intellectual and emotional price one must pay. It is one thing to accept the idea that America must recognize its historic links to Mexico and the linguistic claim that Spanish has on American education (which most acknowledge). It is quite another to assert that only chicanos may teach chicano history or that the true believer must purge himself of "Anglo thinking" and find his cultural values and heroic symbols in his Mexican past, especially in the indigenous resistance to repression offered up in the Mexican experience—Cuauhtémoc against Cortés, the Revolutionary folk heroes (especially Zapata and Villa) against the oppressive Mexican state and its gringo ally, and in modern times, Reies Tijerina or César Chávez against the Anglo capitalists and their "Tío Taco" comrades. For the Mexican American such cultural salvation requires forgetting (or reinterpreting) some historical truths. Many of the Mexican Americans of the southwest are descendants of *mexicanos* who fled the destruction wrought by Zapata and Villa. The modern Mexican now glorifies the nation's Indian past, to be sure, but persists in dominating those indigenous peoples who have survived the reach of the Revolutionary state. In any event, the modern Mexican American who is confronted with chicano pressure is asked not only to forsake his loyalty to American culture but to question the Hispanic ingredient in his Mexican origins. The Mexican American professional who has departed the barrio to fulfill his version of the American dream cannot easily identify with the oppressors of *his* grandparents, Tijerina's invaders, or Chávez's grape strikers, but insists he is just as committed to retaining and celebrating his Mexican heritage.

Modern Hispanic Americans, especially the numerically dominant Mexican Americans, I believe, have largely rejected chicano militancy, especially the separatist tactics its more extreme exponents demand, but want to play a larger role in the country's governance. The inner strength associated with Hispanic culture is no longer sufficient comfort to those Hispanic Americans who know *their* political, economic, and social values are thoroughly American and who deserve a greater share in the shaping of public policy.

For the Hispanic American political aspirant there are often unexpected obstacles. At the outset it might appear that although

Hispanics, like blacks, may not vote in such large percentages as Anglos, they do respond to ethnic appeals. Since a black candidate such as Jesse Jackson can elicit a powerful turnout among small but heavily concentrated numbers of black voters, it has been argued, the Hispanic American ought to be able to generate a similar appeal, especially in those states or cities where the Spanish-speaking predominate. The problem lies in the diversity of the Hispanic population, which can divide along social/economic lines as well as national origin, that is, on the basis of income or profession as well as the country one's immigrant forefathers came from. Even in the southwest, where Mexican Americans far outnumber any other Hispanic group, these divisive elements come into play.

Political analysts speak confidently of a black voting bloc, but Hispanics, particularly middle-class Mexican Americans, have yet to achieve such solidarity. There is a noticeable determination to make their vote count for more but a reluctance to identify with the blatantly factional politics of the more strident chicanos. In regions of heavy Mexican American population, such as San Antonio or Los Angeles, the Mexican American political candidate in the past has weighed the potential gain of bloc voting against the possible damage and found the risk too high. A good example is Henry González of San Antonio, who was a beneficiary of the Viva Kennedy movement in Texas in 1960 and whose electoral victory appeared to herald the beginning of Mexican American political power. Yet González shrewdly avoided identification with the bloc-voting political organizations other aspiring Hispanics were seeking and instead concentrated on broadening the Democratic Party to support Hispanic candidates deserving of political office and building his constituency on economic rather than ethnic issues. To this day he is suspicious of the chicano movement and its purpose, though of course he is not so critical as to alienate the Hispanic vote that comes his way because he is one of them, nor so chummy with fellow Hispanics as to lose traditionally Democratic labor.

Until Reagan came along the Mexican American (and the

Hispanic American, with the exception of the Cuban refugee) was in his rhetoric the most individualistic and independent of voters but, in practice, one of the Democratic faithful. The reasons seemed clear enough: the Mexican American may have liked the self-help philosophy of the more conservative political order but as part of the economic downtrodden failed to benefit much from it. Democrats promised more, sometimes could not deliver, but at least provided the fundamental necessities in their political commitments. In this way, it can be argued, Hispanics and blacks are similar in their politics.

Yet for the former, Democratic loyalty is more tenuous because it is explained less by the candidate's program—''Here's what I'm going to do for you''—than by what the candidate stands for, or, more precisely, how well he can project his sense of self-worth to a mass audience. This involves a delicate blending of verve, determination, and chutzpah with religion, tradition, and philosophy. Democrats field more attractive (i.e., charismatic) candidates, the theory goes, so, given the Hispanic's emotional typology, Mexican Americans vote for them. In the 1960 campaign Kennedy and Nixon more or less pledged the same things to Mexican Americans but Kennedy got more than 90 percent of their vote, not so much for his appeal as a Catholic but because of the skillful projection of his inner strength. Some years later his brother Robert was able to garner considerable Mexican American support and the Viva Kennedy movement revived.

But it is not a vote that Democrats can take for granted, as Reagan has proved. The signs of political independence among Mexican Americans began a generation ago. Nixon may have offended them in 1960 with his self-characterization as the quintessential Anglo middle-class American, the Protestant symbol of the nation's cultural standard, and Kennedy certainly charmed them. But their defiant streak began to appear in the late sixties. It is often remembered that after Robert Kennedy died, George Wallace inherited a not inconsiderable amount of votes from those populist Anglos and ethnics who would have voted for

RFK. What is rarely mentioned is that Wallace picked up some of Kennedy's Mexican American constituency, notably in San Antonio with its "Viva Wallace" boomlet, and Nixon's "Brown Mafia" of the 1972 campaign effectively neutralized the Hispanic vote by making grand promises in order to counter McGovern's appeal.

What could explain such a conversion? Wallace may have been the antiestablishment figure for a generation of low-income Anglos, but the Spanish-speaking "little people" could not have found much in his economic or political program to identify with. The standard theory is that Wallace exhibited a defiance that Mexican Americans found appealing. His strutting about and "bus 'em to Kingdom Come" and "law 'n' order" rhetoric were the antithesis of charisma, but his style, if less than captivating, kept an audience in a mood of near frenzy and his responses to "highfalutin" queries usually combined his inner rage with whatever issue he believed was uppermost on the minds of his listeners. He had an ability to provide an emotionally satisfying answer that might or might not bear any relevance to the question. In Nixon's case the shift to the Republican camp was momentary, a result of assiduous cultivation of "friendly Democrats."

To characterize the educated and ambitious Hispanic American voter as merely a more sophisticated variety of the grape picker from the California vineyard or the Kansas railroad laborer of earlier generations is to deny a fundamental truth about Hispanics in politics and about American political culture. Presumably quantitatively precise studies have shown that Hispanics vote less than blacks and blacks vote less than whites.[7] What often is not so apparent is the qualitative measure Hispanics bring to the political process. For them, the social context of politics is a critical factor. In a society in which language, religion, and skin color have been sometimes insurmountable barriers to political participation, what is surprising is their reticence in accepting past discrimination and not their small turnout on voting day.

The political dilemma faced by the Hispanic American goes

beyond numbers or color. It is ultimately explained by what America wants the Spanish-speaking to be and what the Spanish-speaking believe they can implant in American political culture.[8] There can be many ways in which a minority can leave its imprint on the larger society—in its music, its food, its language, its predominant religious beliefs. Shielded by America's constitutional safeguards of individual rights and its professions of commitment to a culture of diversity, the Hispanic American can persevere. But he cannot implant his cultural values in the larger society until Hispanic Americans accept their rightful place in the centrality of American political culture. In this struggle the Hispanic American, and especially the Mexican American, is at war with the Anglo; and clearly, and perhaps more important, he is at war with himself. If he accepts the self-imposed limitation of reconciliation with himself as he is and with the larger world as it is, and with no commitment to changing either for the better, then the Mexican American who is intelligent and ambitious yet feels himself an outcast probably deserves his isolation and political marginality.

His is a dual battle—to get the Anglo to value his political strength and, ultimately, to value what he can bring to American politics. It will mean the Hispanic American will have to go beyond the tallying of numerical strength in Florida or Texas or California. The Mexican American, the quantitative and, I would argue, deservedly qualitative barometer of Hispanic politics in the United States, must somehow translate his Mexicanness into the Anglo's political world. He must assert his political influence not only because the numbers warrant it but because, at bottom, the Mexican American is as American as his Anglo detractor. He must be taken seriously in American politics, and to achieve that he must take his obligation to the political culture more seriously.

Catherine Rocha was right: she is just as white as I am. And now I know she was not referring to skin color.

5
Rocky Mountain High

≡≡≡≡≡

It is springtime in the Rockies. At the ski resorts higher up the last bands of jet-setters from back east are sipping white wine and Perrier in their end-of-season parties in Aspen and Vail. But down on the flatland that begins abruptly on the Colorado Rockies' eastern slope, in Denver, the city that has long prided itself for being at 5,280 feet above sea level, the Census Bureau is sponsoring a roundtable on Hispanic Trends in the Eighties. The bureau's resident analyst, Edward Hernández, talks authoritatively about an Hispanic American population of twenty million by 1990 and follows with tentative comments about the bureau's accuracy in determining who are the Hispanics U.S.A. In the 1980 census, apparently, some 200,000 whites and blacks, expressing either uncertainty or indignation at the listing for Mexican American on the form, drew a defiant circle around *American*. Presumably, then, the count of 16.9 million people of Hispanic descent in the United States in that year should be 16.7 million, *más o menos*.

Denver has an Hispanic mayor, Federico Peña, a migrant from Texas who has joined the ranks of "seminatives," outlanders who chose Colorado for environmental as well as economic motives. Some years back their escalating numbers prompted the true natives to join an antidevelopment movement, largely on the belief that Colorado confronted an ecological disaster if it continued to absorb more people. Peña was only thirty-six when he came to Denver and plunged into politics. Some of the old guard did not like his record as a civil rights lawyer and antiwar activist, but Colorado has developed a reputation for political tolerance. The uncertainty the establishment felt was due to its not really knowing just *how* his Hispanic roots would affect his politics.

He soon won over the more suspicious barons of Denver's business elite and, like Henry Cisneros in San Antonio, managed to retain his Hispanic base. Since his first election Peña has been preoccupied with the inevitable problems a politician creates when he tries to blend his cultural heritage with American political realities. More than a century ago big-city mayors from New York to Chicago created urban political empires, tainted with graft, on the swelling numbers of ethnic votes, but the modern mayor who elects this course runs a risk, particularly if he is one of *them.* If Peña accommodates the promoters of a more vigorous economic development he may alienate the ecologically minded Denverites whose first priority is controlling pollution. If he shifts too much toward either, he faces the challenge of more militant Hispanic Americans, especially the chicano activists whose vision of what *their* mayor ought to be derives from the historical experience of the chicano in "occupied America." Denver has a smaller Hispanic base than does San Antonio, so Peña cannot hold the dominant Anglos as hostage to a Spanish-speaking mass, as can Cisneros. Yet as Peña learned in his 1987 electoral triumph, the Hispanic vote can make the difference in a narrow race.

With their newfound political muscle, Hispanic Americans ought to be more confident about their future, yet here and elsewhere in MexAmerica Norte they have not resolved a debate among themselves about who they are and what they want in America's political culture. More urgent, apparently, is their inability to fashion a political strategy to express their frustration. Denver's director for Human Rights and Community Development blends American idiom with Hispanic indignation: "We're not getting a fair shake. If you watched television, you'd think we were not part of this country. We want our people brushing their teeth on commercials, too.'' But he recognizes that, at bottom, the visibility of people named García or Rodríguez promoting dental hygiene on the tube may not mean much if Hispanics don't get out and vote in large numbers or if their vote is diluted by some artful political redistricting. He speaks angrily about what happened in Colorado. ''All the areas you can think of that had significant numbers of Hispanics, we were gerrymandered out.'' For Castro the issues are clear enough: Hispanic Americans have the numbers to warrant a larger political role, perhaps decide a presidential election with a large turnout in half a dozen key states, but they must be given a ''fair shake.'' What he does not readily acknowledge is that inner feature of the Hispanic American character that yearns for acceptance but resists dilution.[1]

For many of Denver's Hispanics and Anglo natives and ''seminatives,'' the symbol of an Hispanic political culture lies to the south, in the arid reaches of impoverished New Mexico. There the Hispanic equivalent of the founding fathers call themselves Hispanos and speak disdainfully of the *mestizos* who outnumber them. They claim that they descend from the sixteenth-century Spanish conquerors who were blessed with generous land grants from the crown. By the time of the American conquest of a large chunk of Mexico in the mid-nineteenth century, they were already beginning to lose out. In the aftermath of the Mexican war, the Anglos, mostly cattlemen and dryland farmers, moved onto the Llano Estacado, the Staked Plains, of eastern New Mexico, where the Hispanos had extended their sheepgrazing, and built what New Mexico's Hispanos call Little Texas. In the southeast Mexicans predominated. So the Hispanos had to retreat to the upper Rio Grande Valley and the northern counties.

They could not shield themselves, culturally or economically, from the outside. The Anglos pushed ever inward with development schemes and a more aggressive legal system that, in time, swept away the Hispanos' tenuous hold on the land. Later, they lost even their identity. In the 1930 census, "whites of Spanish ancestry," much to their dismay, found themselves lumped under "Mexican." By the sixties the Census Bureau was categorizing whites with Spanish family names as persons from Indian to Spanish heritage, mostly *mestizo*. The Hispano has been redefined, and the elitist "whites of Spanish not Mexican ancestry" gather in lonely social clubs to bemoan the passing of the "true race."

Yet Hispanic-dominated politics has produced victory at the polls but not a settled Hispanic *political culture*. In the late fifties Senator Dennis Chávez, irritated at a fellow Democrat, sarcastically noted, "If they [New Mexico's Hispanos] go to war, they're Americans; if they run for office, they're Spanish Americans; but if they're looking for a job, they're damned Mexicans."[2] What Chávez matter-of-factly expressed as a political reality—the growing power of the Hispanic in a state where his numbers have been steadily drifting downward for two generations—exists nowhere else in the United States.

To the north, in Denver, there is an apprehension that the cultural winds of American politics are shifting and forcing the political order to set a new course. But much depends on precisely which New Mexico the nervous Coloradans are looking at: the traditional Hispanos who have accommodated Anglo-America's political system but carefully preserved their cultural influence in a region that possessed deeply rooted institutions long before the Americans came storming in, or, in our times, the explosive militancy of Reies Tijerina and the land-grant movement, which threatens not only the political but the social order.

Ironically, it is the first, not the second, that seems to be more troubling, perhaps because its impact cannot be so easily measured. Coloradans should not reproach themselves for not readily understanding New Mexico's politics. Sociologists, anthropologists, historians, and political scientists have been studying the state's political culture for generations. Even a few imaginative literary types have joined in. None, lamentably, has produced a social-scientific assessment of New Mexico's Hispanic politics.

One astute student, assessing the myriad scholarly and popular analyses, morosely noted that all of them amply catalog how the Hispanics maintain their power but none can say with certainty for what larger purpose they intend to employ it. A possible exception to this befuddled group would be the politicians who know how to count the vote.

In other heavily Spanish-speaking regions of the United States, Hispanic politics follows a different pattern. In the Rio Grande Valley of Texas the Hispanic voter does not vote in large numbers and when he does he is readily controlled; in the Rio Grande Valley of New Mexico he has voted in large numbers for generations. Hispanics in New Mexico have built, on both the rural and urban level, a more durable two-party system. It is true that where New Mexico's Hispanics have the numerical edge they run community political affairs. But they do so not because their political behavior has some driving power from the admittedly influential heritage of the family or the church or the village boss or even the language. Their habits reflect the commitment they have acquired to a competitive two-party politics—in other words, their commitment to American-style local politics with an Hispanic flavor.

Despite its poverty and dependence on infusions of federal money, New Mexico has shown it can adapt its Hispanic culture to Anglo-Saxon political institutions. Colorado has yet to accommodate its politics to the forces of cultural change and, especially, to the ever-growing pressures of its Spanish-speaking. In the nineteenth century it had as tumultuous an image as any western state or territory, and its economic livelihood, grounded largely on herding and mining, depended on what the newcomers from the east learned from the Hispanic pastoral culture of its valleys. In its mythology of western settlement, however, the Anglos gave precious little credit to the Hispanos. What the former brought to the cattle industry, for example, was not so much expertise, which the Hispanos largely provided, but the capital to develop it. Even the west's much vaunted range-law principle of "first in use, first in law" owed much to Spanish practice. At

Bent's Fort they spoke mostly Spanish, as did Kit Carson, who married an Hispana. Until the twentieth century, Spanish (and German) stood alongside English as the official language of the state.

Yet Coloradans, who endlessly debate the environmental costs of economic development and champion a tradition of political tolerance, have yet to accord their Hispanic past its rightful place in their political culture. Theirs is an increasingly unsettling confrontation between Yuppie America and MexAmerica (which has its share of yuppies). Their quarrels over language and immigration policies mirror the nation's uncertainties about Hispanics, those who are already here and those who want to get in. Theirs is the fundamental debate about what kind of society we want to be.

The squabble over bilingual education—its benefits and draw-backs—has created sharp divisions in Denver and throughout MexAmerica Norte and illustrates what this larger debate means. Former Colorado governor Richard Lamm, who has plunged into the immigration controversy, places language at the center of the assimilation process for immigrants. Testifying before Congress on the Simpson-Mazzoli immigration-reform bill, he spoke eloquently of an America that is a "rainbow of colors but not a tower of Babel." Like other liberals, he is willing to accommo-date the country's "fair share" of the world's refugees but unwilling to yield on the centrality of English in public life. More than a practical necessity, he argues, English in this nation is the closest unifying embodiment of what American culture repre-sents. Merely learning enough English to get by or survive in school is not enough—the immigrant has to learn to *think* in English before he can really be an American. Citing the poor performance of Mexican American schoolchildren, a disturbing national trend amply documented by pedagogues, Lamm has taken sharp issue with LULAC and other groups which contend that the cure is *more* bilingual education.

Lamm has been joined by such diverse supporters as former California senator S. I. Hayakawa, who heads up an advocacy group determined to make English the official national language; James LeMare, a scholar whose studies of Mexican American schoolchildren in El Paso revealed an unsettling limited political commitment to the United States—though they praised the American life-style—and the chicano writer Richard Rodríguez, who has persuasively argued that teaching the Spanish-speaking in their native tongue in the schools of this country is tantamount to learning to swim by putting one foot in the water. It is a less frightening experience and certainly eases one's apprehensions but makes more painful the inevitable plunge later on. Down in McAllen, Texas, a Rio Grande valley town with a large Mexican American population, the school board, dissatisfied with bilingual education in the early grades, has experimented with the "total immersion in English" philosophy and raised test scores.[3]

The controversy is not susceptible to any facile educational solution. Bilingual education, if it keeps Hispanics in school, improves their marketable skills but frustrates the schools' objective of molding the citizen. A society that bases its distinctiveness on its political philosophy and historical defense of its political creed—as the United States rightly and proudly does—has come to believe, apparently, that such lofty ideas can be conveyed in only one language. If the ultimate goal of the schools is to shape an educated adult citizenry and the most fundamental demonstration of one's citizenship is the exercise of the vote, then the printing of ballots in any language other than English, to use an example often raised by the opponents of bilingual ballots, diminishes the Americanism of the person who is voting.

Critics of the proliferation of Spanish not only in schools and in the voting booth but on road signs or in rest rooms—to listen to a few irritated commentators on this subject, "everywhere you go"—point to the Latinization of the country, or, more precisely, to the assault on the use of the English language. Regions historically untouched by Hispanics, and even today sparsely populated with them, have succumbed to pressure to raise the linguistic flag of defiance. The examples of "what can happen if

85

we don't do something" are, for most of the critics, Miami and southern California. In Miami, it is argued, the old social structure, molded from within, has been overwhelmed by Hispanics, mostly Cubans, who have transformed the city into the capital of Latin America. They insist on retaining their native tongue, which the original Miamians don't particularly mind as long as official discourse remains in English.

A few years ago, after Dade County had gone through a spirited debate over this issue, I reentered the country through Miami's international airport. With the glibbering throng packed into the customs baggage claim area, I must have listened to a dozen different languages. Most of the arriving passengers were blazing away in staccato Spanish. Here English may be the *de jure* tongue but it is definitely the *de facto* minority language. As I impatiently waited to get my battered suitcase, the young black attendant retrieving suitcases from the conveyor suddenly whirled around and yelled at the chattering mob: "You people are in America now. Talk American!" There was a five-second silence followed by the resurrection of the tower of Babel. I grabbed my bag and scooted away for a three-minute grilling from a ponderous and officious customs agent who wanted to know, in descending order, why I had gone to Nicaragua, why Jimmy Carter had "given away our Canal," the future of University of Georgia football after Herschel Walker, and, finally, my mother's maiden name. I got two out of four right, and the reader may be assured that I "talked American."

Actually, there are not a few Hispanic Americans who firmly support the view that, as one of them said during the debate over California's 1986 election proposal to make English the official language of the state, "if they're citizens of this country, they oughta speak English." In New Mexico, this is an old debate, reaching back half a century or more. During the thirties the Spanish-speaking residents of the northern communities, their language shielded by numbers and by tradition, found little need to learn more than basic conversational English. But after the war they began moving to larger towns, where Anglos dominated.

State law, anticipating the necessity of English for economic advancement, *required* educational instruction in English even though New Mexico was, for all realistic purposes, a dual-language state. Confronting Spanish-speaking pupils, teachers often lapsed into using very little English in class. Dennis Chávez was one of the Hispano firebrands in the 1930s who demanded the law requiring instruction in English be enforced. English was essential, they believed, to compete with the Anglos. So strong were their convictions that they resisted teaching their children Spanish. Throughout MexAmerica Norte an entire generation of middle-class Hispanics grew up with only an embarrassingly paltry knowledge of Spanish.

In the sixties, when Reies López Tijerina raised the chicano flag of defiance in Rio Arriba County, the linguistic battle was joined again. Tijerina had been a Catholic migrant worker who converted to Protestant fundamentalism, then moved to California to spread the gospel. In the early fifties he went to Mexico and plunged into a prolonged search of ancient Spanish and Mexican land grants to the Hispanos who once reigned in New Mexico. In 1963 Tijerina founded the Federal Alliance of Land Grants, a militant chicano organization. The "Alianza's" standard was the recovery of ancient lands granted to their ancestors and "stolen" by the Anglos. The dream was the creation of a millennial kingdom, an independent Hispanic community of communal villages and farms.

Only three years in New Mexico, Tijerina rallied twenty thousand to the cause of the Alianza, most of them angry young chicanos who rallied to his cries of ethnic identity and demands that New Mexican schoolteachers speak Spanish as well as English. Neither was as threatening to the established order as the Alianza's demand for the return of ancestral lands, several million acres, and the secessionist chicano battle cry. In the beginning Tijerina tried using the courts and gaining support from government agencies. Frustrated when these initiatives produced few results, the Alianza activists began erecting no-trespassing signs on lands they claimed. On Independence Day

87

1966, Tijerina commanded a protest march from Albuquerque to Sante Fe, the state capital, where he delivered a petition on behalf of the land claimants to the governor. A few months later, the chicanos camped out in Kit Carson National Forest, which, they said, lay on ancient Hispanic lands, and declared it an independent republic, San Joaquín del Rio de Chama. Forest rangers moved in, arresting Tijerina and four of his followers.

In Rio Arriba County, where the movement was centered, the Hispanic ruling order began rounding up his followers and tossing them in jail. In June 1967, a band of Tijerina's followers raided the Rio Arriba courthouse to rescue their comrades. In the attack, two deputies were wounded. With Tijerina now in command, the chicano band took their leave, with two hostages. The state mobilized a pursuit force of two hundred state police and twice that number of national guardsmen, tanks, and helicopters. With such an army they soon captured Tijerina and his Alianza band. This time he had to stand trial, first for the confrontation with the rangers in Kit Carson National Forest. Found guilty, he was sentenced to two years in prison. He appealed and posted bond, and in the troubled days that followed one of the principal state witnesses for the courthouse raid, Eulogio Salazar, was murdered.

Tijerina headed east for a meeting with Martin Luther King, Jr., and black civil rights leaders. They soon fell to quarreling over Tijerina's charges of lackadaisical black support for the chicano movement. But the chicanos, mollified, later participated in the Poor People's March of August 1968. Tijerina descended on Foggy Bottom, where he lectured State Department bureaucrats on the Treaty of Guadalupe Hidalgo, which ended the Mexican war, and the legal basis of the Alianza's land-grant claims.

Back in New Mexico, Tijerina declared himself a candidate for governor but then had to withdraw because of the court conviction for the confrontation with the forest rangers. In the trial for the Rio Arriba courthouse raid, he defended himself and was acquitted. But in 1969 he lost on his appeal for the Kit Carson conviction and went to prison, then lost again on separate charges stemming from the courthouse raid. He resigned his Alianza office and went to prison. A year later, pledging he would never again take part in the Alianza or its activities, Tijerina was paroled. The movement had fallen on hard times, but a determined core of Tijerina's old followers, even without his fiery leadership, continued the battle for the return of ancient lands to the Spanish-speaking people of New Mexico.

So the confrontations on the linguistic battlefield go on, in New Mexico, Denver, and wherever English is under attack. For the "Official English" defenders, the war goes beyond the schoolyard and reaches across the country. And for the vigorous champions of the "cause," the confrontation has less to do with Spanish and its teaching than with the generally implied and occasionally stated assault on the culture the language represents.

I have no solution for this dilemma. But I can report the opinions I heard on this controversial issue in my wanderings through MexAmerica Norte. Hispanic Americans, especially Mexican Americans and even chicanos, I believe, do not require instruction in Spanish to reinforce cultural pride or reassert their _identity_. For the most part, the exaltation of language as a source of cultural pride is a response of enthusiastic pedagogues who are striving to make a statement or curry a following. Hispanics don't need a validation of Spanish as a substitute for English in order to retain their cultural pride. In many respects, they are more realistic about the economic payoff that comes from bilingualism than their Anglo-Saxton compatriots. Even in California, where the English-language amendment passed by an overwhelming majority, those whose native language is Spanish have displayed a remarkable advancement in idiomatic English. They have to in order to get ahead—and to watch _Dynasty_. But they do not accept that Spanish is some kind of mongrel dialect nor that English is the miraculous key to political salvation. They are saying, "Pay more attention to the ideas and sentiments I am conveying than the particular language I express them with."

*   *   *

A better education, greater economic incentives, a heightened political awareness—these are at the center of Hispanic goals in Denver. Traditional Anglo obstacles to Hispanic advancement have fallen. Not only does the city have an Hispanic mayor, it boasts an Hispanic business elite. Persons accustomed to servile labor in the past now run companies that cater, in a reversal of cultural roles, to an Anglo clientele.

The heavily Hispanic west side has become a center of community development, much of it the work of the West Side Economic Development Corporation. New housing and supermarkets now occupy blocks once dotted with junkyards and dingy factories. The corporation's head, Veronica Barela, grew up in Lincoln Park, an ethnic melting pot of the forties and fifties that ultimately was transformed into a Denver barrio. In Denver she sees a quiet revolution in Hispanic aspirations. But on the north side, also heavily Hispanic, another outspoken chicano, Phil Hernández, a history professor turned state representative, runs down the list of "triumphs" and cynically remarks, "Are we going to be lace-curtain Mexicans?" Barela talks of changing dingy neighborhoods into model communities; Hernández, of Hispanic unemployment, drug addiction, and the astronomical school dropout rate.

In Barela's youth, Lincoln Park, separated from downtown by Cherry Creek, was a domain of low-income housing where residents had to sign a loyalty oath affirming their commitment to the "American Way." But Lincoln Park had community spirit, a sufficient number of Hispanic, locally owned stores, and parents who encouraged their children to get a college education. In the 1960s the neighborhood altered dramatically—the developers began moving in and those who could afford to move headed for the suburbs. The builders of the Auraia Higher Education Center, a complex of three colleges, razed one Hispanic church and turned another into an auditorium. Hispanic residents still bitter over the loss of their churches now complain of students parking in their driveways.

Barela fears the real estate speculators but speaks confidently of a development strategy guided by Hispanics who have joined middle-class America and want their fair share of what it can offer to those with aspirations. But there exists among Denver's Hispanics a militant cadre who resist paying the cultural price to join. For them, "identity" is cultural identity. Many wound up in the chicano movement of the sixties.

One of their leaders is a retired boxer, Rodolfo "Corky" Gonzales, the "Denver Battler." He first gained political notoriety in 1958 when he prevented a Denver policeman from using his nightstick on another man by knocking the cop out, breaking his leg and nose in the process. Gonzales was found not guilty, the first chicano, he continually bragged after the trial, to batter a cop and beat the rap. In 1965, when most Americans thought blacks were the only legitimately disgruntled minority, Gonzales founded the Crusade for Justice and organized an enthusiastic following of angry young brown brothers. True to the faith of molding a new generation, he began a school, the Escuela Tlatelolco (named for a site founded by Aztec dissidents), which taught the history of the southwest from a chicano perspective. At its height the school had 350 students and occupied an impressive building on Downing Street. Gonzales, with the other chicano leaders of MexAmerica Norte—César Chávez, Reies López Tijerina, José Ángel Gutiérrez, Abelardo Delgado—spearheaded what some enthusiastic observers were calling a movement that would accomplish for chicanos what black power had tried but failed to do for its constituency. "Corky's Commandos" invaded school board meetings to demand courses that incorporated the chicano experience into the curriculum. For a few years Denver's Hispanics rallied to their cause or at least timidly acknowledged their assertive presence.

Today Corky's Commandos are largely forgotten or overtaken by a younger generation of Hispanics more interested in adapting to middle-class ways than in glorifying chicano culture. Delgado, who electrified the movement in 1969 with a poem, "Stupid America," which aroused chicanos with its vilification of Anglo domination and glorification of the suppressed chicano, lost

91

much of his poetic fire and joined the liberal establishment. He is nowadays the executive director of the Colorado Migrant Council. Gonzales retreated to a tiny office on East 16th Street and lamented the decline of the Escuela Tlatelolco to a paltry twenty students who occupy a few rooms on the second floor. He now excoriates the commercialization of Hispanic culture. The chicano, he still believes, doesn't sell his honor and pride for money and a few steps up the social ladder.

Fighting the battle for chicano identity can be a frustrating cause, however, given the appeal of a material culture and its ability to incorporate Hispanics who dream of a better life. As Corky told a *Rocky Mountain News* reporter in 1985, "There isn't one thing the American—the gringo, the Anglo—can't make money off of."[4]

While Gonzales talks about writing a book and dismisses his compatriots drawn onto the public payroll as "boomerang chicanos," other Denver Hispanics have become the Latino variation of Reaganites. They praise home, church, and a balanced budget, and warn against too much dependence by minorities on social welfare programs. And the go-getters among them, irritated with Democratic Party leaders who take them for granted, have been defecting to the enemy camp. Joe Nuñez, a former lieutenant colonel in the Air Force, now chairman of the Colorado branch of the Republican Hispanic Assembly, speaks openly about freeing the Hispanic from social aid programs. To him (and other Hispanics who have shifted into the GOP) the Hispanic's reliance on welfare programs will mean continued dependency on the Democrats. In 1984 the largely Hispanic G.I. Forum held its convention in Denver. Neither Walter Mondale nor Geraldine Ferraro showed up, but Vice-President George Bush did. In the election the Reagan-Bush ticket garnered 30 percent of the Hispanic vote. Even in the heavily Democratic (and poor) Rio Grande Valley of Texas the Republicans have been making significant inroads.

Denver's Hispanics may often disagree, certainly on what it means to be Hispanic in America, but they seem most baffled about what has to be the most disappointing and frightening number on their statistical chart—the heavy dropout rate of their children from the schools. Few students of this phenomenon, here and elsewhere in MexAmerica Norte, can point with certainty to one explanation. In Denver the dropout rate for Hispanics is double that of whites. Some observers identify economic factors—Hispanic students who quit school come from poor families, have poorly educated parents, and live in public housing. Their parents do not have to remind them of the value of education for survival in a rapidly changing and more complex economy, yet still they quit school. Their explanation is sometimes expressed as the "west side attitude," which the Hispanic dropouts explain vaguely as a "problem of motivation." They lack even the sports-hero role model with hortatory inspirational speeches. Tragically but understandably they attribute to themselves the laziness the Anglos long ago attached to their culture— "Sleep all day, fight all night," the more derisive Anglos used to say—yet they bristle at suggestions they're not as capable as any Anglo. Given time and opportunity, they believe, Hispanics can make it in business and the professions. Certainly, at least in Denver, they have role models—not only an Hispanic mayor and several Hispanic councilmen but even a few notably successful chicanas like Linda Alvarado, who employs Anglos in her construction enterprise and regularly advises women's groups on corporate opportunities.

But for every potential Linda Alvarado or Veronica Barela or Federico Peña there are hundreds of Hispanic teenagers in Denver's schools who drop out to party, to get high and stay high on drugs, to labor at menial jobs that lead nowhere, to have a baby—the explanatory chant, familiar to guidance counselors, goes on but rarely dwells on bilingual education. Greater stress on a curriculum that demonstrates the contribution of Hispanic culture has made a difference among those who left the barrio to enter the Anglo-dominated world of higher education and learned for the first time about Spanish literature and the Hispanic roots of North America. Denver's Hispanics do not appear persuaded,

93

as is former Governor Lamm, of a melting pot speaking one public language with different accents. Rather, they seem to be resisting middle-class Americanism, not by demanding bilingual education but by retaining their belief that America can be a multicultural society that reflects its diversity in many ways, among them the acceptance of a language deeply rooted in MexAmerica's past.

For those who want to address the "Hispanic agenda," the task can be frustrating. They must confront the MexAmerican yuppie who worries much less about passing on Hispanic culture to his kids than about making it in modern America and who speaks about "letting go" from one culture in order to enter another, the English-speaking melting pot. But moving up and moving on can exact a price that may linger. Denver's Hispanics are discovering that adopting the Anglo's social, economic, or even political philosophy does not automatically bring a new identity. In a culture that continually reminds the individual that "you are what you do," a slogan that has even begun to penetrate MexAmerica Sur, Hispanics are getting a message earlier generations of immigrants received. In a society with a philosophy that exalts ambition, determination, "get-up-and-go," you can have more than your parents, and the fundamentally American (and revolutionary) notions that "you can get anything you want if you've got the bread" and the individual should have, not what he needs, as Marx said, but what he wants, the Hispanic often feels he must relinquish his cultural identity to benefit. Some, like Corky Gonzales, have refused and cling to a once proud and dominant culture, which they believe never sacrificed its creed for material gain. Others, like Joe Nuñez, whose parents were janitors and farm laborers, have joined Denver's yuppiedom and are justifiably unashamed of living in exclusive neighborhoods, driving Mercedeses, and sending their kids not to Escuela Tlatelolco but to private schools. Who can say which is the "typical Hispanic"?

The continually shifting debate over language and culture in New Mexico and Colorado has left a peculiar legacy. For

Hispanic Americans, and especially for Mexican Americans, it has meant a tradition of uneasy choices. In New Mexico the "true" Hispanos who possessed social and economic influence before the American conquest may have lost out, but the Hispanic character of the territory did not. The Mexican American majority persevered in the political and economic life of the territory, even sharing the spoils of southwest development that elsewhere went largely to Anglos. And when New Mexico became a state the framers of its constitution shielded the Spanish-speaking by including a provision that the right to vote, hold public office, or sit on a jury would not be denied because of "religion, race, language, or color, or the inability to speak, read, or write the English or Spanish languages except as may be otherwise provided." When the federal government insisted on the exclusion of the last for admission into the union, the still powerful Hispanic legislators framed a response in another part of the constitution in such a manner as to satisfy Washington yet retain their intent.

Yet their victory spawned another debate, in which Chávez and a Depression-era generation of Hispanic Americans waged the battle that Governor Lamm and his fellow Coloradans have only recently begun. A half-century ago the New Mexicans were pressing the cause of English instruction as a necessity for economic advancement in a state in which the political and cultural influence of the Spanish-speaking has remained strong down to the present day. Of the southwestern states that once formed northern Mexico, California, where the Mexican American found himself virtually excluded from political power and his language continually under attack, is the richest, and it is there the Mexican American enjoys a higher quality of life. New Mexico, where his culture, language, and political influence have persevered, is the poorest, and it is there he endures the lowest quality of life. Colorado, less secure in its cultural identity and more committed to the primacy of English, provides (after California) poor southwestern Mexican Americans with public services and benefits above the national average.

95

The comparative evolution of Hispanic American economic advancement and political culture in New Mexico and Colorado does not always offer a reassuring portrait of the future of MexAmerican political culture. Where the Spanish language possesses a *de facto* equality with English in public life and dominates in numbers who speak it, where Hispanic social and political leaders have long exercised considerable economic and public sway, and where a cultural legacy from an Hispanic past still occupies a visible presence in the life of a state—as each of these does in New Mexico—then a political and cultural model for the remainder of the country should result. In New Mexico, lamentably, it does not. There not only have Anglo, Hispanic, and Indian combined to produce a mosaic of southwestern culture, it is argued, but Anglo and Hispanic have fashioned a political culture of common respect. What has really emerged is not a political culture of common respect among Anglo and Hispanic but a political and economic understanding among Anglo and Hispanic elites dictated by expediency. They have ruled the state together, developed it together, and, frankly, despoiled it together. Anglos have exploited Hispanics, as elsewhere in America. But in New Mexico Anglos and Hispanics have exploited their own people.

The Hispanic American dispossessed migrate north from New Mexico to Denver. There they encounter a more politically enlightened state and greater opportunity. And in a city long under the domination of Anglos they find an Hispanic mayor, a political aspiration not yet fulfilled in Albuquerque. Yet even in progressive Colorado, where the social benefits they will receive far surpass those of the state where their numbers *and* culture have triumphed, their inner turmoil over who they are and what they want persists.

Language occupies an important place in this inner debate among Hispanic Americans but it is not, I think, crucial to its resolution. The reason why bilingualism has become a bitterly divisive issue is that Anglos *and* Hispanics have made it one. Understandably concerned about America's fundamental political unity and the shaping of its citizenry, Anglos have reasserted the primacy of English. Understandably concerned about economic realities, Hispanics have advanced the pedagogical cause of English instruction. Regrettably, for each the centrality of English or the visibility of Spanish in the schools has become a symbol in a larger battle—a conflict of cultures. The emergence of a victor in the struggle for linguistic supremacy will not resolve the issue—for either Anglo or Hispanic.

As a voluble *mexicano* told me in Puerto Vallarta: "Of course I believe my people in El Norte should learn English. But I also think the Anglos should give us respect. You don't have to like Spanish. You don't even have to like us. But you'd better respect us."

I liked what he said. I didn't like the way he said it. Frankly, I didn't like him. But he has my respect.

6

The Great Valley

In a rented Mustang I speed east on Interstate 8, the highway flanked by San Diego's scattered commuter suburbs. After thirty minutes or so the road begins its winding path into the foothills, and soon the dense sprawl of southern California yields to sparsely populated valleys and forbidding mountains. An hour out of San Diego, cars and recreational vehicles are pulling over into the rest stop, the drivers raising car hoods to cool engines overheated by the winding climb into the mountains. This rugged terrain continues deep into Mexico's Baja California, but only twenty miles east, through the final cuts in the rocky slopes, past the water faucets on the opposite side of the highway installed to refill depleted radiators of vehicles headed west, the terrain levels. Brownish desolation changes to a patchwork of irrigated farms and small towns.

I have entered the Imperial Valley, a world vastly different from the urban sprawl of southern California. Driving over the farm-to-market roads that crisscross the county and into its diminutive agricultural towns—Holtville, El Centro, Heber, Imperial, Brawley, Seely, Westmoreland, Calipatria, and Niland—I am reminded of diminutive Texas Panhandle towns with modern placid self-images and turbulent pasts. Relaxing in the comfortable dining room of my motel, trying to escape the 111-degree summer heat, I join a dozen or so patrons who are speaking "American" with distinctive midwestern drawls, talking about the weather and crops and upcoming social events. Only occasionally is there a verbal reminder of the border twenty minutes down the road in Calexico. A young Mexican American woman, a motel employee, sarcastically comments about a rumor that Mexican officials in Mexicali, Calexico's "other side," have begun assessing special charges on mining companies dispatching teams into Mexico. The _mordida,_ the time-honored "bite" by which Mexicans at every level of authority supplement their meager incomes, is nibbling again at the pocketbooks of Valley inhabitants. Wisely, I refrain from uttering a comment about wretchedly paid stoop labor from the south. "Honestly," she says in a tone of obvious disapproval, "sometimes I just don't understand my people."

Her Anglo coworkers, as confidently knowledgeable about her "people" as she, believe they do. After all, their ancestors trooped into this valley when geographers called it the "great Colorado desert." With the diversion of water from the Colorado River they labored to transform the flatland from the Salton Sea in the north to Mexicali on the border on the south into an agricultural heartland. An early promoter, Geoffrey Chaffey, called it the Imperial Valley. Its heart, El Centro, was in the first thirty years of the century a melting pot almost as varied as San Francisco in its ethnic makeup: Anglos, Japanese, Greeks, Armenians, Chinese, a smattering of Filipinos and Scandinavians.[1] When Chaffey imposed his own version of Puritan rule by banning liquor, Mexican entrepreneurs just across the border happily provided booze to his neighbors. In 1940, when the All-American Canal was completed, the Imperial Valley's agricultural future seemed assured. All the Valley growers needed was a dependable and cost-efficient—i.e., "manipulable and cheap"—labor supply. Mexicans would provide it.

By then the early waves of immigrants, mostly small farmers, had increased California's rural Mexican population in Los Angeles, Orange, Riverside, San Bernardino, and Imperial counties from 8,000 in 1900 to 350,000 when World War II

99

commenced. By then their Mexican American and Anglo bene-
factors had exhausted themselves in efforts to organize rural
workers. Neither the American Federation of Labor nor local
Mexican consuls showed much interest in addressing the special
problems of rural labor. More militant organizations, like the
International Workers of the World, the Wobblies, strong in the
mining and lumbering camps of the west, had come in only to
promote the unrealistic cause of world revolution. The Trade
Union Unity League, a branch of the Communist Party, lost
much of its enthusiasm for the rural workers after a series of
debilitating strikes in the thirties. By then their living conditions
had deteriorated to such a depressed level that even official
observers, generally sensitive to growers' interests, wrote disap-
provingly of the squalor and human degradation.

Today the Valley is dotted with prosperous farms, heavily
mechanized, requiring far fewer workers to harvest the cotton,
truck crops, or sugar beets or tend the livestock. The irrigated
flatland has become part of the vast domain of California
agribusiness, politically, if not always economically, secure.
How agribusiness rose to such prominence in the Imperial Valley
is an often stormy history of confrontation with a generation of
determined union leaders in the forties and fifties. What happened
in these often tumultuous struggles between labor organizers and
large growers says much about the tormented rural past of
MexAmerica Norte, from the Rio Grande Valley to the vineyards
of inner California. It is a tale of Mexican Americans pitted
against powerful western-state agribusiness, which knows there
is a ready supply of stoop labor from across the border, and, in
our time, a painful familial quarrel between Mexican Americans
and their cultural forebears from "the other side."

With the All-American Canal to irrigate their crops and the
bracero program to supply Mexican laborers, the Valley farmers
grew wealthy. In 1951, one embittered chronicler of California
agribusiness has written, they produced seventy different crops
on land worth $600 million. In an upside-down economic
pyramid rivaling the social structure of their counterparts in

Sonora or Sinaloa, 7 percent of the landowners controlled 40 percent of the acreage in the Valley. Their success, according to their own proud assessments, lay in their unrelenting efforts to make the desert blossom. Their critics, of course, attributed their wealth to federally subsidized water and cheap labor. The Irrigation District provided 3,000 miles of canals and 2,500 miles of electric power lines; the state of California offered expert advice on pest control and the available labor supply; and the U.S. Department of Agriculture kept them informed about the market and delivery conditions from an office at the Planters Hotel in Brawley. To the north, Border Patrol surveillance assured them that none of their Mexican laborers would wander into the interior. And to preserve the political, economic, and even social order, the growers relied on the Imperial Valley Farmers Association, dominated by half a dozen or so huge growers and efficiently administered by an Imperial Valley agricultural boss, B. A. "Big Daddy" Harrigan, who supplied the growers with braceros and, on occasion, the braceros with a steer for their fiesta barbecue.

The fifties brought not only prosperity but power to the Valley's entrepreneurs. For the "locals," the domestic laborers who settled in "Messcan" sections of Valley towns, the growth of agribusiness meant backbreaking toil in the fields, where entire families gathered before sunup to pick melons or whack off onion tops with clacking shears. During the harvest season they migrated north to the vast interior of California, to work as migrants, but always returned home to the Valley. They were citizens: they paid taxes, sent their children to school, and despite their precarious situation lived better than the braceros or the "illegals."

In 1952, when the bracero program was firmly established with Public Law 78, thus assuring a ready _legal_ supply of laborers from Mexico, the growers found clever ways to check the demands of the "locals" for better working conditions. They began firing Mexican Americans, starting with the women, then terminating males who belonged to the National Farm Labor Union. They introduced short-handled hoes and more arbitrary

101

working assignments, which irritated the males. When they complained the Mexican Americans found out that the braceros and "illegals," while usually less efficient, were nonetheless more acceptable to the growers because they were more docile. To the growers, the free-market rules of agriculture and its insatiable demand for cheap labor justified these practices. But to the Mexican American displaced by a bracero the villain was not the market but an arbitrary system justified and sustained by the state and federal governments and middle-class consumers who argued that less expensive garden crops were, quite frankly, more important than the working conditions of *American* farm laborers who happened to be of Mexican heritage. After all, the consumer can apportion only so much of what he pays for a head of lettuce to improve the working conditions of the person who harvests it.

In time, naturally, even the compliant braceros would, as university students choosing a major like to put it, "get smart" and begin making demands of their own. But by then the growers had learned to fall back on the endless supply of "linejumpers" and "wetbacks"—people always on the move but gathering in sufficient numbers to provide border agribusiness with the un-complaining and fearful workers it required. During Valley harvest time Mexicans on the other side sometimes paid to be spirited across the border and housed for a few days until farm trucks came by to collect them. The Border Patrol adopted an informal policy of relaxing its vigil when the growers needed field hands.

Unlike the "locals" or the braceros the linejumpers tolerated the most primitive conditions, digging caves or erecting wretched little shacks outside Valley towns. Heber, south of El Centro, had its linejumpers' shanties hidden just outside town. Driving through on the way to Calexico, I was reminded of the remnants of New Deal in 1950, wind-swept fading stucco houses set down on the plain. The linejumpers would never have dreamed of occupying one of these "shotgun" abodes, their three or four rooms set in a row from front to rear. If lucky they camped underneath the rotting floors of an abandoned farmhouse or in a straw hut. Still, their lot was often better than that of their rural brothers in Mexico—in the fifties even a newcomer could make thirty-five cents an hour and, if he was able to stay on, might aspire to seventy-five cents per hour as a tractor driver.[2]

Mexican labor thus assured the success of southwestern agribusiness not only in the Imperial Valley but northward into the San Joaquín and Sacramento valleys of interior California. But it also sparked powerful conflicts among Mexican Americans and in part explains the appeal of the chicano movement. As an American citizen the Mexican American laborer feels entitled to the economic and political rights of any other American. In the division of this country's economic rewards, he has demanded the opportunities offered to other citizens. The "Mexican" in him helps him identify with the stoop laborer from south of the border who can feed his family only by seasonal employment in the rich agricultural valleys of California, but his sometimes acute sense of his entitlements as an American dictates that his economic interests must take precedence over the needs of a melon picker from central Mexico.

The Imperial Valley melon grower may legitimately respond, "What does this have to do with getting my melons picked?" To that proverbial query of the agribusinessman, whose last concern may be the country of origin of his melon picker, the chicano response has both an economic and political bite. Before the braceros arrived, it can be argued, Mexican Americans provided all the labor required by Valley farms. In the old days there were five thousand "locals" in the Valley, and at harvest time, when the demand was for four times that many, Mexican Americans from other regions of California came down to meet it. The bracero program drove them out with its lower wages and altered working conditions, destroying the social fabric of the rural Mexican American community and effectively denying the American of Mexican cultural heritage his rights as a citizen. Ending the bracero program, displaced Mexican Americans insisted, would bring them back to the fields. The Valley farmers predicted its termination would ruin them.

Actually, when the Johnson administration ended the program in 1964, neither the economic collapse of California agribusiness nor the social regeneration of the rural Mexican American community occurred. California's governor, Pat Brown, and the state's congressional delegation used their considerable political clout in Washington to retain the supply of legal Mexican labor, won a few concessions, but accepted the political reality that Public Law 78 was doomed. A year later, when Congress was considering a similar measure, another intense debate over the merits of the bracero program erupted in California. But by this time the growers realized that changing technology and a porous border would keep their accounts in the black. California's technical and educational establishment had already started to develop machines capable of picking tomatoes, lettuce, asparagus, grapes, and melons. The future lay in mechanical harvesting and cultivation, not human labor, but until the growers mechanized fully there would always be ways to get stoop laborers from Mexico. From their viewpoint, the big drawback was, of course, the enormous initial investment in machinery and the hardier varieties of plants that had to be developed to withstand the less delicate tug of the machines.[3]

And for the displaced Mexican Americans, who had long resented the owners' preference for undemanding Mexican *campesinos,* the end of the bracero program may have signaled a triumph for the coalition of religious, union, and chicano protesters who had condemned the exploitation of stoop labor— but it did not revitalize the rural Mexican American community. By the mid-sixties the Mexican American was mostly an urbanite with a life-style and language as distinct from those of his rural compatriot as from those of Anglo society. Driven from the agricultural domains like the Imperial Valley, they migrated into the barrios of the cities, into Denver, Albuquerque, and especially Los Angeles. It is a pattern of migration that rural Mexicans have adopted.

A few years after Public Law 78 expired, one rural cause, the grape strike in Delano, California, provoked Mexican American wrath and even reached into liberal America, until then largely detached from the chicano cause. The strike leader was César Chávez.

Chávez was an improbable candidate for this role. In the beginning he was reluctant to commit himself to a cause that at first glance seemed hopeless. The son of an impoverished Mexican American migrant, he had spent most of his life moving about the southwest following the harvest. As did other Mexican Americans in the forties, he found a way out of stoop labor by volunteering for military service, but, unlike many of them who had joined up to fight in the war, after it was over he returned to the fields. His shift into union organization was gradual and calculated. As a union promoter in southern California he survived the long struggle to organize its distressed labor into a coalition, learning in the process about the hazards of such crusades. He was operating in the Imperial Valley in the late forties when the National Farm Workers' Union waged a year-long strike against DiGiorgio Fruit Corporation, only to give up when DiGiorgio brought in strikebreakers from Mexico. Later strikes in the early fifties brought similarly disappointing results; in some of them the growers resorted to violent tactics.

When Chávez failed to organize Valley workers he decided to move on to Delano. There he began laboring in the vineyards, and in 1963 put together another union, the National Farm Workers' Association. Rejecting the traditional American union structure, Chávez elected to construct NFWA on the model of Mexican "mutualist associations," which were built around cooperatives and cultural organizations. NFWA was still in its infancy but had over seventeen hundred members when Chávez got an urgent call from Larry Itliong, who had led thirteen hundred Filipinos on strike when Delano growers began employing Mexican Americans as scabs. On Mexican Independence Day, September 16, 1965, Chávez committed NFWA to the strike, commencing a battle that eventually brought him to national prominence.

From the beginning Chávez sensed that a local strike might end as ignominiously as earlier labor protests against California's powerful agricultural interests. But he was aware of the rapidly changing public attitudes toward the social causes and grievances of minorities in the 1960s. The Delano strike, he told church gatherings, civil rights activists, and university students, was more than a union cause in a California vineyard; it was manifestly a crusade for social justice. Soon not only the unknown but the prominent were trumpeting the Delano strikers' creed throughout the west. Chávez shortly identified the movement as a religious undertaking, invoking the revered Virgin of Guadalupe as a symbol. Even ordinarily aloof urban chicanos trooped out to Delano to lend their numbers to the cause. When the U.S. Senate Subcommittee on Migratory Labor began investigating the strike and Chávez' call for a grape boycott, all seven Catholic bishops in California voiced their support for the strike and urged the government to protect farm labor by including it in the nation's basic labor law.

There were, of course, the inevitable charges, emanating mostly from Delano townsfolk, that few of the grape pickers really wanted a union and only two hundred or so had walked off the job. Chávez proudly announced a strike force of five thousand. His count must have been more accurate, because the growers had already begun importing strikebreakers from other California towns and, eventually, from Texas and Mexico. But by then Chávez' support network reached high into the domain of WASP America, and the Delano strike became one of the "happenings" of the sixties. I well recall the intense reactions, a thousand miles north in a placid valley in central Washington, where students were ordinarily more concerned about the snowfall on the ski slopes in the nearby Cascade Mountains. Before Kent State riveted attention on the Nixon White House, the grape boycott inspired a small but vocal number to march outside supermarkets hoisting placards with crudely lettered appeals to support the Delano boycott. The "Great Silent Majority" began eating more grapes.

Chávez had enjoyed an initial success but suffered a few blows to his prestige. Using tactics developed by the community organizer Saul Alinsky, who always stressed the importance of bringing local grievances to national attention, Chávez turned his unionizing zeal on Schenley Industries, which owned vineyards in Kern County. In faraway Boston his followers held a "Boston Grape Party" by dumping grapes into the harbor. The strike against Schenley culminated in a march on the state capital in March 1966, twenty-five days and three hundred miles away, scheduled to arrive in Sacramento on Easter Sunday. Schenley capitulated. But the DiGiorgio Company, which had beaten off unions in the Imperial Valley but had reluctantly agreed to let its Kern County workers vote on joining Chávez' union, suddenly invited the Teamsters into the contest. Chávez angrily took the NFWA out of the vote, got a state investigation of grower tactics, and forced the issue in a new election. To counter high-pressure Teamster activity, he formed another union, the United Farm Workers Organizing Committee (UFWOC), an AFL-CIO affiliate. When the vote was finally tallied, the Teamsters were victorious among the shed workers but Chávez' new union won over the field workers. Schenley later agreed on a new contract with UFWOC and abruptly sold its vineyards, which nullified Chávez' accomplishments.

Eventually, Chávez and the Teamsters agreed to split the terrain, and the combative Chávez turned his attention to other California growers who were still fighting the union. But these battles had begun to take a toll on him; his prestige had eroded even among other chicanos. He maintained his commitment to nonviolent tactics, but some of his followers, embittered over grower-inspired violence, retaliated. In early 1968, during a long siege against Giumarra Company, he went on a month-long fast. When he resumed eating there was still no agreement with Giumarra. The growers announced the formation of a farm-worker right-to-work organization. Chávez retaliated by making the boycott an issue in the already turbulent political climate. He found a champion in Robert Kennedy. When Kennedy was assassinated in June, the cause suffered, and when Californians entered the voting booths in the fall election, the grape boycott and the social concerns it represented were far down on their list of priorities, well below Vietnam and the manifest need, as Nixon was telling them, to have "law and order" in America.

Chávez persisted, however, and following another grape boycott campaign in 1969 appeared to have won another victory when three growers in Coachella recognized his union. In late June, Giumarra acquiesced and with twenty-five Delano grape growers signed what was generally acknowledged as a concession of victory to Chávez' five-year struggle.[4] It was a stupendous but momentary victory. Mexican American agricultural laborers who benefited from the new contracts would be assured of a higher wage and improved living conditions. They had touched the liberal conscience of Anglo-America. They had alerted their urban chicano compatriots to the lingering social and economic injustice of rural California.

But a hundred César Chávezes could not have overcome the relentless drive of labor-displacing technology in southwestern agriculture nor derailed the powerful consortium of growers in their quest for cheaper labor. When the bracero program ended, they created an impressive alternative labor pool. They turned to "commuters," workers with green cards who regularly (and legally) crossed the border to work in the fields. When these began showing a noticeable reluctance to pick melons or grapes if, for example, they could get jobs as maids or gardeners for an Anglo "missy lady," or some other employment in town, the growers began importing a generation of Mexican field laborers who regularly (and illegally) entered the country.

In the argot of the Immigration and Naturalization Service they are known as "border jumpers," most of them itinerant males who leave their families in Mexico before sunup and cross over to work on a farm in the United States for a few days. Some have worked out a system to remain for a week, though the majority, according to one study, elect to cross daily. Growers dispatch trucks to isolated spots on the border to pick them up. They are, like the Mexican American rural laborers in the towns, men with families, but they cannot demand better working conditions, nor are their families a visible presence in town. But on average each is sustaining five persons in some dreary hovel deep in Mexico. The gap between wages paid to Americans and those paid to border jumpers in the border towns has narrowed significantly in the past decade, but it has not closed nearly as much in agriculture nor in those small nonunion factories seemingly beyond the reach of federal fair-employment practices.

The Mexican American's cultural affection for the family and the obligations it can impose permits at least some tolerance for the border jumper who must work in the United States to sustain his *familia* across the border. But it does not often extend to yet another class of farm migrants, "adventurers," younger males with no familial obligations in Mexico who enter illegally and will accept atrocious working conditions and live in barns or chicken coops. They will labor long and hard, accumulating as much money as they can in the shortest time, and they have virtually no concept of what is a just wage. Fearing detection, they tend to stay on the farm, safe from the *migra* (their term for the feared Immigration and Naturalization Service), but when they do go to town their intent is to quench a sexual or alcoholic thirst. Mexican Americans who already resent them because they depress wages have yet another reason for scorning these footloose migrants, who, as one irate chicano told me, "give us a bad name."

But a month's work in the United States out of every year can be a powerful inducement to run the risk of deportation. A day's labor in a vineyard can bring as much as $75, and in four weeks the adventurer can earn several times the yearly wage for his Mexican counterpart. And he can do so with the virtual certainty that the INS agent is not going to show up at the vineyard to check for "illegals" until after the grapes are picked. By then he is a willing deportee.[5]

The "illegals" are still coming, but most of them are not headed for the Imperial Valley. They are going to L.A. or San Francisco or Chicago . . . into an urban caldron where they will become a part not of the mythical American melting pot but of modern "third-world" America.

The *legal* migrant agricultural worker has achieved in the 1986 immigration bill a status denied to earlier generations of Mexican American farm workers. Not only is his economic usefulness to southwestern agribusiness validated, but the country of his labor has accorded him a special place in the categories of those who may apply for permanent resident status. His *mexicano* rural comrade who is here without proper papers must somehow wrestle with the personal conflict induced by a culture that does not want him as citizen or as permanent resident but does covet his labor. Perhaps it is less an emotional inner turmoil than the constant uncertainty that comes with hiding in America.

Just as the 1986 immigration reforms were making their tortuous way through the American Congress, a sensitive West Coast journalist made his way along the rich coast of southern California, only fifty miles from the Mexican border, into the tomato and melon fields of Carlsbad and Oceanside. There he found living conditions so miserable as to sicken even the insensitive: wretched men living in ravines in cardboard shacks, surviving on beans and more beans, on a farm in the garden of plenty, picking tomatoes and melons and whatever needed picking for the stupendous wage of $30 a day, work that in Mexico may bring them only $2. They live like this not because they want to but because they have to. Many have wives and five, six, seven children—the numbers sometimes run to double digits—back in Mexico, so they will live without electricity or running water or a toilet and put up with rats and mice and sleep on urine-soaked mattresses in conditions most Americans believe exist only in some other country but never in America. Only a faded portrait of Jesus hanging on the wall may offer reassurance that man may have abandoned them but God has not. Not "only in America" would one encounter such social and economic injustice, but, it must be said, "only in America" would it be tolerated with the casual response "Well, they're a lot better off here than where they came from."

The jaded observer would of course point out, quite rightly, that with Chávez and the grape boycott, at least, came the victory after the long rural battle for the Mexican American agricultural worker. Not really. When César won his victory in the California vineyards his chicano brothers had already migrated to L.A. East and San Diego and San Francisco. The growers were already mechanizing. California agribusiness continued to expand its production and its profits. Even Saul Alinsky, the fabled organizer, recognized Chávez' limitations. The Mexican American, he told a chronicler of the grape boycott, is an urban squatter with all the attendant social and economic and political troubles of the city. Chávez' victory has symbolic value, but the battle he won in Delano is a battle which began generations ago, before there were machines to harvest garden crops and before labor unions joined middle-class America. Besides, Alinsky said, in a tone of cynicism, Chávez was too mystical, too antiunion, too wrapped up in his own _causa_. Alinsky's advice must have been disturbing: avoid too much identification with the civil rights movement and the churches. Go after a big-name labor organizer who needs to polish his image, like Jimmy Hoffa—somebody who can really produce results. Chávez got the Teamsters involved, of course, but as a rival.

In Delano they came to hate César for disrupting the town's social placidity and for compelling its rural aristocracy to sit at the bargaining table with a "Messcan" troublemaker. Paradoxically, the grape boycott probably did Delano more good than Chávez; the town gained a fame it would otherwise never have achieved. On the day Robert Kennedy died, César was roaming L.A. East rousing the chicano vote for the second Kennedy in a decade to inspire the Hispanic American who can give his heart to Anglo or Hispanic but rarely his vote to either. Out in the vineyards, he had won a victory, but it was a triumph of no real lasting significance, unless one attaches much to symbolic victories. The growers blame him for speeding up automation, and there is a curious logic in what they say. They speak in nostalgic reminiscence of the old days when their "children" tenderly plucked the grapes and how the machine can never replace them. But it has.

And in L.A. East, on vacated stores and fences, politically motivated graffiti artisans, laboring in the dead of night, scrawl the defiant words attributed to the Mexican revolutionary Emiliano Zapata:

"It is better to die on your feet than live on your knees."[6]

7
L.A. East

≡≡≡

In 1970, before the word "chicano" had acquired any widespread use outside the southwest, an ambitious East Los Angeles singer named Bobby Espinosa had a group called El Chicano. The band had a hit song, "Viva Tirado" ("Long Live the Outcast"). Not content with the dizzying local success that often accompanied such bands, Espinosa dragged El Chicano back east. The Big Apple proved less *simpático*. The group's first bookings were at the Apollo Theatre, a Harlem institution, where the gaudily clad chicanos scarcely blended with the Apollo's repertory of soul brothers. But Espinosa was enterprising, so he got El Chicano an agent, convinced the New Yorker could open doors at more fashionable midtown clubs. When the chicanos appeared in his office, the agent insensitively queried: "What are you guys—Indians? What's a chicano?"

Nowadays, booking agents no longer ask such idiotic questions, but the chicano bands still suffer from lasting stereotypes. Latino bands are multiplying at a geometric rate, and the moguls of the music business have accurately calculated the profits that are buried in the rapidly growing twelve-to-twenty-year-olds of the Hispanic population, their most enthusiastic followers. But almost all of the new groups are still born in East Los Angeles, are discovered by one of the chicano-oriented stations, and immediately get stereotyped as a clone of Santana (if they employ congas and timbales) or one of the salsa bands that have proliferated in southern California.

Some chicanos have made it big as entrepreneurs, but they have had to sacrifice a few Hispanic traditions (one of them a cultural antipathy to incorporating business matters into one's social life). In summer 1984, the *Los Angeles Times* conducted a survey of half a dozen very successful Latino entrepreneurs. All had somehow managed to beat the Anglos at their own game, but they had to mix business and pleasure. An Angeleno supermarket owner, pressed for funds, asked his New Mexico brother for a $50,000 loan. The brother responded with $57,000 and explicit instructions on what to do with the unrequested excess: $2,000 for a party (no mariachi bands) with a live band and valet parking and the remainder as a down payment on a Mercedes to drive prospective lenders to lunch. Within a few weeks the once financially strapped chicano had generous creditors who had been habitually turning him down.

The appeal of the Latino market, which is expanding rapidly throughout the country, has prompted some of the major firms to try to break into the market, and the new breed of Latino broker is getting rich helping them to do it.

One of them, an enterprising young chicana from Dallas, quit college, moved to L.A., and started her own company promoting everything from balloons to bumper stickers to small businesses the big companies have overlooked. She has created a network of loyal *mamá y papá* stores whose proprietors are fiercely loyal to her, in the best Hispanic tradition, and translated that familial connection into a remarkably successful operation.

Studies show that a new Latino entrepreneurial class is emerging in this country, using mainstream techniques but able to push into businesses where, in the past, few of their ancestors dared to venture. Its members are now getting the venture capital they need and the expertise they must have for engineering and high technology, and they have done so by breaking the old-boy Anglo network and, of course, by being very persistent. The connections of the greater *familia* that reach across the border have worked not a few entrepreneurial miracles. One of East Los Angeles' most dynamic businessmen, an auto-parts-store owner, came to southern California in 1970 with his parents and five brothers. He never graduated from high school and even after fifteen years of residence has yet to acquire much more than halting English. Yet along the way he got solid advice from a Latino architect who encouraged him to buy his own building instead of leasing, assistance in getting a small-business loan from a Latino accountant, and the money he needed to open the store from a Latino banker.

Their fiery chicano brothers often accuse them of selling out to the Anglos, with scorn like that with which blacks of the sixties hurled accusations of "Uncle Tom" (in chicano idiom, a "Tío Taco") at fellow blacks who worked too closely with a dominant white society, but they seemed determined to persevere. The young chicana who promotes wares among small Latino businesses dreams of heading a multimillion-dollar public relations firm.

Though the new Latino entrepreneurs run into the same problems that impede all businesses just getting under way, their numbers are increasing faster than those of risk-takers in the marketplace among any other American minorities. A decade ago, the prospects for Latin businesses, even in southern California, were depressing. In 1977, when the Department of Commerce conducted a survey of minority-owned enterprises, it found that Hispanics constituted more than 6 percent of the population but owned less than 2 percent of American firms, and 80 percent of Latino operations were family affairs. But, a decade later, Hispanics have begun to catch up. In California, the number of Latino businesses has risen from a relatively unimpressive 67,000 a decade ago to a quarter of a million. At the prestigious Bank of America, Latino borrowers have suddenly begun to get more business loans than blacks.[1] The dynamic Latino entrepreneurs of Los Angeles who constitute the vanguard of intruders into the city's business elite are in fact reclaiming a lost status. On the northern fringe of MexAmerica, it is the Anglo and his European brethren and not the *mexicano* who is the newcomer. The modern chicano, especially the aggressive variety, sees the resurgence of *la raza* as a modern *reconquista* of land and influence that once belonged to his ancestors.

The Spanish, priests and conquerors side by side, drove up the Pacific coast in years when the forefathers of their Anglo conquerors were raising the flag of revolt against George III. They founded Los Angeles in 1781. Until the American conquest it remained a quaint village in a valley dominated by wealthy *rancheros* who also had houses in town. The gold rush, California statehood, and the influx of Anglos, Orientals, and blacks, most of whom settled on the outskirts of the old Spanish *plaza,* threatened the rigid social structure.

Before long the newcomers outnumbered the Spanish-speaking old-timers, the Californios. Still, the Californios retained an influence in social and political life their countrymen elsewhere in California were rapidly losing. They had a church vigorously active in a country in which the separation of church and state was constitutionally enforced and anti-Catholicism was a natural reflection of the ordinary citizen. They maintained bilingual schools. But in the 1880s, when the railroads finally pushed into southern California and boosterism swept the region, they began to lose out. The old families lost their money and, in a culture where class was purchasable, their social standing. By century's end, the village was a city of 100,000, and the Spanish-speaking portion, once its center, had deteriorated into a barrio known derogatively as Sonoratown.

Thirty years later, as the Depression settled on America's industrial northeast, Los Angeles had a million people. It had already taken on the character of a sprawling metropolis with no definable center. Yet its excellent harbor, its easy access to petroleum, and the assurance of adequate water supplies (made possible by engineering feats and political skullduggery that brought water in from the Colorado River and the Owens Valley in northern California) meant that Los Angeles could become the west's version of Pittsburgh and New York. It also meant that business and living space were at a premium, and Sonoratown, once denigrated by the commercial tycoons, had since World War I begun to look more attractive. Across the river, in what is today East Los Angeles, the old European ethnics began leaving for less crowded surroundings. When they abandoned East L.A., the _mexicanos_ of Sonoratown and the refugees from the Mexican Revolution of 1910–1920, who had crossed what was still a virtually unguarded border, moved in.[2]

After that, the L.A. Latinos became increasingly isolated in an Anglo and, after World War II lured them to the booming shipyards of Long Beach, Anglo-black cultural ambience. True, the city's Latinos never suffered the indignities hurled at the West Coast Japanese after Pearl Harbor, but to those demanding wartime conformity they were a troublesome presence. Though Mexico was a steadfast wartime ally (and even contributed a squadron of pilots to the cause) the teenage chicanos of L.A. showed their defiance when they fought with servicemen, who resented the swaggering style of these _pachucos,_ Mexican tough guys. In June 1943 gangs of servicemen roamed L.A. looking for fights with the _pachucos_ in a confrontation known popularly as the ''zoot-suit'' riots. Historians and sociologists have attributed the origins of these clashes to everything from fifteenth-century bands of Hispanic gypsy thugs to the rapid coming of age of a generation of wartime adolescents.[3]

The _pachuco_ legend, which in its personified form is the knife-carrying (nowadays, small-arm-toting) adolescent male violently defending his turf, has served as sociocultural explanation for L.A.'s numerous chicano gangs. No less an authority than the brilliant Mexican philosopher Octavio Paz has attributed the rebelliousness of L.A.'s _pachucos_ to their aimlessness and inability to identify with either their Mexican ancestry, which is denigrated, or American culture, which ferociously tries to break their will. Until age mitigates their violent dispositions (or they die in one of the frequent gang wars) they wander the barrio, flaunting their defiance of social customs. The _pachuco_ is a rebel because he has lost his heritage of language and custom and beliefs. Everything—clothes, idiom, walking style—is an exaggeration. He is an orphan, long ago abandoned by the Hispanic paternalism of the centuries, not yet adopted (nor willing to be absorbed) by a culture that has always regarded him as inefficient, lazy, degenerate. American culture will not have him as he is, and Mexican culture will not accommodate him no matter how hard he tries to be Mexican.[4]

For a great many Americans, it seems, the Los Angeles chicano image is not the go-getter entrepreneur described above but the tattooed, shotgun-wielding teenage gangster. Los Angeles County, it was estimated in 1982, has thirty thousand "homeboys" (as members style themselves) distributed among some three hundred gangs. Each has its own code and insignia, its designated turf to defend (often only one block), and, in several instances, its own speciality in crime. The only common behavior of these three hundred unions of adolescent criminals is their gruesome commitment to defend the gang at all costs, to protect its domain, and to retaliate for the slightest intrusion. Gangs have been known to shotgun or beat senseless any rival who merely steps over the dividing lines of territory. In the early 1980s the bloody gang wars of Los Angeles achieved a death toll seven times greater than the ferocious Philadelphia gang conflicts a decade earlier.

Of all L.A.'s gangs those of the chicanos have the longest history, reaching back to the zoot-suiters, the *pachucos*, of World War II. Explanations for their permanency—their existence over so many years has spawned a subfield in chicano social studies—range all the way from the psychological (the identity crisis every adolescent chicano endures) to the economic (the deprivation wrought by generations of impoverishment and poor education). L.A. County has, of course, its representative share of black gangs and Oriental gangs, but the chicanos have the numbers and, more important, the rituals and codes that make chicano gangs a seemingly unchangeable feature of the city's social character.

Why are they so intractable?

Some blame the schools, America's historic institution for shaping social behavior. Early in this century the public schools, dominated by stern Waspish types, drilled into the Italian or Irish or Russian immigrant kid some presumably lasting values about survival and opportunity in this country. We now know the melting-pot concept was a myth, but over the years the European hyphenates merged into something called polyglot U.S.A., and the schools helped them (sometimes by denigrating their culture) to make the journey. In modern America the schools no longer are able (in large part because we no longer possess that nationalistic self-assurance about what an American is supposed to be) to perform this function.

The schools today accommodate many more students and for more of their formative years (California requires school attendance until age eighteen), but their ability to transform the chicano into the all-American boy has noticeably diminished. In Los Angeles, where dropout rates parallel those of other large urban school systems, the casualty rates among Hispanics easily surpass those of America's other minorities. Some pedagogues condemn an insensitive educational bureaucracy that fails to provide a meaningful school experience for the city's largest minority. In this debate, bilingual education has become a sustained battle of the Anglo-Hispanic cultural war.

Still others, more sympathetic to the chicano's assertive pride, point to the idiosyncratic nature of chicano culture: Mexican Americans trapped in the Anglo's world and not accepted as Mexican by the Mexicans, drawn to the inner world of the barrio, its rules, its tempo, its reassurance. Some Americans doubtless believe the chicano's occasional aberrant behavior (_la vida loca_, the crazy life) can be modified by a relentless economic logic of the pursuit of the American dream, in much the same way the black power movement of a generation ago was transformed into a relatively bland social agenda.

But they forget the inherited strengths of Hispanic culture, which is in no sense superior to but is certainly different from America's other minority cultures in that its geographical and cultural roots lie very near. ''Mexican Americans of Los Angeles are lucky,'' Truman Capote observed. ''They have their own culture.'' Here their numbers are so overwhelming, wrote an enthusiastic business analyst for *Advertising Age* in 1985, that the newcomers from other Latin American countries, especially Central American refugees, must accommodate their life-styles to the rhythms of the 80 percent of Los Angeles' Hispanic population that is of Mexican descent. And here the Mexican American assimilates not only the newcomers of Mexican descent but those of the other Hispanic nationalities, creating in the process an Hispanic subculture in which the Spanish-speaking are becoming more alike than different. By the year 2000, some of the political forecasters are saying, L.A.'s Hispanics will be the dominant *political* culture of the county. What this means for the Anglos is uncertain, but it may force them to blend into another culture in order to survive. In other words, the Anglos will have to ''Latinize.''

Until now, they have not shown much inclination to yield in either the economic or the political arena. The corporate tycoons of modern Los Angeles may not be blood descendants of the city's first boomtowners from back east, but they have inherited their developmental philosophy. *Their* Los Angeles is not the second-largest conglomeration of Spanish-speaking peoples in North America but a modern commuter culture put together by go-getters. A generation ago, when Los Angeles was rapidly changing into a ''suburb in search of a city'' with a center dominated by insurance companies, banks, and corporations with international reaches, Los Angeles' ruling elders had created a Community Committee to discuss public policy items with important community leaders. Ostensibly the committee was a civic-minded group of economic planners who would listen to community representatives before bringing in the bulldozers. In actuality, it offered the city's business and political establishment a means of making sure that its control and authority still extended over L.A.'s quilted sprawl.

The Community Committee's first crisis was a potentially explosive encounter with chicano militants from East L.A. led by

an outspoken chicana, Gloria Chávez of the United Neighborhoods Organization (UNO). For many the confrontation symbolized the torment of the Mexican American who has cultural
presence but too little political influence.

The origins of this crisis lay in the vigorous postwar development of Los Angeles and the increasing frustration of Hispanics,
particularly the returning veterans, at their inability to bring about
social reforms in East Los Angeles. When they pressed their case
through the church, the archbishop of Los Angeles, James
McIntyre, responded by opening more parochial schools. By the
sixties the malcontents were leaving the church, but a new
generation of more activist priests and chicanos renewed the
struggle. When McIntyre still refused to budge on the issue of
social activism, they organized the Católicos por la Raza (Catholics for the Race). Their specific goal was the improvement of
East Los Angeles' deteriorating housing.

McIntyre soon denounced CPLR as too political, but in early
1970 a new archbishop, Timothy Manning, more attuned to the
liberation theology that was then sweeping across Latin American
Catholicism, offered them his support. He counseled the more
militant chicanos and to show his identification with the cause led
a pilgrimage to the Shrine of Our Lady of Guadalupe in Mexico
City. Ultimately, he believed, Saul Alinsky's Communities
Organized for Public Service (COPS) offered East L.A. a means
of getting the attention of the ruling elite on the west side of the
river. When Chávez signed on she began to organize local action
committees that circulated through East L.A. and compiled a
long list of grievances that went beyond the area's poor housing—
sharply escalating auto insurance rates, too few streetlights and
stop signs, gang warfare, drugs, poor schools, and absentee
landlords. Chávez soon channeled the disconnected committees
into a more vocal UNO operative. Through UNO, in 1970 the
100,000 residents of East L.A., most of them living in a large
unincorporated area of Los Angeles County, gained the temporary attention of the power brokers from downtown.

Chávez made it clear that the Community Committee should

121

listen to what East Los Angelenos were saying before they began another round of development. The Anglos who dominated it decided to invite her to speak, anticipating, perhaps, that she would erupt "like some crazy Mexican" and validate their preconceptions of the emotional and illogical Hispanic. Instead, she presented a concise and effective summary of East L.A. problems and the area's general neglect by L.A.'s political and business rulers.

When she finished, the committee's members tried awkwardly to respond. The chairman, Edward Carter, declared, "I guess I never focused on East Los Angeles. I am vaguely aware that thirty-one percent of the city is now Mexican. And I guess Watts would never have happened had we paid more attention." This turned out to be a mild reaction when contrasted with that of Fred Hartley of Union Oil, who embarrassed even his colleagues with the remark "My chauffeur is a Mexican." Expanding on his general sentiments about Hispanics, he queried: "Do your people have jobs? Do they have money? Are they the kind of Mexicans that clean up after themselves? If you had any rich Mexicans where would they live?" He finished with a warning about "another Quebec" in the heart of L.A.[5]

The separatist movement among the French-speaking in Quebec is only partly analogous to East L.A. and what it represented that crisp December day in the Los Angeles Chamber of Commerce. More properly, the confrontation was one of the third world with the first, both of them inhabitants of the same city.

The chicano historian Rodolfo Acuña has described East L.A. as a "community under siege." It has always been known in largely negative terms—the locale of the *pachuco* riots, the chicano school boycott of 1970, and, in the same year, the chicano moratorium, a protest by Hispanics against the Vietnam War. It forms a part of Greater Los Angeles that has long strived for local political and economic control and never achieved it. Somehow, through manipulation or domination or political gerrymandering, L.A. west of the river has always managed to control L.A. east of the river. Even its geographical boundaries

122

are imprecise—"any Mexican barrio in or around the Civic Center," argues Acuña, can refer to what is known as East Los Angeles. If East L.A. has a core it is Boyle Heights, part of the sliver of East L.A. that is incorporated into the City of Los Angeles. Mexicans first settled here in 1830, were pushed out a half-century later by more moneyed intruders, and moved back in the twenties when the developers putting up the Civic Center shoved them east of the river.

Until he stepped down a few years ago, Boyle Heights, along with Eagle Rock/Highland Park and El Sereno/Lincoln Heights, was the political domain of Arthur Snyder. It is now the domain of Richard Alatorre. An Hispanic has supplanted an Anglo in the city's most populous Spanish-speaking council district, but Boyle Heights remains a community under siege. To the west of the river the developers still control its future. With Snyder they had a political ally, in large part because Snyder had powerful and influential friends among Boyle Heights chicanos less interested in preserving community ties than in the employment new construction would generate. Since the exodus of middle-class Mexican Americans to Monterey Park and other heavily Hispanic suburbs, Boyle Heights has continued to deteriorate. The chicano militants who speak of _la raza_ and _comunidad_ and the unbreakable bonds with Mexican culture point to Boyle Heights' persistent clinging to community. Here, they believe, development means the destruction of a community.

In the mid-seventies those who ruled L.A., somberly assessing the precarious social structure of Boyle Heights and the unincorporated portions of L.A. East, put forth a "master development plan" for the region. It was an ominous sign for those chicanos who believe that real community control, expressed with the same conviction that Mexicans display when they talk of real democracy, must be achieved in L.A. East. In the eighties this largest of Spanish-speaking communities in the United States has yet to take control of its future. By every statistical measure, it appears, L.A. East has continued to deteriorate—in its single-family housing, its educational levels, its employment, its

123

income. Only in the surge of population, much of it represented by aliens illegally in the country, has L.A. East risen sharply on the statistical chart.[6]

Who then is to blame for the decline of L.A. East? Outsiders, mostly Anglos, who have exploited its labor and given little in return? The developers, who have coveted its land and strived to "maximize its utility" with multiple-family dwellings that erode any real sense of community? Or Mexican Americans themselves, in such a frenzied pursuit of the better life that they have abandoned L.A. East for middle-class America and in their flight have deprived it of the foundation it so desperately needs?

More crucially, why cannot Los Angeles County's Hispanics, who amount to almost 50 percent of California's Hispanic population and almost 30 percent of Los Angeles City's Hispanic population, wield greater influence in California politics and in L.A. politics? Is it because they are too young, too poor, too uneducated; because there are too many who are not citizens and cannot vote; because there are too many who are citizens but don't vote? California's blacks, who are far fewer in number, have had more success at the polls. Black candidates attribute this to the role black churches have played in politics and, more concretely, to the status of blacks as citizens and their turnout on election day. The more outspoken chicano leaders blame their political debility on discrimination against the Hispanic voter by the "system." More arguably, it derives from the disagreements among Hispanics themselves about the purpose of Hispanic politics, if there even is an "Hispanic agenda," and who best can articulate Hispanic needs in the political system.

For the chicano activists of East L.A. the device employed to deny L.A. County's Hispanics their "rightful" share of assembly and senate seats was the 1982 reapportionment drawn up by a legislative committee headed by David Boatwright and Alatorre, Snyder's successor on the Los Angeles city council. Alatorre had committed himself to advancing Hispanic interests, but he also had to acclimate his cause to the reality of California politics, especially Democratic politics, which includes many non-Hispanics. When the plan was debated in local town meetings, the president of the East Los Angeles Community Union, David C. Lizarraga, interpreted a just reapportionment to mean, in effect, an "affirmative action gerrymander." Declared Lizarraga, "Quite simply, we expect what everyone else expects: fair representation. We would expect a plan that gives us some parity with our population."[7]

Affirmative action gerrymanders serve to balance the presumable evils of either _compactness_—when a minority is crammed into an electoral district in such heavy numbers that its influence is diminished in adjacent districts—or _dispersion_—when the minority is scattered in several districts. In California, Hispanic votes fall into the second category because they are more dispersed than black or Asian voters. Affirmative action gerrymanders, argued a spokesman for the Mexican American Legal Defense Fund (MALDEF), provided the Hispanic community with a "fair opportunity to . . . have some _palanca_, or political influence." In California, the Democratic Party has historically favored dispersing minority votes among adjoining districts in order to provide candidates with "gold" votes, minority voters who vote the Democratic ticket. This practice has well served Democratic Party interests but ill served the candidacy of Hispanic political aspirants. Thus, the latent bitterness among chicano activists against Democratic politics. One student of California politics summed up the grievance: "The Democratic political leadership during periods of redistricting has deliberately dispersed chicano voters throughout many districts in order to maximize the number of Democratic candidates who would be guaranteed a significant number of chicano 'hip-pocket' votes." The conservative Republican opposition in recent years has _favored_ compactness because it reduces minority voting strength. But with an affirmative action gerrymander the Republicans would not be able "to lump [Hispanics] into one district so that [they] could fatten up in the suburban political districts."[8]

Ultimately, Alatorre had to devise a reapportionment strategy that reflected California's Democratic political realities, among them his legislative alliance with the new assembly speaker, Willie Brown, a black. Asked about the prospects for creating new Hispanic seats even if it adversely affected a Democratic incumbent, Brown had declared: "You cannot, and I don't think the house will support, dismembering any incumbent just to achieve a racial minority district. [Hispanics are] fine people, but if they're not registered to vote, they can't help you very much. If you draw black lines, you're drawing a black seat. If you draw chicano lines, you're drawing a chicano seat—maybe." Some of the chicano militants, bent on publicizing the Hispanic cause on radio and television, engaged in a sit-in at Brown's office. The less aggressive decided to apply subtle pressure on Alatorre to come around to their view that non-Hispanic Democratic incumbents had to make some sacrifice to accommodate Hispanics' demand for another seat in Los Angeles County. They went to Brown and got his approval on collapsing two seats, one of them Democratic, to make way for an Hispanic district. But, working outside the California legislative inner circle, they had no way of adapting to the changing political realities inside the assembly. Once he lost Republican support for his reapportionment plan, Alatorre could not afford to antagonize any of L.A.'s non-Hispanic Democrats. To placate the L.A. Hispanics, he pushed more vigorously for consolidating Hispanic communities in less populated regions of the state. When he finished, the result was a reapportionment that increased the number of districts one-third Hispanic from ten to sixteen, mostly at the expense of Republican incumbents.[9]

Undaunted by the approval of the plan by the California supreme court, the Republicans got behind an initiative to submit it to California voters, who rejected Alatorre's work. The Democratic-dominated legislature modified it and resubmitted what remained a pro-Democratic districting outline. California Republicans renewed the battle in 1983 with another initiative, but this time the state supreme court, with the lone Republican dissenting, declared that another vote was improper. Two chicano battlers for "fair representation" for L.A.'s Hispanics, sensing betrayal, filed suit in 1984 against Governor George Deukmejian, Willie Brown, Richard Alatorre, and David Boatwright. The plaintiffs charged that L.A. County has 27 percent Hispanics but remains underrepresented by Hispanic candidates. In 1986, the United States Supreme Court, in an Indiana case, in effect sanctioned gerrymandering that favors one political party over another as long as the principle of "one man, one vote" is maintained.

For California Hispanics, largely Mexican American, and especially for L.A. East, the battle for "just representation" goes beyond the traditional horse-trading and backroom maneuvering that are fundamental ingredients of American politics at any level. For chicano militants who talk about _la raza_ and the "once and future majority," who decry the political injustice of a state that from 1879 until 1970 effectively denied California's Hispanic Americans the franchise by denying the Spanish language its rightful place as a native California tongue on the ballot, and who resist accommodation to "political realities," Hispanic political power, if victorious in California, may exact too heavy a price. To rule, a minority must effectively become a majority, either by uniting its own people or by accommodating other minorities—or cleverly dividing them. Whatever the option, California's chicanos will have to mold their "once and future majority" in traditional American fashion if they intend to Latinize California's political culture. Californians, with some outspoken Hispanics in agreement, voted overwhelmingly in 1986 to make English the state's official language. Mexican Americans may take considerable pride that for political and especially economic reasons, Mexico is no longer regarded as a "colony" of the state, but they divide, often very bitterly, over the intrusion of Mexico into the state's politics. More fundamentally, California's Hispanics disagree on whether or not it is desirable, let alone possible, to mold a political culture from _la raza_.

Yet there is the tantalizing appeal of becoming the "future majority" or at least the balance of political power. When Howard Finn, who represented District One in the east San

Fernando Valley on the L.A. city council, died suddenly in late summer 1986, the Hispanics finally got their second district, carved out in jigsaw fashion in the near downtown section of the city, including Chinatown. The political futurists, listening several months later to a Census Bureau official predict that the Hispanic population of the United States will rise from 17 million to 36 million by 2020, were stirred by his figures on California's share—from 7.5 million to 20 million. In the six counties of southern California, their numbers will be almost 8 million in 2010.

The economic impact of these numbers may be more precisely measured than the cultural, for understandable reasons, but their *political* legacy defies any categorization. Hispanics and Asians, the state's most rapidly growing ethnic groups, are still more reluctant to exercise their political clout than are blacks, whose population figures are less dramatic in their rise but whose voting habits are far stronger. This explains, I believe, the tentativeness of political analysts who hesitantly point to the amnesty provisions of the new immigration bill as a spur to Hispanic registration because it will offer the prospect of citizenship or still others who identify the Hispanic movement to the suburbs as a retarding force on Hispanic political power because it dilutes their strength.[10]

California is dominated politically by whites, who compose more than 80 percent of its *registered* voters, who retain control of its wealth, and who set its social standards. But they rule in a mosaic of white, brown, black, and yellow and in an economy that is linked irreversibly to the labor of color, particularly in minimum-wage jobs in manufacturing and service. They preside, proudly, over America's most populous state. But they rule, fearfully, over America's first third-world state.

8

"This Is Our Country"

The flight from Puerto Vallarta to Tijuana on AeroMexico took more than two hours, but my fascination with the afternoon sun on the west Mexican coast and the California Gulf from thirty thousand feet seemed to shorten the time. I had just finished a few days of interviewing in Puerto Vallarta and was already weary of the bleached-blond surfers and suburbanites who have "discovered" the Mexican resort. We landed at Tijuana airport, twelve miles east of the city on the Baja flatland. A band of California surfers went ahead of me—young athletic symbols of Anglo California who can afford to escape its crowded beaches. We shunted past a desultory Mexican official collecting tourist cards and into baggage claim. Though this was a domestic flight, several of the passengers were subjected to a baggage search by an officious customs agent. My countrymen collected their surfboards and designer luggage and headed off to waiting cars.

I intended to reenter the United States, but I elected to remain with eight other passengers who lined up for a shuttle bus to San Ysidro. I was the only gringo. We wearily tossed our bags into the rear compartment of a commuter van and handed our tickets to a tough-looking driver with slick hair and a half-buttoned Hawaiian shirt that could accurately be described as "shitty chic." He had the look of a man who had run this course a hundred times. For a moment I regretted not having joined some of the others who elected to take the air taxi to San Diego airport. Seated inside, I saw none of the logos or inscriptions that Latin American bus and taxi drivers use to inspire them through an otherwise tedious routine or, I am told, to reassure the passengers of their personal or religious convictions. But after a brief comment, he said nothing and kept the speed down to fifty-five miles an hour. It was welcome behavior after so many terrifying experiences with Mexican taxi drivers.

We crossed at Otay Mesa, a new station with manicured grounds and several sprawling buildings. From here to San Ysidro, ten miles away and toward the rolling hills westward, the Border Patrol confronts nightly what has been described as a third-world invasion of the wretched and dispossessed across no-man's-land into America. Along these ten miles of border, it is said, there are more attempts at illegal entry into the United States than anywhere else. For some the Chula Vista hills have become a nocturnal battle zone, for others a reminder of the depth of the despair to the south.

My companions were a young man of perhaps twenty, a fortyish woman with delicate features who told us that she was a schoolteacher, an overweight girl with waist-length black hair who had squeezed into grotesque yellow pants and covered the upper bulge with a faded loose-fitting shirt, and a family of four. The man was fighting the losing battle of middle age. He had a wrinkled face that had been too long in the sun. His wife, younger, had the stoic Indian gaze that conceals the pain of life and conveys nothing to the Anglo observer. Their children, a boy of nine or ten and a girl of perhaps six, chattered in barely comprehensible border Spanish, what cynical linguists call Spanglish, the despair of border teachers who must first teach such students correct Spanish before they can be tutored in English. They were excited about the trip, but Papá had a fearful look in his eye. I soon learned why.

After the first checkpoint, where the guard asked the driver a few questions, the van pulled to the curb. We carried our luggage into the building, the petite schoolteacher struggling through the glass doors with her oversize suitcase. We lined up as a mustachioed INS officer went through the daily routine. The schoolteacher was ahead of me. She had a "green card," which the agent held up toward the overhead light. Satisfied, he nodded his approval. I followed, flashing my passport, and got only the standard question "Do you have anything to declare?" He was, apparently, unsuspicious. There were no queries about my mother's maiden name or where I'd been or about University of Georgia football now that Herschel Walker was no longer around. The young man and the girl in tight yellow pants followed. They had *papeles,* papers, and responded in a way that indicated they had made this crossing before.

The family passed the yellow line and entered together. The agent was suspicious because the man spoke halting English— this is in itself no barrier to entry, but he had no green card. He managed to give seemingly passable responses to the agent's questions, uttered in textbook Spanish, but his American interrogator was not satisfied. He looked down at the children, darting about and hanging on the rails that lined the passageway into the luggage inspection area. "Where do you go to school?" he asked the boy. The fretful *papá* tried to answer for him, but the official pointed a finger and in an authoritative voice told him to be quiet. He passed to the girl, who had stopped hanging on the rail and looked bewildered and frightened. Again, "Where do you go to school?" and again the father tried to respond for her.

They did not pass into El Norte. The survivors hauled their bags to the waiting driver, who was sympathetic to their plight but could do nothing. The teacher began to weep, and the fat girl explained what all of us knew—"They didn't have *papeles.*" Suddenly she darted back into the building, returning a few minutes later with a hair dryer one of the detainees had borrowed. Emptied of almost half its human cargo, the van headed toward California 125, across the treeless landscape dotted with an occasional building, passed a racetrack for dirt bikes, and turned onto the highway to San Ysidro. By the road there was a sign

131

expressing a reassuring sentiment in both cultures—*Siempre viva,* "May you live always."

Fifteen minutes later the driver pulled into a parking lot adjacent to a two-story stucco building full of small offices catering to the needs of the migrant/tourist trade. Again we deplaned, but this time my fellow passengers and I parted company. They filed through a side door in the stucco building to change their money and to make sure their papers were in order. When I politely inquired about their destination, the driver gave me that querulous look Mexicans adopt when they believe they're talking to a stupid gringo but know they have to be polite. "This van is going to L.A."

Sighting a motel across the street, I picked up my suitcase and travel bag and walked out of the lot, past the terminal station for the San Diego trolley and a Jack-in-the-Box and a McDonald's, where they take pesos or dollars and speak mostly Spanglish. The motel, managed by a short, affable chicano, serves as a border way station. Americans who shop in Tijuana but don't want to take their cars into Mexico park here for $2 a day and walk across. Or the motel manager will arrange insurance if you do want to take your car into Mexico.

I paid the first night's rent and lugged the suitcase along the narrow walkway, passing a shirtless chicano doing a brake job on a sun-faded Porsche. At the foot of the stairway leading up to my second-floor room, I was distracted by a Datsun that zipped past and screeched to a stop. At the top of the stairs I looked down and in the dim light saw a man seated on the passenger side unfolding a pouch on his lap. The contents were whitish. As I fumbled with my door key, two men rushed up to the car. Thirty minutes later, there was a frantic banging on the door. Three officers wanted to know if I had seen the driver of the Datsun. I could vaguely describe only the man with the whitish substance. Below me, he sat on the asphalt pavement, obviously in custody. Annoyed that the driver had eluded them, the border patrolmen thanked me politely and left.

Next morning, the motel manager was outside looking on as a

tow truck removed the Datsun and made room for paying customers. Later, arranging for a rental car to go over to the Imperial Valley, I inquired about the previous night's drama played out beneath my room. As I had surmised, it had been a drug exchange. The driver of the Datsun had aroused the suspicion of the agent in the booth at the San Ysidro crossing and had been waved over to the secondary checkpoint. He had slowed down as if to comply, then pressed the accelerator sharply down and sped on, headed, his pursuers had believed, for Interstate 5. Instead he had whipped the Datsun into the parking lot beneath my room.

The drug smuggler had made it into El Norte, illegally and transporting an illegal substance; the middle-aged man and his family at Otay Mesa had been turned back, legally. But if they persist they will make it into the Promised Land. They may have to pay dearly for a "coyote" to spirit them across no-man's-land and risk the loss of their money to one of the marauding gangs on the border, but they will probably get in. Even the new immigration law, unless it is rigidly enforced, will probably not keep them out. Both, the *narcotraficante* and the middle-aged man and his desperate clan, represent the modern symbol of "illegals." Tragically, the narcotics transporter will have an easier time of it because Americans seem to value much more what he is bringing into this country than what that Mexican family can contribute.

Over the next days I thought often about what might have happened to them after they were turned back at Otay Mesa. Maybe the parents had refused to sign the paper the INS agents employ to hustle detainees quickly back across the border. Maybe they had gotten a hearing and the man had been able to convince his captors he had been born in a California melon patch. Maybe he had told them he was Guatemalan so they would be required to detain him. Or perhaps he had watched enough border television to know about a few essential rulings in American courts that benefited his case, such as a recent ruling by a California judge that in the eight or nine months the INS

133

requires to check out a detainee's claim to be in this country he cannot legally be denied the right to work.[1]

Still, the incident at Otay Mesa that summer day and my fears about what happened to the Mexican family stayed with me during the rest of my trek across MexAmerica. I was not angry with the INS official, who was merely carrying out his legal mandate to ensure that all entrants into the United States have a legal right to be here. Nor, if the terrified Mexican family had to cross the Chula Vista hills, could I be angry with the border patrolman who intercepted them. Nor was I angry thinking about how the family, if finally successful in crossing the border, might be exploited in an L.A. garment factory or worse—at least in this country they would have more of the material blessings of life, more opportunity, and a legal system that guarantees certain fundamental rights whether they are citizens or not. But I *was* angry about my inability to reconcile immigration law and what I believe is right. The cynic will respond that immigration laws can identify rights but those who enforce the law have no authority to decide what is right. But laws, and especially the enforcement of those laws, can reflect our convictions about what kind of society we want to be.

Central to any understanding of our modern immigration dilemma, I believe, is an awareness of the place of the immigrant in our imagination and the historical experience of the immigrant in this country. It is a bittersweet saga. We have taken the impoverished masses of Europe, we believe, and offered them economic opportunities and political freedoms denied them by their native lands. True, once here, they discovered some harsh social realities about nineteenth-century America. As in the old world, it seemed, so in the new—those who held social prominence in the American democratic community also wielded political power. But here they could do something about it, because, among other things, the political system offered them the vote and the economic system provided opportunity. American political parties, responsive to the numbers of these new voters, ultimately absorbed them. And the vigorously expansive

American economy of the post–Civil War years may have exploited them, sometimes brutally, but they managed to persevere.

In 1986, during the centennial salute to the Statue of Liberty, Lee Iacocca perhaps best captured our fascination with turn-of-the-century immigration when he spoke eloquently of his Italian ancestors who were a part of the vast wave of immigrants who entered the country from about 1880 to World War I. Theirs was a quarter-century tide that by their numbers and cultural makeup profoundly altered American society and frightened the country's political elite. But the Italians and Poles and Czechs and other southern and eastern Europeans who dominated that era's immigration, who stood with bewildered expressions in the madhouse pens of Ellis Island waiting to pass inspection from often insensitive immigration officials, who had their names arbitrarily changed from an unpronounceable Slavic to something "American," who were routinely cheated in their currency exchanges, and whose welcome consisted of a sign on a door that read "Push to New York," persisted. They got jobs and the vote and well into the twentieth century maintained a cultural link with the old country, speaking the language of their forebears and living in the network of neighborhoods that once shaped the character of America's cities from New York to Chicago. Nowadays, reflecting on their ordeal and what they contributed to the country in peace and what they sacrificed for it in war, one may rightly ask, How could Americans of two generations seriously have doubted their loyalty or commitment to what America professed to stand for?

After World War I the country turned away from the League of Nations, and in the twenties the government, responding to such anti-immigration groups as the American Protective Association, imposed an immigration quota that not only severely restricted the numbers of legal entries but stipulated that quotas for each country must be proportioned according to the ethnic makeup of the United States in about 1890. This was blatantly, and intentionally, a racist policy aimed at keeping out Orientals, theretofore the only group to have suffered from the imposition of quotas, and eastern and southern Europeans—peoples who, it was widely argued, could not be easily assimilated and whose presence somehow threatened traditional American social and political values.

The western hemisphere countries, however, were excluded, which meant that Mexicans, who had been crossing the border in significant numbers from the onset of the Revolution in 1910, continued to enter the United States, migrating not only into the fields but far north into America's industrial cities. They were not subject to quotas because Americans valued their labor and knew that the closeness of their homeland made them expendable when their labor was no longer needed. In the thirties, local and state governments, confronting rising unemployment and welfare demands, readily packed them on trains and dispatched them deep into Mexico. Some unlucky Mexican Americans who lacked papers went with them.

To many Americans an immigration policy predicated on economic needs made sense. Then and, increasingly, in our own time the practical view that immigration from Mexico and other places should rise and fall with the labor needs of the American economy has considerable appeal. Such a hardheaded approach also made sense a generation ago to liberals who argued that we should accept people who could provide a technical or professional skill in short supply. Early in his administration President Kennedy, in a mildly sarcastic reference to the words on the Statue of Liberty pedestal about taking the world's poor and homeless, reminded Americans of their cultural diversity and the patent injustice of our immigration policy. In 1965 Congress finally changed the law. It sanctioned a new quota policy based, not on the ethnic makeup of America, but on a numerical allotment of 20,000 to each country except those in the western hemisphere. For this hemisphere Congress imposed a ceiling of 120,000, with no country limit. This meant, as Congress frankly intended, that Canada and Mexico could easily account for the lion's share. Ultimately, in the late 1970s, the

20,000 country limit was applied to the western hemisphere countries as well.

In reshaping the nation's immigration law, Congress tried to expunge the racist character of earlier legislation, which it largely succeeded in doing, and measure the worthiness of applicants on other principles—their skills, their status as political refugees, and their family ties to Americans. Unwittingly it created other problems by introducing or maintaining certain "special categories" by which applicants may be admitted regardless of their native country's numerical quota. In the 1950s, especially after the Hungarian revolution, Americans accepted the notion that flight from a repressive (i.e., communist) regime warranted special consideration. In the 1960s they incorporated into the law their belief that families should be reunited. Yet within a decade of these reforms immigration had once more become such a politically divisive issue that Congress, almost in exasperation, established a Select Commission on Immigration and Refugee Policy in 1978.

What had gone wrong? There is no consensus on why the reforms of 1965 failed to maintain popular support, but the less sentimental observers of America's immigration policy have a point when they argue we should not have departed from a policy that tied immigration to economic needs. And just as persuasive, in 1965 and today, is the belief that America stands for something *more* than mere economic opportunity, that its strength derives from its credos of political liberty and the centrality of the family, and that its immigration laws should reflect those lasting values. The response to this idealistic approach is, of course, "Well, we did, and look what has happened. We can't control our borders." In other words, we tried to be "fair," in the American sense of that word, by getting away from national origins as the cornerstone of our policy, and now the third world is trying to break down the Golden Door. The newcomers have limited technical skills to justify admission but abundant political reason and seemingly unending family ties to warrant passage.

For example, in the late sixties came the Filipino professionals in preferences three and six. After a decade the skills categories had dropped significantly; then came the deluge of claimants from categories two and five, spouses and children of resident aliens and brothers and sisters of American citizens. Cubans and Vietnamese entered under political preferences. Even in the early eighties, when the select commission issued its report, in a time when public attitudes had become noticeably less benevolent on the subject, Americans retained their faith in uniting families, satisfying labor needs, and retaining cultural diversity. But they qualified these commitments with expressions that American citizens must be protected in the labor market and that newcomers must ultimately "fit in."[2]

From the sixties until the passage of the new immigration law in 1986, Americans have increasingly singled out Mexico as the culprit and Hispanic (mostly Mexican) Americans as their accomplices to explain our inability to "control our borders" and to obtain immigration reform. For one thing, Americans complain, the changeover to a fair system in the 1965 act had limited impact on Mexican immigration, legal or illegal. Mexico and Canada sent almost equal numbers of their people through the American front door in 1965. A decade later, legal Mexican immigrants were ten times higher. Even after the 1978 quota limit of 20,000, Mexico still received (because of nonquota preferences) more than a third of the legal entries allotted to western-hemisphere nations and four times that of Canada, which had fallen below Cuba, the Dominican Republic, and Jamaica. More disturbing, and to some, more infuriating, was the alarming rise in the numbers of Mexicans who entered illegally, from 50 percent of apprehensions on the Mexican border in 1965 to 90 percent in 1982.

Hispanic (and, once again, largely Mexican) American opposition to enforcement provisions of the immigration reform bills of the eighties, making employers liable for hiring those here illegally, prevented passage until Congress stipulated in the 1986 bill that the government must ensure that Spanish-surnamed Americans would not experience discrimination in employment.

138

The occasionally intense debate over immigration reform revealed just how deeply cultural and political considerations remain embedded in our notion of what kind of society we want to be and our fears of what kind of society we are becoming. Mexicans and Mexican Americans know what kind of society we are. And political leaders on both sides of the border who decried the making of a political issue out of immigration reform have, in reality, made it one. At bottom is the interplay between economic and social concerns that is the essence of politics.

Those who enforce the law, the Immigration and Naturalization Service and the Border Patrol, have, understandably, a less philosophical view of things. They will say that their legal mission may be stopping illegal entry into the country but that their real function is controlling it. They have to leave enough holes in the dike so that America, from the owner of the melon patch in Imperial Valley to the union-harassed small manufacturer in Los Angeles to the socialite in Chicago who prefers a Latino maid, can satisfy its economic craving for an uncomplaining, cheap, "reliable" labor force. Some years back the Border Patrol sector chief in southern California, scheduled to get half the five hundred new officers authorized by a Congress apparently determined to halt the "surge of illegal immigrants," lost out when the Office of Management and Budget decided it was too costly— not to the federal payroll but to a service economy increasingly dependent on illegals.

Yet unrestricted immigration, the sector chief readily acknowledged, might provide an unending labor supply but would ultimately exact a heavy toll in mushrooming social service costs if the worker who entered the country illegally decided to stay. And unchecked population. . . ? The legal mission of the U.S. attorney in Southern California is the prosecution of the "undocumented," those who are here without proper papers, but he also knows that conservatives who say that lawbreakers should be tossed in jail are generally people who will hire an "illegal" (which until the 1986 law was not illegal) and that liberals who fear the erosion of "our way of life" by the social impact of the

139

"illegals" also have strong feelings about America's image as the "land of opportunity" and minority rights.

The "undocumented" spend their money in American clothing stores and supermarkets, and they send cash back to their families in Aguascalientes and Jalisco. Unlike much of our foreign aid to governments, which doesn't filter down to the masses, the money earned by the "undocumented" does reach people who need it. Americans benefit, Mexicans benefit. The United States gets laborers and consumers, Mexico gets a "safety valve" for its population.[3] So why single out Mexico for special condemnation? Why not accord Mexico special consideration on this matter? it was argued. After all, the southwest was once Mexican, and we have demonstrated a preference for Mexican labor.

Mexican immigration has not only formed a hefty portion of immigrant labor, it has had an impact on American politics. As early as the late 1960s, Representative Peter Rodino of New Jersey was urging the Congress to take up the issue of illegal immigration. But most of his efforts were stymied by Senator James Eastland of Mississippi, chairman of the Judiciary Committee and the Subcommittee on Immigration and Naturalization. Eastland sympathized with the labor needs of agribusiness, which, incidentally, included his Mississippi cotton plantation, which employed Mexican stoop laborers. A few years later, the INS, wishing to galvanize public opinion about illegal entries at a time when its manpower was inadequate to police the border, declared there were eight million aliens illegally in the country, costing American taxpayers $13 billion. They constituted, the headlines read, "the silent invasion." Alert to the political implications of such warnings, President Gerald Ford had already broached the matter with Mexican president Luis Echeverría. They had agreed, apparently, that something had to be done. When Jimmy Carter became president he turned Ford's initiative into a strongly worded proposal to reduce the number of illegal entries and to deal with those already in the country. Those who were here before 1970 and who had remained would be granted amnesty; those arriving between 1970 and 1977 would be classified as "temporary resident aliens" who could move about (and even leave the country) but would have to wait for five years to get welfare, food stamps, and similar social benefits. Anyone illegally in the country after January 1, 1977, would not qualify for this status. The overworked and understaffed Border Patrol stood to gain two thousand officers. Anticipating the Simpson-Mazzoli bill, the Carter plan imposed a fine of $1,000 on any employer who "knowingly" hired an "illegal."

The Alien Control Bill, as the Carter plan was called, succumbed to that curious American blend of economics and fair play that has generated a political issue of unknown, perhaps incalculable, magnitude. The Simpson-Mazzoli bill ran afoul of congressional approval until, in 1986, an unlikely coalition of liberal reformers and economic conservatives fashioned an acceptable proposal, wrought largely on two issues—special consideration for the labor needs of southwestern agribusiness and a pledge that discrimination against Hispanic Americans would not be tolerated in the enforcement of the law. But the larger issues of immigration reform went much deeper. During the intense debate on immigration reform, Governor Lamm persuasively argued that illegal immigration was a "time bomb." Left unchecked, it would implant in American society a *permanent* subculture of people who deserved but were denied the rights of citizens because they feared deportation if they claimed those rights. A political man with a social conscience, Lamm reflects that practical liberal's concern with not only the economic costs and benefits "illegals" bring to modern America but the social price the nation will have to pay in the future. Employer sanctions, he argued in defense of the Simpson-Mazzoli bill, might be bitter medicine but were the only effective way to fight the exploitation of "illegals" and prevent the nurturing of this ominous subculture. Economists such as Vernon Briggs and Ray Marshall reinforced his arguments.

And on the other side were equally concerned students like the political scientist Wayne Cornelius who perceived an ingrained American nativism behind the demand for immigration reform. It

141

could be scientifically demonstrated, he argued, that in the "era of limits," immigrants, those who are in this country legally and illegally, give more than they take from the American economy. As the Select Commission on Immigration and Refugee Policy discovered, they are assimilating into American society. Despite the evidence, most Americans now believe the opposite: immigrants, especially those who are here without papers, are a drain. They take jobs away from Americans and they tax social services. And they cannot be assimilated at any *tolerable* social or political price.[4]

The Mexican immigrant is an especially critical presence in California. Among those who came to this country in the 1970s, 2.7 million had a job in 1980. In a decade in which the national economy created 21 million jobs (largely through small businesses, especially in the service sector), the immigrant held one out of eight jobs in the country, one out of three in California. Southern California's employment grew by 8 percent as compared with the national growth of 6 percent; its manufacturing employment, 18 percent in a national average of only 5 percent. But in Los Angeles County, two-thirds of the 645,000 net new jobs created in the decade were in white-collar positions requiring higher skills. Yet despite the fact that 444,000 of the immigrants arriving in this country in the seventies went to work in Los Angeles County, almost half of whom were Mexicans, and occupied 70 percent of net new jobs created, the Mexicans proved too deficient in their education, skills, or English-language capability to occupy more than 25,000 white-collar positions. But they were able to handle the job requirements of half the blue-collar jobs that required skills and half the positions in the service industry. Sixty percent of the jobs created in southern California in the decade lay outside L.A. County, yet the immigrant laborer took only 12 percent of these slots. Here the Mexican participation (6 percent) went largely into agriculture and low-skill jobs.

But these statistics do *not* mean that the immigrant took a job that would otherwise have gone to an American citizen. In truth, these newcomers, legal and illegal, created jobs that in all probability would not have existed except for their presence or had a job because they were willing to perform it under conditions and at a wage unacceptable to an American citizen. Again, the L.A. County economy figures heavily in the calculation of the impact of immigrants and especially immigrant labor. According to the census of 1980, one-tenth of its work force was made up of Mexican immigrants, half of them in manufacturing—food, textiles, apparel, lumber, furniture and fixtures, metals, machinery, transportation. Almost one-half of California's manufacturing jobs are here, more than the employment in manufacturing in Idaho, Oregon, Colorado, and Washington. In this area, critical for L.A. County's economy, it appears at first glance that the tremendous influx of Mexicans into the market did in fact result in the displacement of 55,000 jobs held by American citizens. Net employment in manufacturing increased by 113,000 jobs in the seventies, and immigrants occupied 168,000 such positions in 1980. What in actuality occurred, an Urban Institute study argues, is that the presence of immigrant labor and particularly *Mexican* immigrant labor permitted those Americans in manufacturing, an industry that has historically gone through high turnovers, to move into a sector of the economy where there was little competition from Mexican labor.[5] In other words, the Mexican shoved the American *out* of a low-level job but *into* a better one.

Of all the issues in MexAmerica, immigration is the most volatile, even more than bilingualism. If immigration were transmuted into, say, a medical problem, the United States of America would be in intensive care, and the statements about its condition would be "cautious" and "guarded." To vary the analogy, if immigration could be expressed as a national security issue, then the appropriate expression (which the attorney general actually used to describe the surge of illegal entries several years ago) would be: "We can't control our borders." I can think of few issues in the history of the country that have produced so

143

many symbiotic political alliances, that have juxtaposed such profound and idiotic commentary about "what the country stands for" and "what we want to be." As much as the still explosive subject of abortion, immigration in the past decade has precipitated a debate over policy in terms ranging from admirably moral to legally precise to politically and economically expedient to frankly disgusting. In the ambience in which this (and some earlier) confrontations on the subject have taken place, emotion, fear, alarm, and uncertainty have displaced reason, confidence, purpose, and the nation's sense of fair play.

Consider, for example, the commentary emanating from the U.S. Senate in the final debate on the 1986 bill. The general sentiment, common to both supporters and opponents, was largely negative about the law's adequacy, fairness, or enforceability, as if a bad law were defensible because "something had to be done." Hispanics, who had opposed the Simpson-Mazzoli bill on the grounds that employers fearful of prosecution for employing illegal aliens would discriminate against Americans with Spanish surnames, attached strongly worded antidiscrimination provisions, then listened to an approving President Reagan declare that "intent to discriminate" must be shown. Senator Alan Simpson of Wyoming, who had fought a losing battle over an earlier version, declared of the 1986 triumph: "It's a monstrous s.o.b. . . . but it will be as sure as hell a lot better than anything we've got now." Throughout the debate came ominous warnings about "tidal waves" engulfing the borders and massive, irrational backlashes against people already here (legally or illegally) who "look or sound foreign." The manifest importance of reaffirming national identity was articulated by Texas senator Lloyd Bentsen: "One of the tests of a great nation is the integrity of its borders, and we're losing that." He gave, perhaps unintentionally, a moral and ethical definition of the role of the Border Patrol. His Republican colleague Phil Gramm predicted that the offer of amnesty to those here from January 1982 would only induce a massive invasion of opportunists. In the end Simpson was the moralistic cynic who condemned America's economic exploitation of illegals: "Let's go back to what made America great—greed. I think we fought a war about that kind of thing a hundred years ago . . . slavery. . . . If you've got the status quo, you've got a real society of discrimination."[6]

Mexico and Mexicans are central to our dilemma over immigration. Their determinative role has less to do with numbers of Mexican immigrants, legal or illegal, than with their innate capacity to frustrate whatever logic or fairness we try to bring to the question of who shall be admitted into America. If we ascribe a basic economic condition for admission—the need for people with skills in short supply—as we did from the early fifties to the reforms of the mid-sixties and beyond, then the Mexicans are able to redefine "skill in short supply." In its study of the "fourth wave" in California, the Urban Institute found numerous examples of businesses that had filled *affidavits,* as the job category admission required, certifying that identified Mexican applicants for positions as short-order cooks or dishwashers were *essential* to the operation of the business. The truth of the matter was that these persons had entered the United States illegally several times and worked in establishments now willing to certify they were "essential." When the several categories of family preferences were added in the reforms of 1965, Mexicans were able to confound the American sense of fair play—the felt social need to reunite families—because so many of the Mexican applicants (85 percent) already had close relatives in the United States and could more readily take advantage of the law.

Like some cultural specter from the past, Mexico and Mexicans again seem to haunt the 1986 immigration law. In southern California, where, it is estimated, one-third of America's 2.5 million illegal aliens reside, city and county governments, immigration lawyers and INS officials, and social service agencies ponder its impact. A president who signed the law is reluctant to sustain an inevitably costly policy of sealing a porous border but willing to burden the prospective applicant for citizenship with a costly fee. A federal government that has benefited from the taxes withheld from the paychecks of illegal aliens pledges $4 billion nationally to reimburse state and local governments for their costs of accommodating the law's provision. But the initial deductions from this amount to pay for federal obligations will leave southern California and especially L.A. County short of the funds it needs. To be sure, the waiting period for getting on federal relief programs for those eligible for citizenship will be five years, but L.A. County will still have welfare costs that must be borne by local government. In L.A. County the numbers of those in the country from before January 1, 1982, and thus eligible for amnesty and eventual citizenship, range from an official estimate of 800,000 to the Los Angeles Center for Law's prediction of only 100,000 who will actually come forward. It is the Mexicans, largely, who fear that if they appeal for amnesty the *migra* will find some way to deport them—a loophole in the law, too few check stubs to validate their presence in America—or that if they have the check stubs to prove they were here the government will interpret the section on employer sanctions so as to send their boss to jail. Since there is an artful treachery in government officials back in Mexico, they quite naturally—and, given their experience, logically—expect the worst.

Many Americans, looking at our immigration laws over the years, quite rightly point to the evolution of a more humane policy, one that more accurately reflects our historical commitment to the values inscribed on the pedestal of the Statue of Liberty. But Mexicans know that the Anglo one-eyed Jack has a dark side to his face. Our actions have belied our professions. We have willingly—and admirably—taken more than our fair share of the world's poor, wretched, and huddled masses, its skilled and unskilled, and its political refugees, and we have reunited families. We have rid our immigration law of its disgusting racial preferences. In the dispensation of equality of *economic* opportunity in this country to the newcomer, the Mexican has been a rich beneficiary, yet he has, among all immigrants, been noticeably reluctant to praise the country that provides him with a wage ten times what his own country will offer and that protects his individual rights—even if he is here illegally—far more than his own government. All these things we have done. Yet in doing them, we have demonstrated through the years that we value Mexican labor but we do not value the Mexican. We do not value his culture, his beliefs, his heritage, his person. Everything he stands for, save his determination to head north and "work like a Messcan," we ignore and too often denigrate.

This is why, I believe, the Mexican is less inclined to naturalize and less willing to acculturate, yet, perversely, more determined to hamper the immigration law, even when the law appears to benefit him, and more assertive about his valuation of work in America over anything else America might have to offer, including citizenship. It is the cultural flag of defiance from a proud people who have little but who refuse to yield until they are accepted—and respected—for what they are and for their ability to enrich America and not just to make America richer.

9

SuperMex in San Antonio

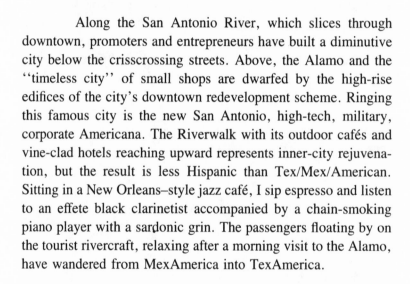

Along the San Antonio River, which slices through downtown, promoters and entrepreneurs have built a diminutive city below the crisscrossing streets. Above, the Alamo and the "timeless city" of small shops are dwarfed by the high-rise edifices of the city's downtown redevelopment scheme. Ringing this famous city is the new San Antonio, high-tech, military, corporate Americana. The Riverwalk with its outdoor cafés and vine-clad hotels reaching upward represents inner-city rejuvenation, but the result is less Hispanic than Tex/Mex/American. Sitting in a New Orleans–style jazz café, I sip espresso and listen to an effete black clarinetist accompanied by a chain-smoking piano player with a sardonic grin. The passengers floating by on the tourist rivercraft, relaxing after a morning visit to the Alamo, have wandered from MexAmerica into TexAmerica.

San Antonio is where America and Hispanic America blend into what enthusiastic observers call *mestizaje, mestizo* culture, the union of the Anglo and the Hispanic, what Mexicans, who *are mestizos,* know is the merging of Hispanic and Indian into the "cosmic race." The distinction, of course, may be important to social scientists but of little consequence to national political power brokers, principally Democrats who are alarmed by the not insignificant Republican intrusion into the Spanish-speaking electorate and who need to find an Hispanic champion.

They believe their man is Henry Cisneros. Across MexAmerica Norte his is a commonly touted name in the directory of Hispanic politicians "on the move," who are "go-getters" in a culture that retains some of its old prejudices about the work habits of the Hispanics. He believes in "honest, progressive city government." He is the new-era Hispanic, educated, ambitious, and, to cite both an articulate middle-class Mexican American in Kansas City and a working-class chicano in Houston, "no embarrassment to us." They did not say "a credit to our race." An old story, oft-repeated, has it that Cisneros once spoke so intensely about the state of Texas at a Daughters of the Texas Revolution gathering that at the end a matriarch of the clan turned to a friend and proudly declared, "He's one of us!" Here is a Mexican American who can deal with Anglos and his own so skillfully that a resentful El Pasoan bemoaned, "Cisneros has sold out to the corporations," while San Antonio's Hispanics know he is one of _them_ but has to cater to the moneyed crowd. He may be "no chicano" or a "cosmetic TexMex," to cite two derogatory characterizations, but there is little denial among politicians that he is SuperMex.

Cisneros is a reminder of the nation's cultural roots in Mexico, to be sure, but more important to his political success, it can be argued, has been his skillful blending of this society's almost mythological belief in America as the "land of opportunity" and its admiration for those who are "go-getters." In Cisneros' case, this has translated into the immigrant's grandson who grew up in west-side San Antonio in the forties and fifties, in an age when the Spanish-speaking in the city had the numbers but not the votes to wield power. Cisneros still lives among his old west-side neighbors, but he has known since adolescence that the aspiring Hispanic in America must, as blacks used to say, "play by the white man's rules." For middle-class Mexican Americans this often meant a difficult choice between _la raza_ and its glorification of one culture, and the opportunity extended by a society that assigns technology a lofty place in its cultural heritage and rewards the individual largely on the basis of what he has to sell.

149

Cisneros' numerous admirers—even Henry himself—continually refer, sometimes in "gee-whiz, only-in-America" rhetoric, to his immigrant's-grandson origins when they talk about his training as an urbanologist at Harvard and Georgetown, his "future-oriented, heavy-thinker" approach to running San Antonio, or his nomination as the first Hispanic American to be seriously considered for the vice-presidency of the United States. "The fact that this is happening," said Cisneros, "is testimony to the openness of American society and is proof that if we have faith in people and give them the tools to work with, they will achieve."[1] True, though a more candid, if politically less effective, comment would have been "I didn't start at the bottom." He did credit the civil rights crusade of the sixties with opening a few doors for other ethnics. In all fairness, he has gotten to where he is because of his persistence and determination, which have much less to do with his Hispanic cultural roots than with his personality.

Often slighted by interpreters of the Cisneros phenomenon (but not by Cisneros himself) is not the education he got at Harvard but the social Americanization he received at Texas A&M University in College Station. When Cisneros was there, in the late sixties, it was still a virtually all-male institution with a firm military emphasis. I began teaching at A&M in 1965, the last year freshmen were required to enroll in the Corps of Cadets, but the military tradition remained strong. It was reinforced by everything from an idiotic World War II–era flick about a spy in the chemistry building (required viewing) to legitimately earned praise for the heroism of its president, a Ranger officer who had parachuted down into German-held territory in the Normandy invasion. At A&M the cadets lived in barracks. If your buddies found out you were a virgin, they tied you up, carted you over to the Chicken Shack (the "Best Little Whorehouse in Texas"), and tossed you in the door with nothing but your pants and a $20 bill. In the Chicken Shack, famous and infamous Texas politicians had gotten to know, in the biblical sense of the term, some of the most sexually proficient working girls of the state. The Aggies, it was said, deserved no less. Known as a "poor boy's school," A&M in those years attracted high school graduates who felt out of sorts at the University of Texas (which Aggies call Texas University), which had begun luring high-powered intellectuals in a bid to enhance its national reputation. The more demonstratively macho Aggies were not anti-intellectual but devoutly believed that determination and action could overcome any uncertainty of thought.

Cisneros became commander of the Combined Aggie Band, in an age when it was still a trying experience for the few blacks and Hispanics on campus. It was an even greater ordeal for the handful of women. The Vietnam escalation of the sixties invigorated the school's military atmosphere. Aggies had an uncomplicated patriotism, like the steelworkers in _The Deer Hunter_. LBJ's exhortation "Bring back that coonskin" was sufficient inspiration. Indeed, the Aggies seemed less perturbed about what the war was doing to the country than what the presence of women in their classes might do to the Aggie tradition. Aggie graduates interviewed in Vietnam were asking incredulously, "Are they really lettin' women into A&M?"

Yes, even in Aggieland. The president of the university fought the measure, yielding only when it was pointed out that only daughters or wives of faculty or female Texans who had to go to A&M because there was no other institution in the state able to provide the education they wanted (and who, professors quipped, had to be "personally scrutinized" by the president) would be admitted. The line of fire was not as deadly as in Vietnam, but the first women in the regular term (summer school was completely coeducational) were on the front line against the male ego. I vividly recall one class in which there were a dozen or so males and a lone woman (the wife of a faculty member), whom the Aggies greeted with crude jokes or coordinated group flatulence right before class began. She persevered uncomplainingly for a few weeks, then one day, just as I was entering the room, she blurted out, "You bastards are goddam crude!" She didn't get to be one of the boys, but the preclass conversation became more polite, and the odor improved considerably.

A&M prided itself on other traditions, of course, one of which was the education students received outside of class. Lacking the intellectually "clubby" atmosphere of the University of Texas, the school looked to the rigorously demanding Corps of Cadets to shape a masculine "go-getter" type. It took in average kids and simply browbeat them into believing they could do more. In most cases the results were beneficial. In a few, I expect, the psychological shocks of a more complex world than the black/white one of Aggie myth may have had detrimental impact. By his own admission, Cisneros was not an intellectually brilliant student, but he got the most out of A&M because he "learned what you can do when you go all-out. Most people don't really know what they can do because they operate within certain restraints."

There weren't many Hispanics in Aggieland in those days, but they had a campus benefactor, an Anglo, Wayne Stark, director of the Memorial Student Center. For reasons only an Aggie could understand, Stark would take the Hispanics under his wing, chew them out in typical Aggie drill-instructor fashion, and watch proudly as their declining grade average suddenly pushed upward to the A level. (I can vouch for this approach. I recall an Aggie in one of my classes who flunked an exam, blamed me, and brought his Aggie father into my office to back his complaint. I began yelling at the kid in my best imitation Aggie-speak for not reading the exam questions carefully. The old man readily picked up on my style. After a while, he turned to his son, "Now, goddammit, don't you see! RTP, son, RTP, like the sergeant always said—Read the Paper!")

Many of "Stark's Boys" went on to high-powered executive positions and still joke about the "Mexican American Mafia" that he carved out of the Hispanic Aggies in those days. Some of the inspiration was, undeniably, the Aggie "go-getter" hyperbole. But the personal determination to "do something" about problems—more important, the conviction that you *can* do something if only you can muster the energy and acquire the necessary skills—is quintessentially an Aggie legacy. Cisneros' absorption of the credo served him well when he went back east and encountered his first humbling experience at a student government conference at West Point. There he sat quietly, the self-confessedly "outclassed" Hispanic, as more outspoken Anglos chirped away. He went away with a sense of inadequacy. A visit to the New York of John Lindsay and a thorough reading of a *Time* magazine story on America's urban crisis transformed him into a "born-again" urban reformer and, ultimately, an urban politician. The years at Georgetown and Harvard polished his style and certainly honed his skills, but he told a graduating class at A&M in 1984, "Probably the most formative years of my life—that really changed me and put me on course—were my years here. . . ."[2]

Determination, perseverance, "teamwork," leadership, cooperation, not confrontation—in Aggieland such credos provided spiritual if not intellectual reinforcement to generations of males trained to act rather than reflect. Such qualities won Cisneros the endorsement of powerful Anglos, and this plus the Hispanic votes generated by the Voting Rights Act enabled him to defeat a well-known businessman for mayor in 1981. He was only thirty-three, the city's youngest, and first Mexican American, mayor.

When Cisneros took over, San Antonio, which dates back to 1690, had been surpassed by Houston and Dallas, not only in population but, more important, in the ability to attract corporate American giants, in oil, banking, or technology. An economic analyst in the late sixties had noted the proliferation of military installations in and around the city and its attractiveness as a tourist center to people who wanted to visit the Alamo or stroll along the Riverwalk before heading on down to Mexico for "some real action." The urban economy had diverse but generally small businesses—the best-known was probably the brewery, Lone Star—but laborers earned less than their counterparts in Austin or Dallas or Houston, and unemployment ran the highest in Texas. Average family income was 65 percent of that in Dallas or Houston. The explanations varied—weak unions, traditionally low-paying jobs—but the most often cited was the city's heavy Mexican American population, whose workers suffered unemployment persistently higher than the state average, and the steady influx of migrants into Bexar County. They clustered in the city's Hispanic barrios, where entire families survived in dilapidated housing (a fourth of it without indoor plumbing), parents were functional illiterates, and children rarely went beyond the fifth grade.[3]

From the mid-fifties San Antonio had been the political domain of the Good Government League, challenged in the early seventies by the Independent Team. Both were less concerned with the city's ethnic majority than with placating the Anglo upper crust, which had shifted its interests to the rapidly expanding suburbs. But even the ruling order sensed change was in the offing, mostly because the black and chicano militants adopted Saul Alinsky's strategy of organizing community-action pressure groups (Communities Organized for Public Service, or COPS) on the basis of economic and social needs rather than politically divisive ethnic lines, and, more important, because the 1975 Voting Rights Act prevented San Antonio from expanding farther out into Anglo-saturated suburbs on the grounds it would deny inner-city minorities their proportionate share of political representation. The Anglos had to accept a city council based on districts, which meant that the Mexican American vote could no longer be diluted with Anglo ballots. It also meant San Antonio would get a Mexican American mayor, sooner or later. For those who were losing their grip on the political reins, the question was: "What kind of Mexican American mayor are we going to get?"

In a city where the Spanish-speaking constitute a historically numerous if not politically dominating force, this was a crucial issue. The Mexican American variant of ethnic political solidarity (brown power), modeled on black coalitions in northern cities, was one possibility. San Antonio's Mexican Americans were an old and established community. They held, the Anglos feared, lingering animosities. Linked with the more aggressive COPS, which had generated considerable interest among the working class (black, brown, and white) on economic and social issues, a militantly chicano leader posed, for the disintegrating elite, an ominous political portent.

In actuality, here and elsewhere, Hispanic Americans had been debating (and continue to debate) the tactical questions raised by Alinsky, the savant of COPS, for years. Alinsky had persuasively argued that the country's urban poor contained a rainbow culture but endured a common economic deprivation. The way out was community organization and community power. In a few places—in some of Chicago's wards, for example—this approach made political sense. In the sixties the more class-conscious Hispanic Americans had marched alongside blacks in the civil rights struggle. Mexican Americans in particular had fashioned organizational structures based frankly on cultural ties but dedicated to righting civil wrongs. LULAC, the League of United Latin American Citizens, dated from 1928; the American G.I. Forum, dominated by Mexican American veterans, appeared after World War II. Both had been active in attacking restrictive covenants, demanding the seating of Hispanics on juries, and, in 1962, electing Henry González, now the patriarch of the Hispanic Caucus, to his first term in Congress.

But the sixties and seventies brought a more militant Mexican American, the chicano, whose political orientation emphasized cultural as much as class ties. Even the names of the new organizations heralded a break with the past—MAYO, the Mexican American Youth Organization; MALDEF, the Mexican American Legal Defense Fund; the Raza Unida party, which had political goals that social conservatives likened to black power and separatism.

Cisneros began his political surge in the early seventies, when San Antonio was just emerging from its cloying political atmosphere of earlier times. In 1975, when the Good Government League was in its death throes, he was one of the three GGL candidates elected to the council. But Henry had no intention of perishing with the GGL. He began making news, riding with city workers to read electric meters to dramatize their complaints about assaults from vicious attack dogs or going out in patrol cars or ambulances to get some firsthand experience. If a club needed a speaker, Henry had speech, would travel.

The touchy issue was growth—more precisely, development for the suburbs or the inner city. The suburbs had the moneyed promoters and the eager new businesses which saw no future in downtown. Against such obstacles, Cisneros would certainly have lost. But his political star rose just as San Antonio's Mexican Americans, inspired by a chicano political militancy elsewhere, began to demand that the city respond to their needs for community improvements. Their leader was Ernie Cortés, a Mexican American Aggie who identified with Cisneros' strategy but disagreed over tactics. Cortés, unlike Cisneros, had traveled the working-class route to organizing America's downtrodden Hispanics into a force for political and economic change. Cisneros had studied urban problems and then chosen to obtain power through the ballot box. Cortés had labored with César Chávez, a disciple of Saul Alinsky.

COPS professed to be politically nonpartisan, even socially conservative if one measured the organization by its strong ties to the Catholic Church. San Antonio's business elites, however, disliked COPS' tactics. In order to dramatize the Hispanic west-side push for business support for a drainage project, COPS "commandos" took all the pennies they could find to a downtown bank and lined up at tellers' windows to change them to dollars. Their friends invaded a fashionable department store to try on clothing they had no intention of buying. They got the attention of the business establishment, predictably, and when Cisneros came on the council he began to identify with some of their causes, especially community development on the west side. But Cisneros made sure he did not get too close.

That innate political instinct—sensing that he could attract support if Anglo leaders feared there was a *mexicano* turmoil churning from below—served Cisneros well. Years before he won election as San Antonio's first Hispanic mayor, Cisneros skillfully crafted a dual image. To the Anglo business elite, which had long run city affairs, he was a threat but not so frightening as the COPS mobilizers or the firebrands of the Raza Unida party because he _understood_ the Anglos' problems. Yet when they pressed him on a crucial issue, he would explode in a manner as characteristically "Aggie" as "Hispanic." In one fiery session in a city council meeting, he turned to an Anglo councilman and screamed: "It's people like you who have had their boot on the neck of my people for generations." The Hispanics cheered, and the councilman, recognizing Cisneros' ability to foment a brown storm from the west side, became a convert.

What Cisneros has is an understanding of municipal politics in an age of expanding civil liberties for minorities, particularly the historically suffocated Mexican Americans of south Texas, and a keen appreciation of the dilemma of their Anglo persecutors. In the sixties the social conditions of San Antonio's Hispanics were so miserable that Peace Corps volunteers found in the city's barrios, it was said, a proper training ground in which to prepare for the squalor of their Latin American destinations. The prevailing order earnestly promoted San Antonio's Hispanic past to capture the tourist dollar, lauded Mexican (in reality, Tex-Mex) cuisine, and adorned their palatial homes with south-of-the-border art, but in the political and economic decision-making the Mexican Americans were excluded—until the seventies. Then came the takeover of the city council and the ominous signs of chicano agitation and the settling of old scores _a la mexicana,_ Mexican-style.

That unsettling protest, some of the old order morosely concluded, was sufficient justification to band together like their ancestors at the Alamo and defend San Antonio against the Mexican horde. Students of the city's rich history reminded them, however, that the only _native_ San Antonians in the Alamo had names like Abamillo, Losoya, and Esparza. Cisneros shrewdly convinced them there were enough Hispanics with the good sense to realize that confrontation politics would do neither side much good. The first time he ran for mayor he convinced several prominent Anglo businessmen (among them Tom Frost of the Frost National Bank) that San Antonio could attract new industry with a Mexican American as mayor because he could provide "stability." Frost joined up and got other prominent Anglos to back Cisneros against one of their own.

When the Mexican American voting power registered on the new San Antonio Council, it produced not a union of militant chicanos but occasionally bitter disagreement over tactics. A few newcomers argued loudly for a politics of race and class, the righting of old social and economic wrongs committed in the name of progress by the Anglo elite. But Cisneros, who served for three terms on the council, was the champion of conciliation and cooperation. In 1981 his political strategy paid off. He put together a formidable if unlikely political coalition of blacks, Mexican Americans, and white liberals who looked for more social programs and money from Anglo developers.[4] His notable success derived less from Raza Unida histrionics than from his ability to mesh old-line Democratic political maneuvering (forging coalitions among diverse constituencies) with middle-of-the-road economics (promoting social reform with a vigorous expansion of the private-sector economy). The strategy came straight out of FDR and JFK, modified to meet the demands of a modern America for curbs on the role of government.

What Cisneros has brought to San Antonio is more government spending (to meet some of the demands of long-neglected Hispanic neighborhoods) and a frenetic promotion of the city as a developer's paradise. In the decade of the eighties, labeled by some as the era of the Hispanic American, San Antonio has a vigorous young Hispanic as mayor who blends a charismatic personality with an urban planner's expertise. Journalists troop into San Antonio to get a closer look at the Hispanic phenomenon. And Henry dazzles them with statistics and plans, wrought by "strategic thinking," such as TARGET 90, an ambitious catalog of goals designed to transform San Antonio into a "future-oriented" metropolis. Little wonder that the Aggie SuperMex has become a media celebrity. A year in office, his imprint already on the city, he justified the emphasis on development because it created jobs. Besides, he told a writer for *Forbes,* the thinking businessman's magazine, "As a Hispanic, I [had to demonstrate that I] would not run the city into bankruptcy [and] that a Hispanic labor force is as capable, and has a strong desire to learn and improve their lives, as any other people in this country." Such inspirational interviews were followed by a whirlwind tour of the west-side barrio, where Henry would, as LBJ used to say, greet his neighbors and "press the flesh." Then he would proudly direct the wearying visitor to a street improvement or sanitation project. A *60 Minutes* profile in February 1984 sent Mexican Americans scurrying for pen and paper to scribble laudatory thoughts about "one of us" who has "intellect" and "personality" and even "charisma" and has "made it."

Perhaps so, but, as a cynical University of Texas grad (what Aggies call "teasips") told me sometime later, Cisneros deserved higher praise because he had proved to all America there were a "few articulate Aggies." When Walter Mondale presented Cisneros as a candidate under serious consideration for the vice-presidential slot in the 1984 Democratic ticket, he was acknowledging, wrote Cisneros' biographers, that the thirty-five-year-old mayor had "style" or "charisma" or "force of personality" or "pizzazz. Call it what you want. But whatever it is, Cisneros has it."[5]

Judging from Cisneros' record in bringing new money into town to shift San Antonio's economy into big-time development, Frost and his renegade Anglo comrades made the right move. In two subsequent elections Cisneros maintained his core of Anglo business supporters, even though the surprisingly diversified Texas economy, still too dependent on oil and gas, has slumped badly in the eighties, and San Antonio has felt the impact. But "oil-patch" cities like Houston, Port Arthur, and Midland/Odessa were devastated, and in retrospect Cisneros' call for a diversified economic base in San Antonio has paid off—at least for the elite.

One grand project that plagued Cisneros since the late seventies is Vista Verde South, one hundred acres of deteriorated housing that Cisneros determined to transform into an urban showcase of new homes, high-tech plants, motels, and a mall. In 1979, Vice-President Mondale informed then Councilman Cisneros that Vista Verde South would be receiving almost $20 million as "seed money." But the developers never came forward with a realistic plan or, more important, with enough funding to carry it forward. Since then, the city's dwindling faith in the project was momentarily revived when Control Data talked of moving in with a plant that would employ a thousand workers (just to start), but it backed out and sold its interests to another conglomerate. Within a few years, the newcomer was in bankruptcy court. With Henry as the project's indefatigable promoter, *something* had to happen. He talked about moving some city offices into Vista Verde, but no one was eager to move. It acquired a hideously ugly pink mall that was euphemistically labeled an international trade center, a tourist center, and a performing arts center, but the wiseacres in San Antonio began calling it Henry's Folly. None of this diminished his enthusiasm.

Nowadays the most vocal complaints come from those Anglos, many of them retirees on fixed incomes, who are unimpressed with the frantic growth of downtown and point to the escalating city budget. In 1981, when Cisneros first took office, San Antonio spent $71 million on capital improvements; four years later, the expenditure jumped to $348 million, absorbing half of city hall's hard-pressed budget. Fed up with rising property taxes, the retirees, led by an antifluoridation conservative, C. A. Stubbs, formed a Homeowner Taxpayer Association. It campaigned for a referendum in 1986 that would link yearly increases in capital expenditures to inflation and population growth.

But Henry proved too combative, even for the cantankerous geriatrics. The old Aggie drive sent him back into the streets. He enlisted business leaders, public workers, civic and social groups, and even ministers and priests in the campaign against the proposition. When it began, the opponents of the ''cap'' trailed badly; when it was over, Henry had led his army to a two-to-one victory margin. Virtually every public official in Texas, a state that confronted a $3 billion deficit in 1986, was relieved. If successful, Stubbs' movement would have doubtless tried to dismember Cisneros' *plan grande,* Target 1990, to transform the old ''San Antone'' into the new. Those who supported the limitation talked bitterly about ''big government'' in which the ''little guy'' no longer gets a hearing from a mayor whose loyalties are to the developers and the Mexican American community action pressure groups. To fight it, Cisneros has refashioned his old coalition of Anglo businessmen who depend on continued public expenditures and the vocal barrio leaders who fear cutbacks in social services and neighborhood improvements Cisneros has brought to the west side.[6]

San Antonio is no longer the placid city of yesteryear, mainly because SuperMex has managed to integrate its disconnected Hispanic middle class into the political inner circle with the Anglo economic barons. What Cisneros has done would have been no mean accomplishment for an Anglo, yet no Anglo would have been able to deal effectively with the rising Hispanic demands in the barrios. San Antonio has fashioned a union of two seemingly incompatible cultures and values—the Anglo faith in human perfectability and progress, which government must strive to support, and the Hispanic conviction of man's desperate need for compassion and understanding, which government must respect. The first demands energy, determination, and a technical vision of the future; the second, an awareness that those who are burdened by the past cannot easily shake off that legacy and commit themselves to the uncertainty of a new order. Cisneros does not preside over a San Antonio that has created *mestizaje,* the blending of Hispanic and Indian, but he has produced a truce between the Anglo-American ruling order and the ambitious yet stifled Mexican American middle class.

*   *   *

In Texas, where conservative Democrats not only support Republican policies but are switching their party labels, political analysts now talk about an Hispanic version of "yellow dog" Democrats, *perro amarillo* Democrats. In the 1986 statewide elections they calculated that the one Hispanic of four Democratic candidates for the court of criminal appeals would win three out of ten votes, solely on the basis of his name. In the pre-election polls the Hispanic wound up fourth in the preferences of west and east Texans but led in Houston, Dallas, and Fort Worth and in the Valley of south Texas. Mexican Americans now really turn out on election day, and in Texas, Mexican Americans dominate the Democratic Party. In San Antonio, a prominent Anglo Democrat running against an Hispanic tried to offset his expected losses in the inner city with a big majority in the Anglo north side. Unfortunately, too many of the north-side Anglos had swung over to the Republican camp to give him a victory.

One troublesome aspect of this party realignment for Democrats is the significant shift of Texas Hispanics into the Republican camp. Hispanic Republicans are not numerous in comparison with the Anglos who have begun to pull the Republican lever in the voting booth, but local Republican organizers in San Antonio and throughout the state have begun to cultivate Hispanic voters. In 1980 Reagan got almost one-third of the Hispanic vote nationwide; in Texas, 30 percent. Though Democratic pollsters place the figure at closer to 20 percent, it was a sufficient incentive for Governor William Clements (triumphantly reelected in 1986) to cultivate the Hispanic vote. In San Antonio, Clements' emissaries approached a Democratic loyalist, Roy Barrera, Jr., the son of Texas' first Mexican American secretary of state, and offered their support for his nomination as a judge if only he would run as a Republican. They were interested more in his experience than in his twenty-eight-year commitment to the Democratic Party. San Antonio and Bexar County can be murderous for an Hispanic who waves a Republican banner, but Barrera wanted to be an "example to the young Hispanics of this county that there is a place for us in the political process, regardless of what political party you're affiliated with, and an example that there is room in the Republican Party and . . . that the Republican Party wants to extend to young qualified Hispanics the opportunity they extended to me.''[7]

In the old days conservative Democrats outvoted blacks and Hispanics in the primaries and then in the general election got their votes against Republicans. In Texas' often combative politics, Democrats need candidates who can turn out large minority votes because on the state level a conservative Democrat can no longer count on the "yellow dog" Democrats. What the Texas Democratic Party must have is a "mainstream" Hispanic who can win in the primary and in the general election. If this analysis is correct, then Texas Hispanics, largely Mexican Americans, may be mobilizing to retake the state that was once the northeastern Mexican frontier.[8]

For the other Hispanic American political opportunists in Texas, the future holds promise, if only the Hispanic voter will crowd into the voting booths and pull the lever of the Spanish-surnamed candidate. In 1986, for the first time in the state's history, with the endorsement of the Democratic Party and 90 percent of the Hispanic vote to sustain his candidacy, Raúl González became the first Hispanic to win statewide office. Barrera, the favored choice of Republican governor-elect Clements, lost heavily to an Anglo opponent for the state attorney general post. Mark White, politically devastated by the state's economic downturn, received 80 percent of the Hispanic vote, but it was not enough. Hispanic political behavior was as it has often been: those in the Hispanic American barrios who had enthusiastically endorsed the victorious White in 1982 dropped a full 10 percentage points in their turnout on election day 1986, down to only 28 percent, less than their showing ten years before.

In November 1986, Cisneros, president of the National League of Cities, hosted the Congress of Cities in the City of Light. It was a gala affair with fiestas and mariachi bands and peaceful cruises on the river and somber sessions of the plight of the cities in the era of limits and budgetary restrictions. Already Henry had put San Antonio and himself at center stage. The city, he had explained proudly, symbolized ''a cultural dynamism born of diversity, a cultural bonding, a model of urban reconciliation.'' Its reputation had lured Prince Charles to visit the city that Cisneros had called ''uniquely special [because it is] a confluence of ethnic cultures, the new and the old, modern architecture with historic preservation, of complementing international communities while maintaining a sense of comfort and regional warmth that is distinctively San Antonio.''[9]

Diversity, growth, revitalization, tourism, a magnificent medical complex, and a Mexican American cultural legacy to sustain it and SuperMex to lead it—how could San Antonio fail? Cisneros validated the image projected on the *60 Minutes* interview. At last, Hispanic Americans had a leader who was ''no embarrassment to us.'' If victorious in state or, eventually, national politics, he would symbolize the triumph of a culture that has long considered itself stunted and abused yet has long yearned for a champion who can breathe the Hispanic fire into the phlegmatic Anglo political body. No matter that Henry is more American than Hispanic. He looks and acts like an Hispanic, and for Hispanics (as well as Anglos) appearances mean a lot.

10

The Aging Chicano from Houston

I have a west Texan's image of Houston—Cadillacs
with longhorn hood ornaments, John Travolta at Gilley's riding
the mechanical bull, freeway maniacs in high-powered rigs
playing demolition derby with cars bearing Michigan license
plates, the movie clips of *Giant,* where James Dean plays an oil
driller who strikes it rich and builds a fabulous hotel and Rock
Hudson plays a traditional Texan who goes from raising cattle to
drilling for oil and who has a son who marries a ''Messcan'' girl.
They have a child who looks more ''Messcan'' than Dennis
Hopper, who plays the father, and Rock Hudson eventually gets
cross-cultural religion and defends his grandkid in a greasy-spoon
restaurant against a Texas ruffian who ''don't serve no
Messcans.'' Hudson loses the fight but he wins the enduring
admiration of Elizabeth Taylor. I remember leaving the movie
believing that Sal Mineo, who plays a Mexican American who
dies in World War II, died for Texas. He really died for what
America had proclaimed to the world it was fighting for, but I
wanted to believe he had died for Texas. Or maybe he sacrificed
his life for what he *wanted* Texas to be. Or, perhaps, in his death
he validated the traditional Texan's belief that a ''goddam
Messcan'' will fight over nothing ''just to show he's a man.''

Naturally, there is "another" Houston: the National Aeronautics and Space Administration, a world-class medical complex, the American city the Arabs know best, the L.A. of Texas in spirit and sprawl, Rice University (a legend in the Southwest Football Conference because it chose mind over football), and something else. In the year 2000 Houston will be an Hispanic city in numbers and character. In the current despair caused by low oil prices and unemployment, empty buildings and bankrupt drillers, John Connally's financial troubles ("Gee, I was only a so-so millionaire but I wanted to be a Texas-size millionaire"), and the want ads lamenting "Have Geology Degree, Will Travel," Houstonians are only dimly aware of the Hispanic *reconquista*, but it is the one certainty of their future.

In 2000 the Anglos may hang on to most of the money but the Hispanics will have the people and the votes—Smith and Jones may retain controlling interests in the banks but García and Rodríguez will populate the schools, proliferate in small businesses, and dominate the manufacturing and low-skill service economy. The Hispanic tide has already begun. In El Mercado del Sol, a sprawling shopping center, Houston's Spanish-speaking have America's grandest Hispanic festival center. In Houston Fiesta Mart, the Hispanic version of A&P, they sell everything from Spanish-language tabloids to personal tortilla makers. Houston has seven Spanish-language radio stations. The classifieds announce "Hispanic flea markets."

Economists speak hesitantly about the Anglo's retention of the "means of production" and political analysts talk about a brown specter in the voting booth. In the Texas state government four of the thirty-one senators and nineteen of the 150 representatives are Hispanics. Citing these statistics, knowledgeable observers comment on how the Hispanics are "closing in." No one is really precise about what "they" are "closing in" on—only that "they are closing in."

No one really knows whether or not Houston can adjust to being an Hispanic-dominated city in the future, but one thing is sure: the city must accommodate its Hispanic past. More precisely, it has to acculturate the aging chicano among its citizenry. Houston and Texas and America must deal with Félix Ramírez and what he represents.

From the beginning of my sojourn across MexAmerica I had trouble arriving at a precise definition of "chicano." I knew it was the preferred identity of more outspoken Mexican Americans (with or without the hyphen), but could not decide whether or not the word carried a political connotation or expressed cultural values more Mexican than American. Even the academics quarrel over the word's meaning. By the time I arrived in Houston, I was still in a quandary.

Ramírez, a graying but still combative chicano (and Howard Cosell's match for loquacity), began our interview by asking me about "chicano."[1] "What do you believe a chicano is?" I gave a thoroughly unacademic response: "An American of Mexican heritage." He seemed pleased. "Back in the sixties," he told me, "some of us wanted another word to describe Mexican American. We got tired of so many Anglo words. So we chose 'chicano.' It has no special meaning, no Indian origin. It's just different." But about their loyalty Ramírez expressed no doubts: "Look, first we're American, then Mexican. Okay?"

We sat on the small patio overhang of my room in a deteriorating motel now under Chinese management on I-45, south of central Houston. It was early evening. The chicano had just returned from a meeting out of town but showed no signs of weariness. Declining a drink, he heaved a brown grocery bag stuffed with fading newspapers onto an empty lounge chair and hesitantly accepted my offer of a Mexican *puro*, a cigar. He seemed reassured by my definition of "chicano."

"I was in the navy," he began. "When I got to Houston this was a rough town for us, so I got involved in organizing people. I even started a newspaper." He reached over and pulled out some fading copies of *Compass,* a product of the chicano press in the sixties and seventies. I had never heard of it but said nothing.

He founded *Compass* as a gesture of chicano pride—in

Ramírez' case, a meshing of strong religious background and determination to encourage political activity. As he talked in rambling detail, I quickly thumbed through one issue (October 1968) which featured scattered articles on the Benito Juárez Mutualist Aid Society (a self-help organization transplanted to *yanqui*-land by Mexican immigrants), a brief appeal to "identity with the bronze brothers in Mexico," an unsubtle plea on behalf of the Delano grape boycott of César Chávez, and an editorial by my guest entitled "No Man Is an Island," which importuned the reader to remember not John Donne but Jesus Christ, the Social Redeemer. Another issue (October 1972) excoriated the Democrats for Nixon as "turncoats" and included a plea from the archbishop of Santiago, Chile, to "understand Third World Christians"—whose needs are as manifestly social as spiritual. Reaffirming the ancient truth that "nothing can withstand the force of an Idea whose time has come," *Compass* importuned the reader to cast his vote for the Raza Unida candidate, Ramsey Muñiz.

In the sixties and seventies there were dozens of chicano *periódicos,* bilingual basement sheets with symbolic titles like *Bronze, El Machete,* and *La Raza,* and still others with such down-home chicano mastheads as *Inside Eastside* and *Qué Tal* ("Hello," or as southerners say, "Hey"). Most have gone under, victims of rising costs and, cynics say, chicano indifference. But in their day they voiced a collective protest against Anglo domination and its *Tío Taco* (Uncle Tom Hispanic) subservience and even introduced a few chicano writers and poets. Most of them were scathingly critical of virtually everything in middle-class American society that symbolized authority—cops, schools, government of all levels—because these represented the oppressors of the chicano community.

Ramírez began *Compass* with tiny donations from friends. The first edition of a thousand copies, given out free to "informed Mexican Americans," cost $50 to publish. After that, he sustained the paper with advertisements from local businesses (pharmacies, cafés, mercantile stores, bars, and barber shops) with Anglicized names and Mexican American owners and managers—the Rooster Lounge, the Englewood Café, the Expert Shoe Shop. _Compass_ struck me as a mild threat to Houston, but in the beginning, at least, even LULAC's elders were suspicious about what gringo demons Ramírez' broadside might provoke. "I went to them to ask for more information on Mexico," he said, "because I wanted to inform the chicano community about their mother country." When the first issue came out, he told me, "I got death threats." I could well believe him. Mexican Americans have been threatened with death for less provocation in Texas. Ramírez went to the police but they wouldn't investigate until he casually informed them that the Federal Bureau of Investigation was interested in his case.

His defiance of polite Anglo society began early. He started school in Boston, moved to Pittsburgh and then finally to Houston at age twelve. A year later he was an orphan and a student at a predominantly Mexican American school where, under Texas law, teachers whipped students for speaking Spanish on school property. In childish retaliation most of his friends chattered in Spanish during recess. They demanded Ramírez' conformity with the playground code. When they discovered he couldn't speak Spanish he suffered considerable abuse. After several unpleasant incidents he began a crash course in the language.

The _puro_ went out because of his ceaseless talking. I relighted it and he continued with his disorganized autobiography. Though sympathetic, I unintentionally displayed the Anglo's irritation when listening to the voluble Mexican American recite life's displeasures. I wanted to say, "Look, man, I know what you've been through, but changes have come about . . . your life is better . . . your children's lives are better." But before I could utter a "what-basically-is-your-gripe" query he was suddenly rehashing the flaws of the school system. In 1970, when the south lost its final legal battle over segregated schools, Houston discovered a way to conform to the law _without_ compelling the whites to attend the same schools as the blacks and the Mexican

Americans. The school board informed the federal government that it was dutifully mixing the races with interschool busing, but the "whites" on the buses were named Ramírez, García, and Rodríguez, not Smith, Jones, and Brown. The Mexican American Educational Council attacked the policy as an obvious sham, and the educational bureaucracy made a few cosmetic adjustments, creating magnet schools and finding more Spanish-speaking teachers. Even today, he told me, the blacks and the Mexican Americans go to the same school.

In a state where *50 percent* of all first-graders are Hispanics and in a city where 50 percent of all Hispanics drop out of school, the centrality of education in Houston's future is obvious. Yet, the Anglos' "system," which clearly recognizes the problem, manifestly offers no solution. The local school superintendent has pointed to the abysmally small number of bilingual teachers, in a school district where they can earn as much as $7,000 in bonus salary, as a critical problem. But the problem is further complicated by the presence of significant numbers of Central Americans (three thousand in 1986) in the elementary grades. My chicano activist with the unlit *puro* spoke persuasively about the paramount need for the Anglo to grant him "dignity" and "recognition" in the educational arena. But the Anglo school superintendent talks about "restructuring the entire system" so that the six-year-old Hispanic, whether Mexican American or Mexican or Central American, can be prepared for the Houston of 2000. In the Central American student the school confronts not only a bewildered child who probably has never been to a school but is also a pupil suffering from disease, the child of parents illegally in this country, a child who has never been vaccinated, who has never been to a doctor, and who constitutes the newest member of America's public school underclass.

With thousands of other Mexican Americans, Ramírez moved up and out from the traditional Hispanic barrio of east Houston to a more desirable neighborhood. He now lives in a north-side area that has become heavily populated with chicanos. His son attends a school with an 80 percent Hispanic student body and a 70 percent black teaching staff. The principal is black. Ramírez has fought the imbalance from a variety of angles, none of which Anglo liberals would consider "fair." In his occasionally bitter remarks he conveys much of the black/Hispanic antagonism. As in inner-city politics, in the urban schools the blacks, in his opinion, have an advantage when they are the majority and even when they constitute the minority. "A year before the state required competency tests," he said, "I was arguing for them." In Texas, LULAC proudly announced, Hispanic teachers did almost as well as Anglos on the tests—and better than blacks.

In a variation of affirmative action, Ramírez demanded more chicano teachers at his children's school, as "role models" for chicano students. The black principal, evidently, did not cite the heavy imbalance in _available_ teachers between blacks and Hispanics but assumed that Ramírez would be satisfied in knowing that he spoke Spanish. Ramírez angrily shot back: "Look at the color of your skin."

His response was not, I believe, intentionally racist, but it does illustrate the tension between blacks and Hispanics in education and employment, where both suffer from the discrimination of Anglo society. His comments about the black/chicano experience make up a rambling catalog of frustration and resentment. As do many chicanos, he bears an enduring grudge over black indifference to chicano participation in the civil rights movement of the sixties, though his anger should more properly be directed at a "white power structure" that failed to respond with economic benefits or perhaps at his fellow Hispanics who don't bother to vote. Common economic deprivation may dictate a political union with blacks, but cultural differences call for separation. For Ramírez, Jesse Jackson's Rainbow Coalition is a chimera. "Jackson was just trying to get _us_ to help _him_. Blacks should work through their _own_ organizations," he said.

I was tempted to interject a remark about the limitations of minority politics. Jackson, after all, was trying to unite different cultures on common social and economic priorities. But before I could say anything, Ramírez shifted to racial problems on the job. After many years he had risen to a foreman's position. It had not been an easy life. But the younger workers, most of them black, didn't appreciate his early labors on their behalf. Because of his position, it was difficult to decide if his critical remarks reflected a cultural bias or simply the irritation with youth that is often second nature to those with seniority or tenure in the workingman's school of hard knocks. The black workers did not make that "extra effort." They lacked "pride in their work" and were "lazy." To their complaints about "illegals" in the Houston job market Ramírez responded much as a California agribusinessman would: "They take jobs you won't do." Once, provoked by a group of young black toughs, he lashed out, "Well, at least the wetbacks aren't on welfare."

In almost every respect, Ramírez personifies the tension between working-class chicano and the Mexican middle-class investors who have sunk their funds in local businesses. Many of these, he asserted, have chicano managers but are really owned by Mexican nationals. Some years ago, getting wind of *mexicano* investment, he whipped out a protest to the Small Business Administration complaining of collusion between Houston lawyers and Mexican investors who were getting U.S. federal funding and, ultimately, citizenship. It is not an uncommon criticism that circulates among laboring chicanos, people whose resentments over the intrusion of Mexican investments stem from the conviction that their own country has denied them their rightful economic opportunity. I was unable to persuade him that he may ultimately benefit from this foreign investment in *our* country. Rather, in an understandably distorted interpretation of things, the working-class Mexican American is convinced that both the American and Mexican governments are sustaining an economic injustice.

Just as I was on the verge of pursuing this riddle of the class-conscious but culturally sensitive working chicano, he digressed again, into a brief account of his political activities in the Rio Grande Valley.

In 1960, Mexican American political organizations were

invigorated and challenged by Viva Kennedy clubs. JFK carried Texas with a solid Mexican American vote, but in the aftermath of his narrow electoral victory the lot of Valley workers had not substantially improved. In 1963 the Political Association of Spanish-speaking Organizations (PASO) stunned the south Texas political establishment when Mexican Americans took over Crystal City. Anglo machines in twenty-six predominantly Hispanic Texas counties grew so alarmed they frantically began organizing to prevent a similar political calamity in other border towns.

They soon discovered that Crystal City had social and political traits most other south Texas towns lacked. Its Mexican Americans were not only numerically strong but stood virtually united against the seemingly ageless Anglo rule. They had the support of a labor union and political leaders who could articulate their grievances. Unlike most of the other south Texas communities, Crystal City did not number among its Mexican Americans a cabal of _vendidos_ ready and willing, as their pejorative Spanish nickname indicated, to "sell out" the chicano cause to the Anglos.[2]

As did other union organizers, Ramírez saw in the fledgling union movement in south Texas the prospect of chicano political opportunity. But the obstacles were formidable. In the Valley towns the labor intruders had to confront not only the political machines of the Anglo growers (who wielded almost total control over large numbers of Mexican Americans largely denied the vote) and their upper-class Mexican American allies (who kept in line the small numbers of their own people who did have the suffrage), but the Texas Rangers. The Meat Cutters Union, operating out of San Antonio, had a momentary success in the Valley towns but paid a heavy price. Its leaders expended huge sums, won a few converts, and wound up in jail for their trouble.

In 1967–1968 the United Farm Workers moved into the Valley and called a strike. The Rangers retaliated by throwing the organizers into jail. And the growers received some timely assistance from the Mexican government, which dispatched strikebreakers across the border to pick the unattended crops. Incidents of Ranger abuses in the Valley provoked even some in the Lone Star establishment. A young San Antonian from a prominent family spoke out so strongly he was thrown in jail and sodomized by his guards. Some time later, he abandoned San Antonio for an Israeli kibbutz.

The more militant chicanos joined with the American G.I. Forum and staged a protest march in Del Rio. The border military went on alert. "We weren't afraid. We had three thousand in that march, and the cops *had* to guarantee our safety," Ramírez said. He remembers those days with proud satisfaction. The *puro* went out again; he relighted it and continued. "The local Mexicans wanted to join us but they were afraid of losing their jobs." His voice displayed no tone of contempt but understanding of their plight.

Their march over and their protest lodged, the chicano activists headed back to the cities. The Del Rio affair and the prolonged union struggles in the Valley had scarcely altered the economic configuration of the border towns. And the seemingly fragile Anglo political machines had demonstrated once again their capacity to survive in a Spanish-speaking world. They had, after all, a political alliance with middle-class Mexican Americans and an economic hold over the stoop laborers and "wetbacks" across the Rio Grande.

I did not say anything but sensed in Ramírez compassion for the job-seekers from the south, a vague awareness that their presence in our country, his and mine, whether in south Texas, the Imperial Valley, or even Chicago, had served the union-busting cause. Perhaps, deep within his still tormented chicano and American spirit, he acknowledges the threat to his lifetime struggle and political labors. Yet his sense of community and identity with others who want to improve their lot overshadows any fear that the illegal immigrant may threaten his economic well-being.

It is this ultimate faith in fair play and social justice that acquits even the most racially conscious of working-class chicanos in any assessment of their place in American life. It is their conviction that there still exist injustices that must be righted and they must lead the way because they are, "first of all, Americans." It is the Mexican connection that is at once reassuring and debilitating. The aging chicano can see the barriers the gringos have erected against his progress. He courageously breaks them down, his battle cry the promise of fair play and justice that America pledges to all its people. Hispanics do not get proper medical care in Houston. They lack insurance, they cannot speak English, they are uneducated in the basics of preventive medicine. Often the *mexicanos* go to the folk healers because the *curanderos* are a tradition in rural Mexico. The Mexicans suffer physical and psychological stress from the agony of acculturation. They rely on the Trabajadores Sociales de Aztlán (Social Workers of Aztlán), one of the myriad Mexican aid societies, to counsel them on back problems, tension, and related troubles associated with living in the gringo's world.

It has to be troublesome for Ramírez that as a chicano he ought to be able to identify more with the Mexican migrant. But the *mexicano* can be as resistant to accommodation to the Mexican American world as he is to the Anglo's. Mexico is nearby, and the chicano, however *simpático,* is no Mexican. He may speak the language (or a corrupted variation), but a chicano is more American than Mexican. In Houston's east end, overwhelmingly Hispanic, a local bus company thrives on ferrying people to Monterrey and back on weekends. (In an analogous example of "home ties," an enterprising businessman once did a thriving trade busing Kentuckians from the Detroit auto factories back to their "Old Kentucky Homes" on weekends simply because a Kentuckian will do almost *anything* to be able to spend some time in the state.)

In Houston the city planner Ephron García talks frankly and a bit cynically about the presence of illegals, who may number as many as 150,000. They are important to the day-labor industry, but Houston does not advertise the opportunities (or social services) it can offer to the undocumented alien for the simple

175

reason that it wants the illegal as a worker—indeed, as does Los Angeles, its "sister" city at the western edge of the southwest—but not as a welfare recipient. Hereabouts they point to New York and Chicago as metropolitan governments that provided generous welfare benefits to the illegals and paid the price in benefits when the word spread in the illegal underground. Illinois and California, more generous than Texas in their social service offerings, get larger numbers of illegals, and the Texans have, shrewdly and callously, looked at the "bottom line" of what Hispanic immigration costs.

For example, Houston officials have been particularly alert to the somber statistics in *Southern California: A Region in Transition,* three ponderous volumes about the white flight from Los Angeles and its portent for Houston. Here, as in L.A., the Hispanics are beginning to make demands, for jobs, for representation in city and county government, and for services. Recently, the Harris County Hospital District board removed the only Hispanic from its membership and precipitated a brown uprising. Fifty percent of the births in the district, a third of the clinical visits, and a fourth of the emergency admissions are Hispanics. Of the four thousand employees of the hospital district, 350 are Hispanic. The Hispanics who will dominate Houston by 2000 contribute only a fraction of its firemen and policemen. The official explanation is that they lack proper skills. The Hispanic response is that Houston does not want to employ them because it *believes* that the Hispanic is unqualified for any except the most menial job, because Houston *knows* the value of Mexican labor.

Those who speculate about Houston's economic future must now apply an Hispanic measure to their calculations. In 1984, the chicano magazine *Nuestro,* studying the employment prospects for Hispanic youth, gloomily concluded that blacks and Hispanics will make a third of the labor force after 2000, but neither is adequately prepared to survive in the labor market. Hispanics are particularly vulnerable. They enter the labor force earlier than whites, and because of that may earn the same or even higher

176

incomes for a few years. But the character of Hispanic, especially Mexican American, employment is such that they are trapped in menial or low-skilled positions with no realistic hope of advancement. Their dropout rate is higher than that of blacks, and the effect of their low educational skills is aggravated by language barriers. In Houston the Association for the Advancement of Mexican Americans has brought pressure on parents and the schools to challenge Hispanic students into doing more, striving for higher goals, and staying in school.

For years Anglos have generally assumed that Hispanic Americans' educational goals reflected their lower aspirations for employment. In large part, I think, our historically modest assessment of the worthiness of Mexican labor and, ultimately, our denigration of the Mexican in this country have had much to do with our general expectation of the Hispanic American. In actuality, as "The Educational Status of Hispanic American Children" revealed, the *aspirations* of white, black, and Latino high schoolers are similar, but their *expectations* are unsettlingly different. Fifty percent of the blacks and whites believe they can get a college degree; 37 percent of the Latinos hold that notion. And, distressingly, the lowest expectations among Latinos are found among Mexican Americans. Even when federal efforts (such as the Job Training Partnership Program) lure them into training sessions where they can acquire the skills necessary for *future* jobs, they often drop out when immediate employment in a dead-end job is available.

Houston's economic soothsayers are talking about almost 700,000 new service jobs in Harris County by the year 2000. They are less gloomy about the skills Houston employees must have to carry out these tasks and cite as evidence the better-trained and better-educated Hispanic immigrant from Central and South America who will join the traditionally more poorly educated and poorly trained *mexicano* from the south. With a diversified Hispanic population, Houston's Anglos not only can retain their economic power but will be able to prevent Ramírez and his chicano allies from creating a unified Hispanic political culture. The Anglos can get a great steak for $20 in a nice restaurant because there's a Mexican dishwasher or cook in the back and still have a ready supply of more skilled labor to operate the computers, drive the trucks, or supervise the men down at the plant.

Once again, as in the past, the Hispanic will serve the Anglo's economic priorities. But in this optimistic forecast there are a few signs that Houston's Hispanics may be planning a different scenario. Predictably, the Mexicans are its formulators. The director of the University of Houston's Mexican American Studies Program, Tacho Mindiola, commented, "We Mexicans have to take the initiative ourselves. History has taught me that our needs are better met by our own people. My concern is, are there enough of us?"[3]

Ramírez' frustration over the years and the verbiage expended in trying to explain what "chicano" means and what the chicano agenda is have left him not so much embittered as weary. I can sense his bewilderment in trying to convey to a gringo "what the chicano is fighting for." The chicanos could not convince the middle-class Mexican Americans of the worthiness of their cause. Henry González, the San Antonio Hispanic stalwart, a symbol of the early-sixties Hispanic American future, remained suspicious of their purpose. Some of the problem had to do with the origins of the word. Ramírez and his chicano friends wanted a word that would solidify the Mexican Americans and inspire their efforts to mold a political culture. But the linguists got wrapped up with the origins of the word (a derivative from *meshicanos,* what the conquering Spanish called the Meshica Indians), and the larger Spanish-speaking community that presumably would be *united* under the rubric began quarreling over the social and political implications of the word. Some older Mexican Americans associated the term with socially unacceptable behavior; others, with radical politics that simply could not be accommodated in the "American system." Ultimately, the Hispanic American middle class became the beneficiary, as had the black middle class in the black civil rights movement of the sixties and the black power movement that followed.

People like Ramírez have invigorated the trade union movement in the still antiunion atmosphere of the southwest, and the college students who gloried in the movement in the sixties and seventies have achieved an identity in the academic establishment. But the chicanos have had to come to terms with an unsettling reality about _political culture_ in this country. They have been able to articulate the social and economic grievances of the Hispanic American in a vague Marxian class analysis, and they have been successful in identifying, by an angry summing-up of the historical record since 1848, the cultural and political ordeal the Mexican American has endured. But the chicano has been unable to forge a chicano political culture except in a very narrow sense.

Here, again, the intrusive and disturbing element is not the chicano invigorating spirit in the Mexican American, but the Mexican in both. Middle-class Mexican Americans like Henry González and Catherine Rocha who disdained identification with the chicanos did so, I believe, because as mainstream Americans they feared and rejected the Mexican intrusion into the shaping of a political subculture with no likelihood of general acceptance by _their_ America. And, similarly, it was the Mexican presence, symbolized by _mexicano_ janitors at the University of Texas who remained largely indifferent to the chicano campus activists, that ultimately nurtured in the students a determination to head for the Rio Grande Valley and march on behalf of Mexican agricultural workers. And it was this gradual, subtle process that ultimately brought the chicanos around to calling themselves _Mexicans,_ because, in a technical sense, ''chicano'' excludes the Mexican-born who come to America. After all, the _plan_ is solidarity.[4]

Ramírez' continued bewilderment at not being ''understood'' even among those who may be sympathetic to what he has been struggling for, has its origin in the intrusion of Mexico and Mexicans into MexAmerica Norte. He proudly calls himself chicano yet just as proudly believes he is ''first an American and then a Mexican.'' He portrays Mexico as a corrupt government ruling an oppressed people who must venture north to find opportunity; his social conscience dictates that America should accept them even when, as a working-class American, he may pay an economic price. Yet he suffers an inner conflict wrought, I would argue, by the unyielding demands of the Mexican within him. Just as the chicano activists have found, the *mexicano* does not subordinate his cultural instincts and priorities so readily to the chicano who professes to champion and lead his cause. Rather, just as America will tolerate, even encourage, Mexican American subculture, it does not willingly accommodate its political culture to extraneous pressures. Neither does the Mexican. In their striving for solidarity among Mexican Americans, the chicanos have discovered they must include the Mexicans among them and the Mexicans coming north.

Some chicanos have even begun to call themselves Mexicans. America may tolerate Ramírez' self-description as ''American first, then Mexican.'' But Mexico will not.

Part II

11

Pittsburgh, Mexico

≡≡≡

In *Another Mexico,* written in an age when the Mexican state and Holy Mother Church were locked in mortal combat, Graham Greene entered the wonderful country from Laredo. Nuevo Laredo was different, he thought, but when he got to Monterrey he imagined himself back in the United States. He found a hotel that looked American and food prescribed for the American palate. Monterrey, he decided, was a stopover for Americans headed for Mexico City, so the Mexicans had long ago decided that it was worthwhile (and economically advantageous) to make the Yankee traveler feel right at home, 150 miles deep into Mexico.

Speeding into the night from the Monterrey airport, headed for the Pittsburgh of Mexico, my voluble taxi driver offered me a choice of hotels. "We offer two nice places downtown," he said. "You can stay at the Holiday Inn Aurola or the Hotel Ancira. The Aurola is very classy, with a nice bar and floor show every night, and it has those glass elevators, the kind you can see from. But a lot of people who come here like the Ancira. It looks a little run-down from the outside but it is very nice, very traditional. If you want a woman you get a better selection there."

I did not ask but presumed that the Ancira's reputation as a trysting spot rested on its longevity. It was built, I found out later, in the early years of the Revolution and somehow managed to survive the battles that plagued northern Mexico. Knowing neither, I decided on the Aurola. There is something about name recognition. The driver was correct about the bar and the floor show. About nine on my first evening I headed downstairs, joined a throng gathered for hors d'oeuvres and margaritas, and waited an hour or so for the predictably high-powered and predictably loud singer to make her appearance. When I left three hours later, walking in a noticeably labored way, she was still bellowing. In Mexico there are night people and day people. The *cantante* persevered until three or four o'clock in the morning. Those who truly qualify as nocturnal professionals probably didn't start arriving at what is billed as northern Mexico's most fabulous night spot until about midnight. In the Ancira, doubtless, they were going to bed at that hour.

The next morning, strolling through downtown "Pittsburgh," I could understand the taxi driver's description, however brief, of the Ancira. It is an Hispanic edifice in a world of physical and human deterioration. Monterrey is Mexico's industrial, not its cultural, symbol, so the faces here, particularly in these hard times of high unemployment, have the look of despair. Greene came looking for monuments to God in a country at war with the true faith. He found one just outside Monterrey, the Bishop's Palace, erected at the end of the colonial period. It had survived even Pancho Villa's machine guns. I came a half century later, to a city in a country still "far from God and so close to the United States," and found another church, much weathered by the years, near the Central Market. It is a citadel of faith surrounded by diminutive row houses and small shops and businesses and yelling sidewalk vendors with peppers or bananas or melons. Someone has scrawled on the stone entryway into the churchyard: "Don't close the Fundidora."

In Monterrey the working class and what passes for the middle class coexist. They are economically but not socially or politically interdependent. In the Pittsburgh of America you cannot differentiate between middle and working classes by looking at what people wear (except to work), what they eat, or even where they live; in the Pittsburgh of Mexico, a stroll through the downtown mall (modeled on those of American towns) and a hike "uptown" toward the Central Market and beyond to the dingy bedlam of the bus station, a distance of less than a mile, is a migration from one world to another. You can move up in the world in Pittsburgh, U.S.A., and live in the same house and eat the same food and keep the social and political values you have always had. In Pittsburgh, Mexico, you are what your father was, you have what your father had, and you believe what your father believed.

Even before the Porfiriato—the thirty-five-year rule of the authoritarian don Porfirio Díaz, who is largely credited with initiating the modern Mexican industrial state—Monterrey had emerged as a vigorous commercial center. In the eighteenth century, its entrepreneurs fashioned a contraband trade in defiance of an economically stultifying Spanish bureaucracy. After the war with the United States, the availability of foreign goods advanced the city's reputation as Mexico's internal commercial center. During the American Civil War, years when Mexico endured European intervention and French occupation, Monterrey's commercial vitality persevered. Southern cotton, destined for European markets, passed through its trading houses and enriched its commercial classes.

A few years later, Monterrey began to shift to small manufacturing and industry—hats, soap, and *mezcal*, the poor Mexican's substitute for tequila. But its leading entrepreneurs, inspired by the American example, dreamed of bigger plans. They dispatched eager representatives to expositions, in San Antonio, New Orleans, and even Paris, promoting Monterrey's reputation as a producer of clothes, furniture, cigarettes, and bricks. By the end of the century more than a hundred new companies, mostly small industries that produced for local consumption, had sprung up in Monterrey and the Mexican state of Nuevo León.

The move toward an industrial economy in Monterrey required both political inspiration and economic calculation. Bernardo Reyes, the governor of Nuevo León from 1885 until 1909, was one of Mexico's most avid promoters of development. Very early

185

in his gubernatorial tenure, Reyes recognized that U.S. tariff barriers and Díaz' encouragement of a national railway system doomed Monterrey's domination of north Mexican trade. The legendary capitalists of the city who had built their fortunes on commerce arrived at similar conclusions. Among the hundred new ventures of the last decade of the nineteenth century were two giants—Cuauhtémoc and Fundidora de Fierro y Acero (Iron and Steel). The first began in 1891 as a brewery organized by a German and three Mexicans, Isaac Garza, Francisco Sada, and Jose Mugüerza. A decade later, Cuauhtémoc had expanded into the production of glass, paper, cardboard, and cork-lined bottle caps. In the twentieth century it diversified into metallurgical and chemical sectors. By the 1980s the Cuauhtémoc Conglomerate was an impressive network of mining, manufacturing, finance, and commerce.

Fundidora also counted foreigners among its founding fathers—an Italian, a Frenchman, a Spaniard, and an enterprising American, Eugene Kelley—but its driving spirits were *mexicanos,* Ernesto Madero, brother of the martyred heir of don Porfirio's presidential chair, and Isaac Garza, one of the triumvirate of Mexicans who had established Cuauhtémoc. They began a familial dynasty whose descendants and various incorporated clans have ruled the Pittsburgh of Mexico down to the present time. In the postwar Mexican miracle, Eugenio Garza Sada exemplified the modern breed of dynamic Mexican capitalist. Abetted by a succession of national politicians who spouted Revolutionary slogans but who championed economic growth, even at the expense of social reform, these financial dynamos transformed the Mexican economy.

Monterrey, more than any other emerging Mexican industrial center, stood as hallmark of the private-development model, and its entrepreneurial magnates proudly boasted they could show the "socialists" in the capital what the aggressively proud *norteños* were capable of achieving. In the process Garza Sada and his associates, bound by familial ties and marital alliances, built an empire. They transformed Monterrey into a company town with little regard for traditional Hispanic urban ambience. Save for a few sites downtown—the rectangular mall with its flowery gardens, walkways, a statehouse constructed in the ornate nineteenth-century architectural style, a modernistic congressional building, and the rust-colored Lighthouse of Commerce rising above the green carpet—Monterrey, like Pittsburgh, exudes a working-class image.

Monterrey represents the economic dilemmas of modern Mexico. Here the promise of an industrial society took hold: migratory rural laborers who found employment in the mills of Fundidora and a presumably benevolent shield of grand enterprises presided over by men of business acumen and a paternalistic affection for their hardworking and mezcal-swilling labor force. The dream was a symbiotic union of modern industrial strategy, emulating the faith in technology and a consumer society that has flourished to the north, and the cherished traditions of Hispanic familial culture. In such a world, the Monterrey wizards believed, a vigorous middle-class Mexico could thrive, supplying the laboring armies with more than adequate supplies of cheap products.

Because Mexico inherited from Spain a tradition of political interference in the private economy, the threat of government meddling, especially after the Revolution, has always been present. Given the integration of labor into the Institutional Revolutionary Party (PRI) and the complicated labor code, the Monterrey industrial magnates have always had good reason to fear the long (and usually forceful) reach of the federal bureaucracy into their affairs. But they have always had an advantage over the other industrial urban centers. Monterrey's economic moguls started out in the nineteenth century with capital generated by the city's dominance in north Mexican commerce. Early on, the captains of industry and the managers of high finance joined forces. By the time the Revolution triumphed and began trumpeting the cause of "social redemption," they were readily capable of resisting the socialist tide most Americans believed was engulfing Mexico.

Mexico adopted a leftist constitution in 1917, and some of its post-Revolutionary leaders, especially Lázaro Cárdenas in the thirties, waxed enthusiastic about social reform, but the Monterrey clans survived. In 1940, when Mexico's industrial economy began to expand rapidly, bringing about the postwar "economic miracle," the Monterrey chieftains insulated themselves against state interference on behalf of their industrial armies by the expedient of co-opting the potential leaders of any worker rebellion. Fundidora and Cuauhtémoc began constructing workers' housing, located near the huge plants, before World War I. Cuauhtémoc adopted the motto "Everybody His Own Home," for its cooperative society, and by the 1960s, it was estimated, had subsidized 2,300 houses. In the early years of the Alliance for Progress, U.S. aid, channeled through Cuauhtémoc's Patronage Center, financed the construction of another 2,500 homes for laborers of "modest financial capability." The center also established a system of company stores to dispense food and clothing, deducting the cost from workers' paychecks. In paternalistic fashion, the companies even declared their responsibility for the recreation and education of their employees.

None of this signaled the millennium for the city's industrial toilers. Rather, it enabled the companies to quiet most potential unrest by rewarding a selected few, a management practice not unknown north of the Rio Grande. A laborer who received one of the tiny houses in Lomo Linda, the Levittown of Monterrey, a mansion in comparison with the wretched shacks down the road, more often than not was a *skilled* worker so beholden to Cuauhtémoc for his mortgage that he dared not risk ejection from his home by causing any trouble on the job. And such practices reinforced the familial domination of the founding fathers. Among old *regiomontanos,* as Monterrey's residents call themselves, circulate stories of their habit of strolling through the factories, calling on José or Rodrigo or Abelardo and in paternalistic concern inquiring about personal problems or dispensing a trinket.

Their heirs are of necessity more sophisticated. They identify workers who are "men who can be trusted" and boost them in rank to act as go-betweens with the unions. The reward can be anything from a mortgage loan or a scholarship for a child to attend Monterrey Tech to the institutionalized _mordida_. When labor activists become more threatening to industrial order, they are fired and then blacklisted. If too numerous, they may be locked out.[1]

Mexican labor codes are, at first glance, protective of workers' rights, but in the reality of Mexican judicial practice the courts generally favor those who stand for economic (read "social") order. The system gets more arbitrary in the smaller companies because, among other things, the labor code makes small demands on plants employing fewer than a hundred workers. A company will subdivide to avoid the government's requirement that employers assist an employee with a year's seniority in purchasing a house, or, quite frankly, in order to contain the unions with a strategy of divide and conquer.

Where have the Revolutionary heirs in the capital stood in these struggles? A disgruntled worker expressed a not uncommon bitterness in a labor periodical:

"I am one of the millions of exploited workers in this country asking for justice. We all know that the humble people are not listened to, but perhaps my plea will change the hearts of the leaders who instead of making politics should be defending the worker and not deceive him. At the moment they help the capitalist because they are well treated by him. Always when the worker claims something, they will call him an agitator and the capitalists, the government and the union leaders feel very offended. . . . Leaders and government have rendered us to the capitalists. . . . In the absence of decent government we will continue to be controlled by those who determine our misfortune. . . . I hope . . . we will turn into reality the real aspirations of those who made the Revolution and about whom the government is talking so much."[2]

His lament, written in 1970, came toward the close of an era of probusiness governments more concerned with developing Mexican industry than with dealing with the social costs it had

the Monterrey of the privileged lived its economic and social elites in houses of such grandeur they were unequaled in any other region of Mexico. They lived in splendor while the "other Mexico" lived in hideous shacks with animals and trash. For their pleasure and comfort, the potentates of Monterrey thought nothing of importing a European theatrical group or flying down a musical group on a special plane for an evening's entertainment.[4]

Yet, even accounting for the persistent social rigidity, some regions, including Monterrey, the northern cities, and the Federal District, had fared better, and, everything considered, had provided a comparatively progressive economic climate. And Monterrey had done so with an industrial economy less beholden to the state. Yet its very success now became, in the view of President Luís Echeverría, who took office in 1970, a challenge for a Mexican government determined to restore its badly damaged image.

In his *sexenio,* Echeverría shifted the government to the left. The move was more rhetorical than real, but the Monterrey economic giants began to complain loudly of a government that was less supportive and more obtrusive. They began echoing the credos of the Chicago School of Economics. But in a country like Mexico, where the "free market" is an abstraction, the government had no intention of standing aside and allowing the more dynamic Monterrey families to chart Mexico's economic future. As Echeverría saw matters, the country's economic troubles demanded political solutions. The state could not be neutral in the economic order. With the armies of impoverished *campesinos* pushing into the cities, demanding social services and draining already overburdened bureaucracies, Echeverría declared, the government had to chart a new economic model. More candidly, he announced that Mexico must become a third-world leader, resist the intrusive American economy, and identify with the other "victims" of international capitalism and Zionism. When the affronted Monterrey chieftains objected, he characterized them as traitorous Jewish fascists.

In actuality, Mexico's economic troubles were essentially self-induced. Their origin lay in the state-dominated economy, a politically corporate structure in which politicians and capitalists had fashioned the "Mexican miracle" at the expense of their own people. Import substitution, for example, had enabled the fledgling industries of the forties to mature. From 1957 until 1967, Mexican manufacturing shot up by 120 percent, intermediate goods (chemicals, nonmetallic minerals) by 170 percent, and capital goods by 160 percent. But products of final consumption had actually declined from 62 to 53 percent.[5] All the while a new generation had come of age, expecting more of everything. By the end of the sixties, government economists were saying that import substitution was no longer working, but the addicted were loath to give it up. And, of course, they were even more reluctant to pay higher taxes to deal with the social costs of Mexico's wrenching economic transformation.

Through the early seventies the Monterrey _grupos_ looked disdainfully and somewhat fearfully on the combative Echeverría and his army of state planners who lamented Mexican dependence and energetically pushed ambitious projects. Addressing the country's weak scientific and technological infrastructure, the new political impresarios ordained a National Council of Science and Technology. (In the preceding decade, Mexico had expanded $200 million annually on research and development, which, because of its foreign origin, had permitted an even greater intrusion by the multinationals into the country's economy.) They announced bold new social programs in chronically suffering rural Mexico, and until business pressure compelled him to back off, Echeverría was on the verge of bringing about a revolutionary change in Mexico's tax structure. He did manage to push through a new investment law that limited foreign ownership of Mexican business to 49 percent, but the private sector finally persuaded him to interpret its application in such a manner that foreign investors would not be scared away.

Untroubled by warnings that the state's deepening plunge into

193

the economy—in six years the government doubled its participation in Mexican firms to 845—was really a deterrent to private investment, Echeverría launched into ever grander products. His pride was the huge Sicartsa steel mill in Michoacán, a billion-dollar state enterprise on the coast in the "workers' city" of Lázaro Cárdenas. The Monterrey industrialists called it a monument to socialist ineptitude. From the beginning the Mexican variation of "Murphy's Law" seemed to dictate the course of the ambitious project. The government had to borrow the money to build the plant; it had to go outside Mexico to get basic parts; it built an "instant slum" to house the workers; the plant turned out steel wire, which Mexico didn't need. But in the end its sponsor was able to do what American presidents often do when their economic models founder on the shoals of economic realities. In 1976 Echeverría turned the Sicartsa boondoggle and Mexico's other economic burdens over to his successor, José López Portillo.

When JLP donned the presidential sash he could not reverse his predecessor's economic policies, but he did try to repair some of the damage to relations with the private sector. The government retained its domination in basic industries such as steel and its heavy involvement in mining, tourism, and communication; and it announced its continued "participation" in a myriad array of other enterprises. There were renewed grumblings of disappointment. But JLP reminded critics of the state's intrusion that the government was "protecting" vulnerable Mexican business against the pressures of foreign capital and providing it with support in an uncertain world market. The state and the private sector were allies.

And he assured the International Monetary Fund that Mexico would act responsibly by shaving public expenditures and holding the line on wages. Major industrial and commercial enterprises pledged $8 billion in new investments and the government used its considerable political clout with labor to keep wage increases at modest levels. As the Mexican economy tightened under these controls, the smaller and more heavily indebted businesses had difficulty in paying their dollar obligations. In Monterrey, the government assumed management of the huge Fundidora plant in return for a bail-out loan of $50 million. But generally, the private sector showed improvement, and the IMF was mollified by the reversal of inflation and the government's declining deficit. Those who bore the greatest burden were, predictably, ordinary _mexicanos_ who suffered a declining real wage and a surge in unemployment. This was lamentable, JLP declared, but a necessary price for Mexican recovery.

Then the discoveries of enormous oil reserves in the southeast threw Mexico into a frenzy of expansion by both state and private sectors. PEMEX, the national petroleum company, grew so enormously fast that in a few years it became a "state within a state." It built new refineries, pipelines, and petrochemical plants, and even facilitated the revival of Mexico's languishing steel industry. Every part of the national economy, even historically troubled agriculture, was soon benefiting from the oil bonanza. The psychological impact on the previously despondent national mood was electrifying.[6]

In Monterrey stood the private sector's principal rival to PEMEX, the Alfa Group, created in 1974 by a division of the Monterrey Group (whose chairman, Eugenio Garza Sada, had been killed by kidnappers in 1973) into Alfa and VISA. Alfa absorbed struggling companies, expanding into tourism, real estate, food processing, and auto parts. It soon became the largest conglomerate in Latin America. From the benevolent state came tax credits and inexpensive energy, which the Garza-Sada financial godfathers of Monterrey, who had been fuming about government meddling a few years back, uncomplainingly accepted. They even nodded approvingly when Mexico City announced a new National Industrial Development Plan, which established "trajectories" for national industry and blamed Mexico's industrial retardation on excessive dependence on the internal market, concentration of plants in Guadalajara, Monterrey, and Mexico City, import substitution, and oligopolistic enterprises.

The report, of course, did *not* indict government policy but Mexico's "economic structure," though, clearly, the government's encouragement of import substitution of consumer goods had compelled industry to seek capital goods investment from foreign sources, which preordained Mexican dependence, not independence. But, then, that had been the intention: Give the producers of cheap domestic goods a captive market so they can develop even if they must borrow excessively from the international market—as the report stated, use their "foreign savings"— and neglect the development of a scientific-technological infrastructure an advanced industrial society must have.[7]

A writer for *Forbes* magazine, visiting Alfa group headquarters on Los Angeles Street in Monterrey in 1979, glowingly described its chieftain, Bernardo Garza Sada, an MIT graduate, as more than a successful Mexican businessman. Garza Sada had decorated his office with expensive paintings and imported MBAs from Harvard and Wharton to manage Alfa's far-flung economic empire. Mexico must be transformed, the Mexican told his visitor, but its culture must be preserved. "The government is trying to do the same things we are, produce cheaper goods for the Mexican market and for export."[8]

Since then, the grand design of the oil-boom years has fallen into disarray. Under Miguel de la Madrid Hurtado, the government has retrenched from its domineering role in the private sector, but the private sector wants more. To pay the price demanded by the Monterrey chieftains, de la Madrid must make a political sacrifice: he must acknowledge that the direction of Mexico's economy will be determined by international economic realities, not by the political dictates of the federal bureaucracy and its minions.

There are strong indications that the *jefe* of Mexico, who will choose his successor in 1988, has concluded that import substitution, the foundation of the Mexican economic miracle of the postwar period, must expire. When he took office in late 1982, de la Madrid spoke of "moral renovation," which meant, among other things, a whittling away at the bloated federal bureaucracy. He accomplished a bit of moral renovating, but most of the two million Mexican bureaucrats kept their jobs. The peso rose from 80 to the dollar in 1982 and pushed toward 1,700 to the dollar five years later. But the Harvard man in the Mexican presidential palace made good on his pledges to reduce the government's participation in so much business.

This should please Monterrey's elite and reaffirm the Mexican variation of the economic gospel according to the Harvard Business School. By disdaining import substitution Mexico must look even more to an outside market, a move de la Madrid began several years ago when the country's burdensome foreign debt brought on what Mexico's ordinary people refer to as, simply, _la crisis_. His more enthusiastic supporters speak of a renewed modernization of the national economy. In July 1986, Mexico completed arrangements for its entry into the General Agreement on Tariffs and Trade (GATT), which will eventually mean that foreign companies will be able to penetrate even more deeply into the once-shielded Mexican economy. It will also mean that a multinational wishing to sell in Mexico will pay a tariff established by common agreement rather than a bribe to a Mexican official trying to supplement his monthly income.

The barriers are tumbling elsewhere. Like any good _técnico_, de la Madrid has announced that the old requirement of 50 percent Mexican ownership in foreign companies setting up plants in the country will be "reevaluated" on an individual basis. In a limited way, he has revolutionized the Mexican government's approach to the economy as no other Mexican leader has done since the Revolution. The government is even paying interest rates far above the rate of inflation in order to stem the flow of capital flight.

But the anticipated praise from Monterrey and Mexico's private sector has not been accorded to the _mexicano_ Harvard man's stringent economic regimen. As the government has sold off many of its companies and escalated the interest rate on savings, the shrill litany from the private sector has not quieted

197

but risen in volume. The private economy, along with the public, has been shrinking. When private businessmen line up to borrow money, they must pay interest rates of 100 percent and take what is left after the federal bureaucrats reach deep into the financial barrel. In the "other Mexico," the deepening economic crisis has brought a renewed militancy to organized labor, which is now demanding wage increases pegged to the cost of living.

For the day laborers in the Pittsburgh of Mexico, *la crisis* has wrought more than a burdensome inflation and a seemingly irreversible rise in unemployment. The government has closed down the huge Fundidora steel mill, Monterrey's industrial symbol. Other closures will follow. At the moment Monterrey is trying to project cheerfulness because of the nation's record in the World Cup games, but in the eyes of these weathered faces you can see the look of despair. Up at the bus station, where on a clear day you can see the luxurious dwellings clinging to the hillside, they are forming queues at the window under the Transportes al Norte sign, which offers express service to Laredo, San Antonio, St. Louis, and the end of the line, Chicago. I sit there for an hour, watching the rough-looking males and their emaciated women and their wretched children, waiting patiently. These are people who cannot read but have heard from the governor of Nuevo León, a stern-looking character, that he cannot "create happiness by decree" in face of the reality of more unemployment. A cartoon in a local newspaper shows a man reading the news to his wife: "Monterrey needs sixty thousand employees," he says with a smile. "Yes," responds his spouse, "but you're not one of them."

On my last day I stroll along the mall, headed for Sanborn's and the four-o'clock crowd of coffee drinkers and their ceaseless conversations about *fútbol* and *la crisis*. I try but cannot avoid a bookstall operated by evangelicals. They offer *Corrupción,* a sordid account of the international narcotics industry. "Where are you from?" one of them asks. "Georgia." "We know about your former president," the literary evangelical says. "He was a drug trafficker. And so was his brother. We know. We keep a list.''

I do not ask for the list and walk faster to my rendezvous with the Monterrey small-business coffee club. A half-block from my destination, there is an urchin sitting on the pavement. He has a dingy cigar box in front for the occasional coin tossed his way. But he is not begging. He is singing about the hard times of his life and his father's loss of work at the Fundidora. The voice never seems to tire. He lacks even a fundamental training in voice, and occasionally a passerby will mockingly laugh. But the boy remains undaunted. ''God,'' he reaffirms at the end of every stanza of his improvised lament, ''will save me.''

A half century after Graham Greene came this way, looking for an isolated monument to God's presence, the dispossessed of ''godless Mexico'' retain a glimmer of faith, if no longer in themselves or their government or even their future.

12

Hernando's Hideaway

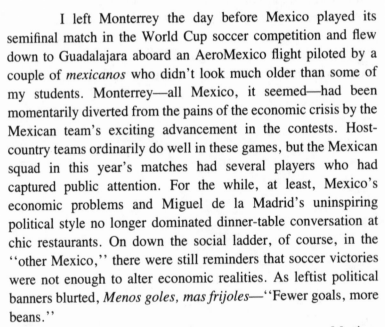

I left Monterrey the day before Mexico played its semifinal match in the World Cup soccer competition and flew down to Guadalajara aboard an AeroMexico flight piloted by a couple of *mexicanos* who didn't look much older than some of my students. Monterrey—all Mexico, it seemed—had been momentarily diverted from the pains of the economic crisis by the Mexican team's exciting advancement in the contests. Host-country teams ordinarily do well in these games, but the Mexican squad in this year's matches had several players who had captured public attention. For the while, at least, Mexico's economic problems and Miguel de la Madrid's uninspiring political style no longer dominated dinner-table conversation at chic restaurants. On down the social ladder, of course, in the "other Mexico," there were still reminders that soccer victories were not enough to alter economic realities. As leftist political banners blurted, *Menos goles, mas frijoles*—"Fewer goals, more beans."

Guadalajara, I anticipated, offered a more prosperous Mexico. If there is a typical Mexican city, with just the proper mix of industrial and agricultural foundation in a traditional ambience, travelers aver, it is this capital of Jalisco state, a jigsaw-puzzle outline in western Mexico. American retirees like Jalisco far more than any other site in Mexico; in 1985, it was estimated, more than twenty thousand had settled in Guadalajara's middle-class *colo-*

nias or in one of the villages hugging Lake Chapala. With a monthly income of $700 or $800 a couple can keep a maid, enjoy eggs Benedict and bloody Marys at one of the lakeside inns, and with satellite dishes watch American television.

Old-timers say that things are not quite as pleasant or secure as they were before *la crisis,* but that the U.S. government has unfairly labeled Guadalajara as Mexico's drug capital. In 1982, when outgoing president José López Portillo nationalized the banks, he effectively halved the dollar savings accounts Americans (and not a few Mexicans) held by converting them to pesos. The impact was not quite as unsettling hereabouts, but the numbers of newcomers dwindled, and some Americans began grumbling about being "prisoners of the Lake Chapala paradise." Then came the surge in Guadalajara's crime rate and the killing of Enrique Camarena, a Drug Enforcement Administration agent who liked to drink beer at the Guadalajara American Legion post. When the State Department issued a travel advisory for Jalisco, the president of the American Society expressed irritation over Ambassador John Gavin's occasionally severe remarks about Guadalajara's reputation.[1]

The American colony here is the largest assemblage of American citizens anywhere outside the United States. They have transplanted middle-class America into a city of 3.5 million, yet, by and large, they remain aloof—even from middle-class Mexico. Their friends are other Americans. They can easily get by without learning much more than a few Spanish phrases to order a meal or give instructions to the maid. They have their own newspaper, the *Colony Reporter,* as thoroughly small-town as any on the Kansas prairie. In the tradition of American communities in the last century they celebrated the Fourth of July in 1986 with an egg toss, watermelon-eating contest, sack-and-foot race, and tug-of-war, listened to the U.S. consul read the President's Independence Day Proclamation, and finished with a square dance. The only concession to Mexican-American cultural unity was the playing of the American and Mexican national anthems by the Guadalajara Municipal Band.

When I arrived the city's hotels were jammed with French and Brazilian tourists who had flown in to watch their national soccer teams compete at the stadium. I had to settle for a deteriorating five-story establishment at the convergence of three streets but only a few blocks from Guadalajara's center. For $12 a night the middle-aged manager provided a dingy room with a "Servibar" crammed with sodas, beer, an assortment of airline-style diminutive liquor bottles, packages of candy and chips, and to finish the evening, Pepto-Bismol. But unlike the proprietors of more fashionable hotels, he did not bother to lock the bar nor require a deposit for its use. At the end of my stay he dispatched a maid up to the room to take a count.

Early in my first day I asked for directions to the bus station. "Maybe you should have breakfast first," the manager suggested. He pointed toward an adjacent cafeteria. "It's a long walk to the bus station." The breakfast offerings turned out to be less elegant than the sumptuous buffet in the Holiday Inn back in Monterrey, where for $6.50 I had enjoyed a Mexican/American/European cuisine. But for $1 in this considerably less pretentious place I could have my ranch-style eggs with hot sauce and generous portions of refried beans. The flies hovering about the melon slices were the only discouragement to an otherwise adequate meal that would sustain me on the day's hike.

And compared to the offerings of the street vendors along my route, it was an elegant breakfast. A block or so from my hotel I passed an "outdoor café." Two fat women had set up three dingy tables to serve their morning clients—a curly-haired taxi driver with a cigarette perched atop his left ear and a wretched man with a battered suitcase tied with rope. One of the women squeezed juice into a bowl, pressing the orange halves between two hands with such vigor that her face reddened in the effort. The other stirred a concoction of beans and bits of meat and chicken in a No. 3 washtub. The taxi driver finished his helping with a gulp from the bowl, wiped his mustache dry with his shirt sleeve, and tossed 200 pesos on the table—a quarter for breakfast. While middle-class Mexico dines on omelettes at Denny's up the way, the other Mexico begins its day at Rosa's Sidewalk Café.

In Jalisco the distance between the middle class and the other Mexico has not diminished appreciably, yet it is middle-class Mexico, Americans believe, which by its success and prospects for a better life will bring about a better society and demand an honest government to preside over it. In this belief, however, we are transferring our own measure of the strength and convictions of middle-class America to a culture that cannot easily accommodate those values and to a nation in which it is the middle classes who are least satisfied with the government but less sure than the "other Mexico" about who they are. I encountered this ingrained and disturbing uncertainty again on the Mexican coast, in Puerto Vallarta.

Bouncing along in a van from the airport with five other travelers from as far away as Chicago and Rio de Janeiro, I am reminded of the hemispheric reach of Mexican tourist promotion. And though P.V. lacks the jet-setter flashiness of Acapulco, my five momentary fellow travelers will find here, as American hucksters say, "something for everyone." They can lodge at one of the fashionable places for a hundred bucks a night and spend their days lying on the beach gazing upward at the hang gliders over the bay and their evenings sipping margaritas in the tropical atmosphere of the hotel lounge, listening to an inevitably monotonous Latin band trying to keep pace with a curvaceous Mexican singer who has uncorrectable vocal mistiming but precisely orchestrated body movements.

When the van pulls up at the first of them the youthful driver asks the Spanish equivalent of "Anybody for this place?" An overweight Brazilian, his shirt unbuttoned to display graying chest hairs nestling a medallion, and his well-tanned bleached-blond companion get out. The others—newlyweds from the midwest who cannot afford Acapulco and a ponderous woman from Chicago—decide to lodge at the Posada, which has a more tropical ambience and joins the international community at the north end of town. The Chicagoan, who has come down on the AeroMéxico milk run, plops out and with a grin informs us that her next days will be spent "soakin' up that goddam sun."

Turning to me the *mexicano* driver queries, "You want to stay here?"

"No," I tell him, "take me to *el centro*"—downtown. After a short distance he turns off the paved highway onto the narrow cobblestone street, P.V.'s main drag, and slows to accommodate the surprisingly heavy traffic. At the pastel-stuccoed city government building the "downtowners" are already lining up at the information desks to pick up handfuls of brochures on everything from a boat ride to Mismaloya to hunting in the hills just outside town. He pulls to a stop in front of a modest two-story corner building with a sign, Hotel del Rey, the King's Hotel, hanging overhead. "This is a good place," he says reassuringly. "My cousin is the manager."

Inside, the "cousin," a polite, ever-smiling fellow who serves as manager/desk clerk/tourist adviser, gives me his choice room— a sparsely furnished single with a rumbling overhead fan and light sockets precariously attached to a wire emerging from the wall. Noting the dangerously rigged lighting, I surmise that the "cousin" is probably also the hotel electrician.

But after a few evenings sitting on the narrow balcony drinking Dos Equis beer and listening to the street chatter I acquire a fondness for the King's Hotel. My only regret is that Ava Gardner is not the manager.

Not until John Huston's *Night of the Iguana* did American tourists "discover" Puerto Vallarta. The movie was not filmed here, but that did not matter. Mismaloya, where Ava Gardner frolicked with two virile *mexicanos* in the surf, is only a short boat ride from the parabolic beach with its high-rise hotels at the north edge of town with their attentive Mexican (and American and Canadian) staff who cater to the fancies of California surfers, *narcotraficantes,* and plain Janes from Sioux City.

Puerto Vallarta's tourist promoters have tried to preserve the town's ambience of small artisan shops and quaint boutiques, but they learned years ago an unalterable economic truth about its livelihood. If the tourists don't come with their dollars or pound notes or francs, P.V.'s curio shops, real estate offices, markets, casual restaurants, and even "Charlie's European Spa" suffer. Old-timer Americans, retirees or winter residents, have invested in bungalows on the hillside known locally as Gringo Gulch. An uncommon alliance between the Gringo Gulchers—here the word is not derogatory—and a vocal minority of the Puerto Vallarta social elite has grown out of discontent with the taxis, buses, and tourist vans clogging the narrow streets. In P.V., you can get virtually anything: a tan, a boat ride, a Texas-size steak, chili (Texas-style), a T-shirt that says "Have a Shitty Day in Puerto Vallarta," and of course the country's leather, jewelry, and handicraft.

I confirmed the diverse offerings with an aging gringo who lived here in the "before-Huston" years. We sat drinking beer at eleven in the morning in an outdoor restaurant, the Fuente de la Puente (Fountain by the Bridge), so called because the owner had erected a crude fountain out of pipes to spray water from the Río Cuale, the fetid creek that runs through P.V. into the Pacific a few hundred yards downstream. He gestured toward me with his half-raised bottle of Dos Equis. "Sure, you can get anything in P.V. But hell, man, you can get laid with less trouble than you can get across that damn street out there!"

The tourists who had wearied from the morning heat or from haggling with the curio dealers across the way were already crowding around us. An all-American family sat down at the next table, displacing two fortyish women—one of whom bore a faint resemblance to a sixtyish Ava Gardner—and a young Mexican male. The American, who spoke with a noticeable midwestern accent, began laughing about his wife's solitary purchase in an entire morning of shopping—a pullover displaying the reddened butt of a fat woman and the unnecessary explanation, "I Roasted My Buns in P.V." "See what I mean?" said my gringo *compañero*.

In this Mexican port the middle class of MexAmerica—the

businessmen from Toledo and Torreón—will find not a tropical paradise but, more accurately, a small-town community overrun by freckled California surfers, "heepies," middle-aged Kansans who cannot endure Acapulco's pace (or surcharge), and those who serve them. In keeping with the down-home ambience, the cops patrol in aged VW Beetles.

But Puerto Vallarta has not been able to exclude the Mexican impoverished, who are less visible here but still present a few miles in the hills that ring the narrow valley in some nondescript village. Occasionally a wandering gringo casually strolling about the cobblestone streets will catch a glimpse of the other Mexico. Once he ceases gawking at the California girls in their cutoffs or the pullovers with their silly inscriptions or mountainous piles of cheap souvenirs, rich man has no trouble finding poor man in P.V. They are people who make do. Turning at one corner, opening on to a block of small boutiques and offices, I came on an aging *mexicano* building a cinder-block wall. He had no concrete mixer, not even a wheelbarrow, only a shovel and water. On the side of the cobblestone street he had formed a volcanic cone with the powdery cement. He carefully poured a gallon or so of water into the ring, then, moving around his creation, he deftly mixed powder and liquid until, after half an hour, he had a mound of concrete dough.

Fifty yards inland from the ocean, the Río Cuale broadens into a small bayou. Here men stand for hours in the darkened pool and toss fishing nets. Looking downstream from the small bridge I observed the "other Mexico" gathering for the noon meal. From a squalid lean-to clinging to the steep riverbank, a woman emerged with a black pot of victuals—beans and rice with specks of meat. She was an entrepreneur with a decidedly limited menu. Río Cuale's below-the-bridgers lined up and extended plastic plates on which the woman ladled generous offerings of the blue-plate special. Two of the customers arrived pulling donkeys laden with bundles of tree branches that country people use for cooking and keeping warm in the hills. A man squatting on the grassy slope nestled the plate of beans and rice in his lap, reached into a brown paper sack, and pulled out a sandwich. The wrinkled restaurateur did not appear irritated with the brown-bagger, but when she looked up at a few Americans on the bridge gawking at a boy defecating by the stream, her facial expression conveyed irritation and then defiance. They had invaded the world of the "other Mexico."

Later that day I headed across the bridge and turned onto a narrow path winding through the sliver of island in the Río Cuale. Here, in a meticulously well-kept setting of shrubs and flowers, stood several garden restaurants and bars. At the bridge the sign announced, "Joe's Place—the End of the Island." I strolled past a fashionable eatery and came on Hernando's Hideaway, a bar/restaurant with a half-dozen tables on a concrete patio and a modest curved bar inside a kiosk replica. It was late afternoon, an hour or so before the beach-weary tourists would start coming in for cocktails and seafood. A three-block stroll in the Puerto Vallarta heat had invigorated my need for another Dos Equis.

From behind a brick divider emerged the proprietor/cook/bartender, a *mestizo* wearing the ubiquitous half-buttoned shirt. He looked annoyed at my interruption of his afternoon labor preparing for the evening customers. But after a few minutes, halfway through my first beer, we began to talk. I took mental notes. "You a tourist?" he asked. "No, I'm writing a book about America in Mexico and Mexico in America." I rattled off a few statistics about the surging Hispanic population in the States and described my travels in the southwest.

A remark about Mexican Americans triggered an irreverent comment that escalated into a mildly belligerent, disjointed critique. "Someday it will be ours again," he boasted, referring to the U.S. southwest, a region that before the Mexican war had been *his* country, not mine. The accounts of its loss form part of the nationalist mythology where factual accuracy is incidental to the unforgettable shame of the gringo victory over the cosmic race. In this Mexican port geared almost exclusively to the American tourist, I had encountered what sociologists have described as the inexplicable feature of Mexican culture: the border cities and the resorts, dependent on the foreign dollar, have spawned peoples with an expressed admiration for American politics and disgust for their own government, which are joined in symbiotic union with an intense, vocal Mexican nationalism.

My expression must have conveyed the torment I was going through trying to ascertain some logic in his remarks. "You CIA?" he asked, a bit haughtily. I assured him I wasn't and produced a well-worn University of Georgia faculty ID. He must have been persuaded. "The American government is the major cause of all the problems in the world." I was on the verge of asking him in a friendly but professorial manner to explain when one of his regular customers, a fair-skinned man with curly brown hair, plopped down on an adjoining stool and ordered a Coke. The newcomer was a travel writer specializing in books on Mexican beaches, some of which have yet to be "discovered," even by Californians.

The bartender now unleashed a diatribe against the P.V. government—its woeful inadequacy, corruption, and meddling in private business. He was unable to get the public services he needed on the island unless he paid somebody. The two began pouring out their disgust, the writer in my left ear, the bartender in the right. I soothed my drying mouth with gulps from another Dos Equis. No one from the local mayor on up to the *presidente* of the republic escaped their wrath. I interspersed a remark about Senator Jesse Helms, who had earlier aroused the ire of the Mexican government by commenting, in a Senate subcommittee meeting, on widespread fraud in the 1982 Mexican elections.

My fellow barfly and his friend reassured me that Senator Helms spoke a truth every intelligent Mexican knew. Almost on cue they followed with a denunciation of the Mexican federal government. "The worst-run and least-safe businesses in this country," said the writer, "are those operated by the government." When he paused to take another sip of his Coke, the bartender, drying a beer glass with a cloth, picked up the theme. "Look," he said, "in this country to make it in business you got to compete with the government. The bureaucrats make sure that their cousins or brothers get licenses or supplies. That's the way things are. If you're not related to somebody in the government you have to pay.'' In a needless gesture he pulled out a 1,000-peso note from his pocket and waved it in the air to signify the time-honored tradition of the _mordida_.

By now the writer had produced additional evidence of the government's stupidity—the ridiculously low fares on the Mexico City subway and buses, 2 pesos. When I reminded him that the fares would shortly be raised to 20 pesos, he replied, in persuasive economic analysis, ''Sure, but the peso has been inflated to more than six hundred to the dollar since the two-peso charge began, so now it's really cheaper than it was four or five years ago. _Es estúpido!_''

My thoughts raced back to the midday scene of the other Mexico and the sight of their countrymen scrounging on the squalid banks of the Río Cuale. ''Perhaps,'' I suggested in halting Spanish, ''corruption has rendered a few social benefits. After all, twenty pesos represents a lot more money to a great many of your countrymen than it does to you.''

They said nothing but glanced at one another in unspoken acknowledgment that despite thirty minutes of persuasive talk they could not make this gringo s.o.b. understand the infuriating predicament of the Mexican middle class.

I trudged back to the Hotel del Rey, stopping only for a six-pack of Dos Equis at the small grocery store on the corner. Lying on the rumpled mattress beneath the mumbling overhead fan, I tried to make some sense of what the two _mexicanos_ at Hernando's Hideaway had been saying. They were obviously middle-class if not part of P.V.'s social elite, yet they expressed a not uncommon Mexican middle-class irritation with virtually everything ''Mexican.'' They resented the government's embrace of business and its piddling gestures of economic benevolence to the down-and-out.

Ironically, they are more the beneficiaries of government largess than the mobs of Mexico City metro customers paying 20 pesos for a ride on the subway. FONATUR, the government's tourist development agency, has financed 90 percent of the hotels in Puerto Vallarta and is directing 70 percent of its funds for Jalisco state into P.V.'s rehabilitation. Meanwhile, scabrous little villages up in the hills have to scratch for handouts from Mexico City to provide even basic social services.[2] Remote *poblaciones* in the countryside, it can be argued, are just as deserving as P.V., but the Mexican middle class has apparently turned its back on the "other Mexico."

Sipping my second Dos Equis I recalled the occasionally devastating psychological explanations of Mexican character by Mexican writers such as Samuel Ramos. The key to understanding the Mexican, wrote Ramos in *Profile of Man and Culture in Mexico,* is to recognize that he distrusts everything because he has no principles and is devoid of ideals. "His distrust is not limited to the human race; it embraces all that exists and happens. If he is a businessman he doesn't believe in business; if he is a professional he doesn't believe in his profession; if he is a politician he doesn't believe in politics."[3]

Though written in the thirties, Ramos' words retain their explanatory persuasiveness about the inevitable failure of well-intentioned gringos who try to *understand* the Mexican, even my middle-class *mexicano* barflies. They were cityfolk and as remote from the life and lot of the people beneath the bridge over the Río Cuale as I. When I had mentioned to the bartender that my literary endeavor was a metaphorical search for a Mexican kid I had met in a cotton field in the Texas Panhandle, his manifest interest had been my incorrect choice of the Spanish verb *picar* to denote the picking of cotton.

He rarely thought of such dreary labors because, quite naturally, he confronted more immediate problems. Had Ramos miraculously appeared to counsel me, he would have responded that the Mexican does not think but acts on instincts in a world in which only the immediate counts. The future may exist but one does not think about it, and what goes on about one is chaotic, devoid, as Americans like to say of "real meaning." (Now I know why it would be futile for me to try to "explain" a hopelessly convoluted scene I had witnessed a few days before in a downtown Guadalajara square across from the towering cathedral. Within three hours, as the priests inside conducted a wedding and two masses, the government staged outside in the square two boxing matches, a performance of garishly clad clowns, and a bicycle race, and concluded with a demonstration of rescue efforts from the cathedral bell tower by the Mexican Red Cross. An American tourist standing near me turned to her husband and asked, incredulously, "Why are they practicing in such a sacred place, Frank?" Frank shook his head. "Goddam if I know." I should have interjected the observation that the Cruz Roja waited until after mass to string its ropes from the cathedral belltower.)

The middle-class Mexican may appear more genteel than the lower-class urbanite (the _pelado_), Ramos wrote, because he is more educated. Unlike the _pelado_ he doesn't make a show of his idiosyncrasies, but underneath, he possesses the same confounding insecurities.[4] These he conceals with boastful professions of nationalism and pride and disdainful comments on everything from the crassness of American culture to the bureaucratic slime running his own country, then expresses indignation at the slightest hint that he secretly admires the materialistic _norteamericano_ life-style.

In truth he may be less Mexican than the people eating their rice and beans underneath the Puente de la Fuente. They are the other Mexico. They are also the real Mexico.

With which Mexico should we identify? The Mexico that admires our politics, mimics our daily habits and dress, devours our television programs and music, yet remains vocally anti-American? Or the other Mexico that conforms to our economic but not our political values, yet, in its lower-class mannerisms and habits, retains a pride in what it represents—even though we hold in utter contempt what it represents? In the two Mexicos we confront a dilemma: the Mexico we admire more holds American culture in contempt while it emulates its cultural style; the Mexico we disdain is, ironically, the "other Mexico" the Mexican middle class holds in contempt, yet the "other Mexico" may hold the political balance of power in Mexico's future and thus may be worthy of the one thing we have historically refused to grant—our respect for the Mexico the "real Mexico" symbolizes.

Initially, my own inclination is that we should identify with those Mexicans who are most like us (even though they don't particularly like Americans). After all, they believe in the benefits of education, professional advancement, the family *a la norteamericana,* where the man pursues a career and the wife dutifully bears a limited number of children, then may pursue a modest career (or may pursue a modest career and then bear the children). At the upper rungs they may wield considerable influence in the private-sector economy and represent the best education obtainable in Mexican (or American) universities, and for the last generation or more they have been (after the *políticos* and the entrepreneurial elite) the major beneficiaries of the "modern Mexican miracle."

If the Mexican middle class has benefited from the postwar Mexican modernization, what explains its collective disgruntlement? If it has reaped the rewards of a better-educated, better-fed, better-clothed, and more politically stable Mexico, why has the middle class of Mexico thrown down the gauntlet against the "system"? The simplest answer is that the inheritors of the power bequeathed by Revolutionary Mexico inspired the maturing middle class of the forties and fifties with the expectations of a more prosperous, more secure Mexico than they were able or, ultimately, willing to provide. What the middle-class Mexican of a generation ago received from the state and its business-elite partners was the promise of more—more of everything. More opportunity, more material wealth, more education, more housing, more democracy. What the middle-class Mexican received was more than his parents had ever dreamed of having but less than he expected to get.

A Mexican sociologist, Francisco López Cámara, in the slim but provocative volume *The Challenge of the Middle Class,*[5] suggests that the ''rebellion'' may have gestated in the forties but burst forth in the sixties with middle-class demands for reforms in Mexico's educational system. At the same time the better-educated Mexicans began making demands for professional opportunities in the already bloated Mexican bureaucracy that simply were not available. One violent manifestation, which cost hundreds of lives, was the grim battle at Tlatelolco in 1968. In other words, the Revolutionary political system and the parallel private economic upper stratum of Mexican society could not accommodate the numbers of better-educated, better-trained, and more ambitious cadres produced by the modern Mexico. More simply, Mexico had produced a middle class but could not satisfy its demands. The economy expanded, to be sure, but the profits raked off the top by the state and the economic elites and the necessary social expenditures for the ''other Mexico'' did not leave enough for those caught in the middle.

In the American interpretation of things, the discontented Mexican middle class provides the only sensible route to a more democratic Mexico. After all, the _American_ middle class, firm believers in education, opportunity, advancement, family, and fundamental political honesty, has shown an admirable charity to the dispossessed and down-and-out yet demanded a government whose leaders respect those credos. But the Mexican middle class, _however persuasive its criticism against the system,_ is not a natural ally because it is, in the broadest sense, a middle class. The Mexican middle class, like that of most Latin America, has not yet shown that it wants a more democratic society, that it is willing to cease its emulation of the rich in order to bring about a more just social and political order. The middle-class Mexican is too often measured against his Hispanic American, especially its Mexican American, putative counterpart, who _does_ exhibit the most admirable of _American_ middle-class values and asks only for opportunity and recognition of his cultural worthiness. And unlike his Mexican counterpart, the Mexican American is not willing to sacrifice the basic needs and rights of those less fortunate in order to obtain the better life.

213

Some years ago, in my third or fourth visit to the City of the Aztecs, I was invited to a *cena* (two-hour evening meal) in the modest apartment of a middle-class Mexican family. One of the sons had been a student in my class at the University of Georgia. He had come to America to get training in computer science but, as I recalled, had spent a goodly portion of his time chasing "good old Georgia girls." When I told him I was going to Mexico City, he asked me to take a pair of ballerina slippers for his sister. He did not trust the Mexican post office to deliver them.

I remember waiting in the Hotel Alffer Century (heavily damaged in the 1985 earthquake) for his twin brother, who had insisted on driving from the northern *colonia* to get me even after I told him I would have been happy to take the Metro. As we sped along Avenida Insurgentes Norte, he talked about his brother's future. The family was worried that the rapidly declining peso would mean that he would have to return to Mexico for his education. When we arrived, the dignified *mamá,* the personification of the middle-class mother, poured me a whiskey. She asked about my *familia.* When *papá* came home from the technical college, the discussion shifted to loftier topics. The meal was not elegant but represented, I thought, a considerable sacrifice on their part. A daughter joined us at the table. She had recently married but her husband could not afford an apartment, so they were living with the professor's *familia.*

In their aspirations they represented the upwardly striving middle-class Mexican wrought by the economic miracle of a generation ago. By any reasonable standard of social justice, economic opportunity, or political right, they should not be denied. But it must not be at the expense of my boyhood Mexican friend.

13

Over There at the Big Ranch

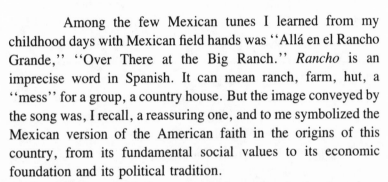

Among the few Mexican tunes I learned from my childhood days with Mexican field hands was "Allá en el Rancho Grande," "Over There at the Big Ranch." *Rancho* is an imprecise word in Spanish. It can mean ranch, farm, hut, a "mess" for a group, a country house. But the image conveyed by the song was, I recall, a reassuring one, and to me symbolized the Mexican version of the American faith in the origins of this country, from its fundamental social values to its economic foundation and its political tradition.

The agrarian myth is entrenched so deeply in American thought that not even the reality of an industrial order could erase it. In the nineteenth century, with farm people suffering from what they considered the oppressive combination of wealth and influence, it nurtured turmoil and in 1896 brought on a tumultuous political campaign. In the end the new industrial order proved victorious, but the rural tradition remained, through good times and bad, and rural constituencies retained a political influence far beyond their numbers. The trickle-down theory of prosperity may not have reached *everybody* in the boondocks, but enough wealth and especially opportunity filtered down to sustain hope.

My father began as a sharecropper in east Texas, migrated to southeastern Oklahoma as a small dryland farmer, and then signed on as a carpenter in a small carpentry shop in the Texas Panhandle. There, for the first time, my school lunches consisted of something more than peanut butter and crackers because subsidies to schools and agricultural surpluses provided a better diet. And the nightly meal, which in the old days on the farm had usually consisted of cornbread and milk (the raw onion on the side was optional), now might include fried chicken *on a weekday* instead of only for the traditionally more sumptuous Sunday dinner. I'm sure my Mexican pal has improved his diet, but if he went back to the *rancho grande* his kids may not be much better off than he was in 1950. (Or they may be eating potato chips and drinking Cokes.) He had little, save pride and hope. His children may have less.

The lot of his children may not have improved significantly, because the Revolution that promised so much has delivered less to rural people, to the *campesino,* than to any other segment of Mexican society, save perhaps the Indian. Yet Mexican agriculture, like Mexican industry, has experienced in the past fifty years a transformation through irrigation, technology, the "green revolution," and often widely publicized government efforts to extend the social benefits of the Revolution to country people. But the principal beneficiaries have not been those on the bottom, but those agricultural producers able to sustain more durable links with the American market, exploit the government's often generous credit opportunities, and through organization and influence command the attention of even the most socially conscious Mexican political leaders—all this despite the *campesino's* position in the ruling party's triad of sectors.

Mexico has brought modern techniques and organization to its agriculture but it has proved unable to extend the benefits and promises of the Institutional Revolution to rural people. They may have more land than their grandparents and more food to eat than their parents, but their share of the benefits of modern Mexico falls far short of national expectations. A succession of Mexican leaders going back to the late fifties have generally begun their tenures with somber references to the "embarrassment" of Mexico's rural condition. Several have inaugurated ambitious programs to alleviate it, but none, frankly, has been able to bring the full force of government intervention to bear on what students of the Mexican economy call the nation's Achilles' heel.

To understand why this lamentable condition exists requires a leap backward to the last third of the nineteenth and the first decade of the twentieth century. In his determination to develop the Mexican economy, the old dictator Porfirio Díaz opened up the country to foreign, principally American, investment and technology. These went into mining, railroads, and industry, reinforcing the agricultural links that had already appeared between the Mexican north and the U.S. economy. Mexican production of basic crops—corn and beans—shifted to export commodities—henequen, vanilla, coffee, melons, _garbanzos,_ cacao. The first constituted the essential diet of the Mexican _campesino_; the second was the money earner for a rapidly expanding agricultural sector. In the center and south of the country the transformation brought greater wealth to those who were landowners and deprivation to those who worked the land. South of the capital, in the Indian state of Morelos, agricultural expansion pushed so many off the land that it sparked what historians call the "true" Mexican Revolution—the Zapata rebellion and its demand for a return of the land to the people.

With the 1917 constitution and its controversial provisions on labor, religion, and land, many believed, Mexico would at last bring justice to what a pre-Revolutionary American writer, John Kenneth Turner, had depicted as _Barbarous Mexico._ But the future of rural people lay with a generation of Revolutionary _caudillos_ whose armies had waged battle in northern Mexico. Here the most ferocious contests of the Revolution had taken place, and the central concern of the "northern dynasty" of Revolutionaries had not been land reform. They were reformers but also opportunists. Venustiano Carranza, the stern constitutionalist revolutionary who became president in 1917, flatly opposed confiscation of land, though he did favor the restoration of land illegally seized from _private_ owners and even created a government bureau to process the return of collectively owned

217

land (*ejidos*) to Indian villages. When Zapata's *campesinos* in Morelos took more direct, and violent, methods to bring about land reform, Carranza dispatched an army into the state to crush them. Zapata was lured into an ambush and murdered. His head was put on a pole in Cuautla as an object lesson of the central government's reach into rural Mexico.

The Zapata rebellion and Emiliano's grisly assassination were an ominous portent of what the Revolutionary heirs would eventually confront in rural Mexico—a people exploited by a modernizing economy, thus deserving of the benevolent protection of the new order, but who defied socialist stereotypes by their persistent clinging to ancient tradition and faith and who wanted not only land but, more alarmingly, to be left alone. From 1920 until 1940 the first generation of post-Revolutionary leaders initiated ambitious programs in the countryside. In the twenties, the education czar José Vasconcelos dispatched an army of pedagogical zealots into deepest Mexico to teach the Spanish language and preach the glories of the Revolution and its rediscovery of Mexico's Indian heritage.

A succession of *presidentes* cultivated trade unions and agrarian reformers. They eventually brought both into the political embrace, and domination, of the state. Every Mexican leader beginning with Carranza in 1917 restored landholdings to Indian villages, a program that reached its zenith under Cárdenas in the thirties, who dispensed 44 million acres, many carved out of large estates, to *campesinos*.

Yet, throughout, there was resistance. And when the Revolutionary state encountered defiance, it responded forcefully, and on occasion brutally, to suppress it. In the late twenties, Plutarco Elias Calles brought the government into a violent collision with the church by demanding that priests register with federal authorities, shutting down monasteries and convents, and secularizing primary education. When the church retaliated by closing down, under papal edict, Calles ordered church property seized. In the tier of states in the north and west (Jalisco, Colima, Guanajuato, Durango, Zacatecas, and Michoacán), Catholic

218

firebrands, calling themselves Cristeros, organized guerrilla bands that burned government schools and murdered Vasconcelos' disciples. Calles retaliated by sending in his soldiers to murder the priests and hound Catholic families. Eventually the new American ambassador, Dwight Morrow (the father-in-law of Charles Lindbergh, Jr.), who had been sent down by President Coolidge to deal with Calles on the petroleum issue, was able to mediate between church and state. The revolt died out, and the churches reopened. But the anticlerical laws stayed on the books.

A decade later, even after Cárdenas' sweeping commitments to reform in the countryside, the church found a new ally in the Sinarquistas (the name means literally "without anarchy"), who lauded the Falangist movement in Spain and made converts among the rural poor of central Mexico. These were people who retained deep religious convictions and had not benefited from the government's policy of collective landholdings. In 1940 the Sinarquistas swung behind the candidacy of General Juan Andreu Almazán, who represented the National Action Party (PAN). Cárdenas' choice, Manuel Ávila Camacho, easily won, in a notoriously corrupt election, then declared himself a "believer." The Sinarquistas continued to grow in numbers, reaching 900,000 by 1944. A central theme of their protest was the economic hardship that Revolutionary policies had brought to rural Mexico.

The Sinarquistas found an improbable symbol of defiance, the Indian governor of the State of San Luís Potosí, Saturnino Cedillo. Don Saturnino was a veteran of the Revolution and commander of the invading army that had fiercely crushed the Cristero revolt in the late 1920s. He did not believe in God. His illiterate followers had lost all faith in the Revolution, whose disciples had promised much to the Indian tillers of this central Mexican state. In the Mexican highlands there were mournful tales about the promises of the government and the agrarian reforms successive generations had been told would bring the Revolution to the country peasant. In one story an Indian peasant, granted a few acres of rocky soil clinging to a mountainside, is said to have uttered his political demurral of the inadequacy of _his_

Revolutionary beneficence and was impolitely told by a government agricultural official that he should be grateful for his liberation from the landholder's grasp. Cedillo's people did not believe in the Revolution's hollow promises, but they did believe in God. And don Saturnino, their patron, gave them his blessing.

For a moment he ruled over another world, hidden within the Mexican mountains of San Luís Potosí. Down in the capital of the state, government agents hounded priests who "preached" revolution when they spoke of the Sermon on the Mount or who "committed" treason by secretly teaching a course in economics. Graham Greene traveled four hours along a tortuous road winding out of San Luís Potosí to interview the man who had defied the Mexican leader who had defied the Americans. Cedillo cared mostly for his crops and his women—"Do not look too fondly at the women here," a Mexican companion told the writer—but in the catacombs of San Luís Potosí the faithful could listen to the priestly recitations as middle-aged men and their children above listened patiently to a government teacher warning of the evils of communism and capitalism. Educated Catholics and the capitalists distrusted Cedillo and placed their faith in God and National Action; the wretched *campesinos* of San Luís Potosí believed in God and the fleeting hope Cedillo would prevail and the Revolution and its godless face would simply go away. Cedillo was kinder, or, at least, more tolerant. Of course, he told Greene, the government's agrarian reform and its educational program can serve these miserable people, but they should not be administered by people who are more interested in disseminating politics or in exercising their authority than in democracy and tolerance. Neither was he much interested in fascism or communism or any of the isms.[1]

Greene had ventured into Mexico to take the measure of a country ruled by Revolutionaries and not God. But in Cedillo he found not El Cid but an aging Indian chieftain no longer receiving ambitious *políticos* who had sensed in his defiance of the Revolutionary state an opportunity to advance their own cause— just in case the Sinarquista cause triumphed. They should have known that in Mexico God may relent but the Revolutionary state does not. And God, apparently, had His plan for the rural _mexicanos_ who clandestinely followed His disciples. He abandoned them. The Revolution gave them land but not liberty, and its armed disciples crushed Cedillo and stripped his rural followers of whatever faith they may have retained that God would protect them against the expanding omniscient Revolutionary order.

Startled by the Sinarquistas' appeal, the government was more restrained in meeting the challenge than it had been in confronting the Cristeros. But, as often happens in Mexico, political expediency intervened, this time from the outside. In 1938 the American and British governments, reacting to oil-company pressures after Cárdenas' dramatic nationalization of Mexican petroleum, had imposed an embargo on Mexican oil exports. But three years later, mired in international conflict, they desperately needed Mexican oil and inter-American security. With such inspiration, the Mexican government needed little more incentive to outlaw the Sinarquistas on the grounds they contributed a fascist menace to national security.

After that, Mexican agricultural strategy and American demands for Mexican labor brought on a great migration from the rural communities of central Mexico. The braceros, including probably my boyhood friend, came mostly from the region of Mexico where the Sinarquistas had been most active. Unintentionally, but in a curiously perverse way, American policy sustained the domineering reach of Mexican central authority into the countryside. The collective farms (_ejidos_) passed out by Cárdenas satisfied rural demands for the breakup of large estates but did little to boost agricultural productivity, principally because the _ejidos_ were too small to permit much more than subsistence farming and were located in regions depending on rain. In the beginning, it is true, the rural population resettled into what promised to be a reborn peasant community, in an age when human capital was more plentiful (and more reliable) than economic capital. But the conditions for creating stable communities in central Mexico could not withstand the external pressures brought on by the declining size of the plot below the fifteen acres or so considered necessary to sustain a farm family, the demand for agricultural workers in U.S. agriculture brought on by the war, and, most important, the vigorous expansion of Mexican export agriculture.

Forty years ago, under the tutelage of the "businessman's president," Miguel Alemán, Mexico chose an ambitious development strategy designed to modernize the economy with import-substitution industry and irrigated agriculture. This heralded an intentional shift from the earlier emphasis on small plots to produce basic foodstuffs, which, at least, had sustained the rural population in the thirties and provided, some have argued, a better life. But in order to sustain its industrial expansion, the government increasingly neglected the agricultural sector. In truth, Mexico's agrarian economy did expand, in some cases impressively, but the large-scale farm enterprises of Sonora and Sinaloa, which marketed exports for the United States, received a disproportionately large share of the government's financial dispensation. Rural villages and small farmers were expected to provide cheap food for the burgeoning urban work force drawn from the surplus labor migrating from the countryside to the city. The dream was "from *campesino* to urban worker to professional." For the rural migrants of central Mexico, the path led to Mexico City, Guadalajara, Monterrey, or El Norte, the United States.

With a strong agricultural base of small farmers the plan might have worked. But by the end of the fifties it had become clear that the unevenness of Mexico's rural development had exacted a heavy, and irreversible, toll. In 1960, government studies revealed, more than half the agricultural plots contained less than thirteen acres, operated with less than 2 percent of agricultural machinery, and produced less than 5 percent of Mexico's agricultural output. At the upper end of the rural balance sheet, 0.5 percent of the biggest farms controlled more than 25 percent of the country's arable land, grew more than 30 percent of its crops, and benefited from more than 40 percent of its agricultural technology. But the agricultural economic czars in Mexico City were unable, or unwilling, to reverse course. Determined to shield the cities against rising maize prices, which had been going up since the 1920s and on which small-plot independent farmers depended, they incorporated in the "Stabilizing Development" program a plan to purchase grains from the United States. This posed little threat to the agribusinessmen, who could accommodate increased yields wrought by the Green Revolution, even though it meant lower prices per unit, but the small farmers were squeezed out.

So, like their forebears they became migrants. But they were _propertyless_ migrants who had to depend on seasonal labor elsewhere, in a Mexico that could not easily absorb them. They became the core of Mexico's wage-labor rural subclass, which had grown from 35 to 50 percent of agricultural toilers in the two decades after 1950, when Alemán's developmental strategy had gotten under way. In the forties, fifties, and even in the sixties they had managed to find work in the cities in industry or the service sector. But since then, with the noticeable decline in employment in these areas, they have poured into what economists call, euphemistically, the "informal sector," work in which the only guarantee is a low wage. In other words, they take what they can get.[2]

Most of this despair had come about in the era of the "Mexican miracle," years when a marginal population, mostly in the countryside, was left behind in Mexico's frantic rush toward modernization. The census of 1960 revealed a discouraging assessment of the widening gap between urban and rural Mexico. In the countryside, more than 50 percent remained illiterate. An equal percentage of rural folk _never_ consumed wheat bread, meat, fish, milk, or eggs. One-fourth of them did not have shoes. More disturbingly, wrote Pablo González Casanova in _Democracy in Mexico,_ the people who could not read and write were usually the same people who never had wheat bread, meat, fish, eggs, or milk, The "marginal" populace may have decreased relative to the numbers of Mexicans who had learned how to read and write, had diversified their diet, and who wore shoes, but in absolute numbers the "marginals" had grown too, "constituting an immense body of Mexicans who had nothing of nothing."[3]

For a time, the economic benefits of the bracero program found their way back to wretched little villages of central Mexico, but they did not rejuvenate its agriculture. The able-bodied males who left Michoacán, Zacatecas, or Jalisco for the north did remit large sums back to their families during the twenty-two years of the program. But precious little went toward the purchase of machinery to make the land more productive. And the returning migrant, his consumer appetite whetted by radio, television, American clothes, and beer or whiskey instead of *pulque,* the *campesino*'s booze, often turned around and headed back for the States or the city.

A generation of talented rural Mexicans—one million—who might have made the difference in narrowing the gulf between the two Mexicos if they had been able to survive on the farm, grow maize, and get a decent price for it was plowed under by a modernizing Mexico.

A decade before they began talking about *la crisis,* Mexicans were gloomily assessing their agricultural dilemma and its consequences. In the sixties the Green Revolution had enabled the Mexican economy to export food, even corn and wheat. But in the following years the once promising statistical charts rendered a depressing verdict. And in the decade that followed, Mexico began importing these basic items in such quantities that by 1980 the country had to rely on a world market for one-fourth of the corn it required to feed its people.

In the early seventies, when Luís Echeverría's leftist impulses were generating a third-world dynamism in the Mexican polity, CONASUPO, the Mexican national food agency, became more aggressive in its efforts to improve the rural condition. CONA-SUPO had been around for a number of years, but the economic dynamos of the fifties and sixties had denigrated its importance in the grand scheme of Mexican modernization. Echeverría, determined to make Mexico a third-world model, invigorated CON-ASUPO with a new purpose. For too long, he said, the agency had served the larger commercial producers with its price supports (a not uncommon complaint north of the border), and the condition of small plotholders had worsened considerably. Local politicians had wormed their way into the CONASUPO network of purchasing programs, warehouses, outlets, and supply houses and transformed another well-intentioned government program into a political boondoggle.

An enthusiastic official lamented in 1971 that the peasants had lost confidence in the program. In late 1969, CONASUPO had begun to construct new granaries for receiving corn, beans, and wheat. Predictably, the government tried to get as much political mileage out of the program as it could. Many of the buildings were thrown up rapidly so that their appearance in isolated villages coincided with the usually frantic presidential campaign. Every six years, when the presidential candidate of the Institutional Revolutionary Party is announced, the government undertakes a variety of well-publicized, usually inadequate social programs to carry the Revolutionary blessing into some of Mexico's most remote villages. In most cases, the good that is done is too little and the promises rendered to the impoverished inhabitants of the real Mexico too grandiose to survive the electoral season.

But the diminutive Echeverría's bureaucrats in CONASUPO tried to change things. An agricultural specter haunted the Mexican countryside. A governmental study revealed a disquieting, perhaps irreversible, trend: Mexico's small independent farmers were increasingly becoming subsistence farmers. Put another way, the rural population was growing but it was not producing more to feed itself and, just as important, to enable Mexico to become self-sufficient in food production. CONASUPO provided price supports for the small farmer's production, but unless he adapted to technological advances, he could not hope to keep pace with the rapidly escalating cost of living. There was a point, the study gloomily noted, where the small producer had to work so much longer to produce the same amount of market crops that staying down on the farm wasn't worth it. The answer lay in picking up and moving to Monterrey or Mexico City or even the United States, where the former producer could purchase what he had once produced.

For too long, Echeverría's agricultural economists pointed out, the Mexican government had equated agricultural development with productivity. This had in turn prompted an emphasis on transportation and irrigation, easier credit to the more efficient producers, and the export market in such crops as coffee, cotton, tomatoes, and strawberries. These earned much-needed hard currency, integrated Mexico into the international agricultural market, and provided the Mexican middle class with more appealing and diversified meals. As in the United States, government policy thus kept the food-basket price paid by the average Mexican middle-class consumer lower by keeping a bootheel on the neck of the independent commercial farmer and transforming a generation of *mexicanos* into a rural proletariat. In the future, they argued, CONASUPO's policies would be directed toward the needs and interests of the producer and not the consumer. Peasants would be getting what they needed at prices they could afford, from clothes and medicine to seeds and insecticides. The government would show them how to market their produce more efficiently and avoid the rapacious grasp of Mexican middlemen who took their meager profits.[4]

Such an ambitious program might have worked in another country with a less pervasive bureaucracy and a government more attentive to the needs of those at the bottom. But not in Mexico. The Mexican agricultural producers who fared well in the seventies were not those small farmers and *ejiditarios* whose quality of life Echeverría had dedicated his government to improving. Those who prospered were the commercial farmers whose irrigated lands produced harvests of wheat and winter vegetables for the international market and, as the decade wore on, the expanding diet of the urban Mexican. In the rain-fed croplands of central Mexico, where more than 80 percent of

226

agricultural laborers were employed, the vicissitudes of weather and the inflationary spiral that commenced in mid-decade combined to deliver a crippling blow to most rural Mexicans.

Thus, at the end of the decade, with yet another leader and another rural development program, the SAM (the Spanish acronym for Mexican Food System), Mexico again turned inward. The goal, declared President López Portillo, was self-sufficiency in basic food commodities and Mexican energy production. Mexico, leftists cried, had become a captive of the multinational agribusinesses which had rapidly expanded their activities in the country in the 1970s. They had purchased Mexican agricultural products, processed and packaged them into the appealing consumer food offerings in urban Mexico's rapidly expanding *supermercados,* and improved the diet of the Mexican middle class. Socialists decried this transformation as yet another indication of Mexico's subservience to the American economy. SAM's director, Cassio Luiselli, a University of Wisconsin graduate in agricultural economics, argued that unless Mexico committed itself to self-sufficiency in food production, by 1990 the government would be paying more than 70 percent of its export earnings for imported food.

As are most new programs in Mexico, SAM was launched with great fanfare. In the beginning, at least, it drew on the seemingly limitless wealth of Mexico's oil and the generous loans it reaped for the government. Luiselli was a technocrat operating in a domain ruled by *políticos.* With newfound oil-wealth monies he instituted a subsidy program for Mexico's food producers; he criticized the expanding cattle-grazing industry for its inefficiency, and appeared to threaten the rich commercial agricultural farmers of the northwestern states of Sonora and Sinaloa. If the rural poor could be saved from a despairing future, Luiselli said, all Mexico would benefit. And with the oil wealth and ready loans to sustain national development, few Mexicans would suffer. But in the end the economic collapse of 1982 doomed SAM and virtually preordained a confrontation between its advocates and those commercial agricultural producers who

227

fumed about subsidies to the small Mexican farmer. The dream of a Wisconsin-trained *técnico,* the SAM, which had, ironically, incorporated the subsistence farmers of rural Mexico into a capitalist agricultural system, vanished in the somber awakening of a Harvard-trained *técnico,* Miguel de la Madrid.[5]

Historians and political scientists and economists write of these wrenching changes in rural Mexico in graphic description or exhaustive analyses or statistical columns. But what they portray is what modernization has done to Mexico, with only a fleeting glimpse of its imprint on the Mexican. If he were to trek through rural Mexico in our time, Graham Greene would encounter again "lawless roads" and an uprooted, aimless people. He would find, as he did a half century ago, people who have *nada de nada* and remain far from God and the Revolution and the promises of both. They are the other Mexico. And their only enduring faith is their conviction that they are the real Mexico.

In its agricultural policies the Mexican government had, quite frankly, measured the "other Mexico" according to a political and economic yardstick. From a practical standpoint, it had no other choice, it appeared. Had the lower rungs of rural Mexico received all the land they had struggled for in *their* Revolution, the Revolutionary order in power by the 1940s might not have survived. Those American critics of Mexico who evaluate Mexican rural development from a comparative perspective sometimes argue (as do Mexican socialists) that the price exacted from the "other Mexico" was too severe. The agricultural modernization of the United States has required a social cost, but it has not been so severe that rural people (unless one dwells exclusively on migratory labor) have not been incorporated into the larger culture. And American political parties still trace their ideological roots to the land and, more important, the values historically associated with people of the land. Our leaders may represent the best and the brightest, they may have entered the political arena through the front door, and they rarely symbolize a "rags-to-riches" tale, but, at bottom, they know the political tunes they sing must play in Peoria to the satisfaction of the "real" America.

Mexico does not follow this pattern because Mexico is built differently. It was constructed from top to bottom, not bottom to top, and those who rule it have to deal with this reality. They may direct their energies and concerns toward a "better life" and "greater opportunity" for the "real Mexico." And they may speak eloquently, as did Franklin Roosevelt in 1936, or crudely but sympathetically, as did Lyndon Johnson two decades later, about "one-third of a nation ill-fed, ill-housed, and ill-clad" or about young adults who cannot hold a job " 'cause they can't spell 'cat.' " They can speak the Mexican variation of these exhortations, but they know a reality neither Roosevelt nor Johnson had to face. When Americans speak of the "other America" they are not referring to a mass so great or so burdened with limitations that corrective measures, either vigorous social programs to relieve its impoverished and educate its children or a vigorous economy to offer opportunity, will make little difference in their *acculturation* into modern America. But when Mexican leaders, even those with power and a social commitment to use it, look at the "other Mexico" and its "problems," they confront another country, another world. And they may have no more in common with the "real Mexico" than the reader of this book. They have neither a political nor an economic commitment to the Mexican equivalent of the "family farm" and its cultural values. They don't have to.

14

The Biggest City in the World

=====

My first encounter with Mexico City, a decade ago, was not especially pleasant. My wife and I had driven across west Texas, a five-hour trip even at seventy miles an hour, arriving in El Paso in early afternoon. After several hours of debate and a few horror stories about the inevitable frustrations and delays on the Juárez–Mexico City run of the national railways, she had consented to an evening flight aboard AeroMéxico. On the advice of a high school classmate, then in the clothing business in El Paso, we left the car at the El Paso International Airport and took the shuttle van that regularly travels the fifteen miles or so to Juárez' pleasant modern airport. (The Mexican government, not wishing to jeopardize its monopoly on air traffic between border cities and the interior, did not permit direct El Paso–Mexico City traffic.) We crossed the Chamizal, the elongated strip of land just north of the Rio Grande that was returned to Mexico in the sixties, passed an indifferent Mexican border guard, and sped by the eastern barrios of Juárez.

The flight to Mexico City was late, and the other Americans milling about had already begun to complain, some in unsettlingly impolite tones. When they finally got permission to head down the narrow concourse for boarding, they formed an insistent knot around an impassive gray-haired guard who had to check their papers. After a few moments, he calmly raised a hand and said, "Patience, patience." But the gringos kept pressing against him. He probably received some mild satisfaction, I later thought, when the AeroMéxico captain kept the plane at the gate for another thirty minutes as we sat strapped in our seats and gasped for cool air.

The flight was direct but did not arrive until after midnight. But the Mexico City airport, close in, was packed with arriving passengers, and the Tourist Hotel Association had set up a makeshift office in the airport lobby. A congenial clerk made a reservation at a hotel near the Plaza de la Revolución, where the bodies of four Revolutionary leaders are entombed. Outside the airport lobby we rejoined our American fellow passengers, by now thoroughly exhausted. The night manager of the taxi stand was yelling into the night, arranging groups with cabs. When our turn came, he directed us to the far corner of the darkened lot toward a waiting taxi scarcely visible from the taxi stand. But we were relieved to be getting underway, even at one in the morning.

We were quite unprepared when three Mexican males jumped into the front seat. I was apprehensive, my wife terrified. Probably every airport in the world has generated its share of tales about unknowing or gullible travelers fleeced by unscrupulous cab drivers or, tragically, spirited away to a remote spot where they are robbed, beaten, and sometimes killed. We should have de-cabbed right then, but the outer darkness was as uninviting as the ominous prospect of heading into the Mexico City night with three unknown Mexicans.

The front-seaters chatted in incomprehensible idiomatic Spanish as the driver whizzed along Fray Servando de Mier, cut northward to the Zócalo, then west again to the Plaza de la Revolución. One leaned back, offering a cigarette. I was then scarcely able to breathe adequately, much less tolerate smoke in my lungs. But in a few minutes the driver pulled up at the hotel and politely asked for the cab fare, payable in dollars or pesos. That night I slept fitfully; my wife did not sleep at all.

Every year thousands of Americans descend on what will be at the end of the century the biggest city in the world. If first-time visitors, they will be surprised to discover that just as there are

231

many Mexicos, there are distinct cities within this sprawling, polluted, overcrowded, and generally bewildering urban legacy of the Aztecs and their Spanish conquerors. Not a few newcomers, especially those with images of Mexico fashioned long ago by brief incursions at the border, never depart from the tourist schedule or rarely wander outside the Zona Rosa, the fabled Pink Zone with its European ambience and fashionable hotels.

I vividly recall my first day, sitting in the modest hotel restaurant, preparing to devour a plate of *huevos rancheros,* fried eggs dashed with sauce and accompanied by refried beans. The waiter had dutifully brought a small bowl of Mexican sauce— cut-up tomatoes, peppers, and onions saturated in hell. Stupidly, and unknowingly, I spooned the *salsa mexicana* on the eggs and began eating. The fiery backlash struck only after the second or third bite, too late for the soothing effects of water, beer, or even warm milk. Since then, when I go to Mexico, I occasionally drink the water, always drink the beer, but I *never* consume the tiny but deadly portions of *salsa mexicana.* Three-alarm chili, which my digestive system can tolerate, is veritably soothing by comparison.

By then I was feeling a tinge of sympathy with a couple of middle-aged Texans, successful but rough-hewn types, seated with their matronly wives at the next table. The men reminded me of deacons in the Southern Baptist Church in my boyhood days. They were arguing about what to see in Mexico City. From their earlier conversation I had learned that the men had wanted to go to Las Vegas, but their more proper wives had dragged them aboard a tourist flight southward to the city of the Aztecs. The women wanted to go to the Pyramids, then the Floating Gardens, Chapúltepec Heights . . . Tourist brochures, richly illustrated, lay strewn about a table of coffee cups and partially consumed platters of scrambled eggs. Finally, annoyed because their husbands did not share their enthusiasm, one of the women said despairingly, "Honey, don't you want to visit all these wonderful places now that we're finally here?" Without pausing for a slurp of coffee he shot back, "As far as I'm concerned, you can have this damn country and every damn Messcan in it!'' Probably, ''Honey'' wound up spending the day trudging around Teotihuacán or Chapúltepec and that evening at one of Mexico City's nightclubs or casinos.

I followed a less predictable itinerary, a practice I have continued in subsequent visits, in search of the ''average'' *chilango,* as residents of the capital are known. Wandering gringos, staring in wondrous amazement at monuments or statues, are easy prey for the flood of *mexicanos* who have descended on the capital and have joined its vast army of underemployed. The first to hit on me was a brownish duplicate of a twenties lounge lizard, his arms laced with cheap watches. Him I escaped. But on his flank came a *chilango* shoeshine artist, who readily hooked me by lowering his price to the point of nonrefusal.

With deftly practiced strokes he began scrubbing off the grime, then pulled out a can of black wax to swab on my shoes. All the while his conversation was alternately inquisitive and informative, in rapid-fire idiomatic, occasionally guttural, Spanish, punctuated intermittently with an American expression. ''You got a woman down here?'' Before I could respond he said, ''Me, I got two women,'' and triumphantly hoisted two fingers.

''My wife is with me,'' I replied.

''It's okee dokee,'' he said, speaking in labored English. ''I can get you a *puta''*—prostitute. ''She be real good. Do anything you want.'' He looked up, grinning, ''You know, fokee or sokee.'' Memories of those high school accounts of Juárez madams with syringes for penis injections following ten furious minutes of ''fokee, fokee'' shot through my mind. I tried to be casually witty and uttered a literal translation of ''My wife is more than I can handle'' into Spanish. He was not amused. He looked up again, this time with a contemptuous gaze that Mexican males have when their conviction of sexual superiority over their gringo counterparts is reinforced.

Assuming I was now an easy mark, he began applying a special (and expensive) clear sheen to the wax on my shoes. The

233

10-peso shine had dramatically escalated to 50 pesos, more than $2 at that time. When I demurred about paying he angrily scrubbed it off. In a few moments, I realized too late, I had punctured that veil of male camaraderie of the urban working-class Mexican whose personality can rapidly shift from amiability to menace. Luckily, we were near the Plaza de la Revolución, in full view of a hundred people, so he had to satisfy his rage with a verbal assault of *chingas tu madre,* which literally means "rape your mother" but can serve as provocation for combat.

The verb *chingar* is as integral to lower-class Mexican speech as "motherfucker" is in the United States. But in its various forms, *chingar* can serve as insult, praise, or an eminently understandable explanation that one has been figuratively "screwed." Here, at least, the Mexican is superior, for his ability to exploit *chingar* as verbal guttural art form far surpasses what his Yankee counterpart can do with "motherfucker." For me, "motherfucker" reached its semantic limits about 1970, when a hirsute student casually queried after class, "Do we have to read all this motherfucking book?" At that precise moment, I recall, I had reached a saturation point of hearing that motherfucking word, and the reader will not encounter it again. *Chingar,* however, may reappear in the narrative.

Later that first day, strolling with my wife in the spacious plaza of the Zócalo, I again suffered the verbal wrath of the lower-class male Mexican. As we stood admiring the ancient cathedral, a wretched man came up to us, yelling incoherently, *"Fuera de mi patria"*—"Get out of my country." His fury, I later surmised, may have been related to a decision by the U.S. Immigration and Naturalization Service to make an object lesson of a batch of "illegals" by putting them on a special plane and unloading them deep inside Mexico instead of following the normal practice of busing them back across the border. Stories of the deportation received wide coverage in the Mexican press and on television. In any event, I again erred by trying to explain that the decision, however extreme, was not my doing. This only unleashed another verbal torrent, laden with *chingas tu madre,* which

234

expressed a simple but for him "logical" explanation: if he was not welcome in my country, then most assuredly I was not welcome in his.

Mexico City is the southernmost outpost of MexAmerica. It is Mexico's political and economic center. Anybody from the hinterland who covets political power and influence must pass muster by those who rule over its byzantine bureaucracy, and even in a country as diverse as Mexico the business tycoon in remote Monterrey or traditional Guadalajara must make the necessary gestures of obeisance to its authority. It is not uncommon for private companies in the nation's urban outposts to establish their headquarters here, often for no other reason than to be near the citadel of real power.

Mexico City's influence encompasses, by comparison, the political clout of Washington, the economic reach of New York, the neighborhood clannishness of Chicago, and the sprawl of Los Angeles. Its _colonias_ are jigsaw-puzzle pieces that do not mesh by any scientific measure. You can head north from the Paseo de la Reforma, the city's magnificent diagonal boulevard, from the Pink Zone, and in a mile or so pass through half a dozen distinct neighborhoods. By the end of your journey, somewhere in the vicinity of the Foreign Relations building, you have entered a domain that would befuddle the most imaginative interpreter of urban society. The Foreign Relations edifice is a modern high rise constructed next to a stone courtyard, where, a carving reads, the Indian chieftain Cuauhtémoc surrendered to Hernán Cortés. "It was neither triumph not defeat," the inscription says, "but the sad birth of the _mestizo_ who is the Mexico of today."

Inside the ancient church that stands nearby, repairmen perched on high scaffolds have been laboring to replace the fallen plaster around a fading engraving of the Resurrection. Encircling the adjoining courtyard is the Foreign Relations archives, once a monastery. To the west and north stand multistoried public housing, much of it in disrepair after the 1985 earthquake that struck the capital, and industrial warehouses. To the south lies a string of low-slung buildings that are home to a working girl's boutique, a *lonchería* featuring the *comida corrida,* the quick lunch, and "cokteles" and "lunchs," in the event you don't know what a *comida corrida* is. By comparison, the Burger Boy, representing the American culinary presence, on the corner is a majestic edifice. Out of business, apparently, is the seedy *casa de mujeres* (whorehouse) that once flourished in this block. To the east is the Plaza de Tres Culturas, with its monument symbolizing the Mexican cultural trinity, where in 1968 a protesting throng incurred the government's retaliatory wrath.

Within a radius of four or five blocks accumulates the cultural, economic, and political conundrum that is Mexico. The city of the Aztecs symbolizes the best and the worst, the noblest and ignoblest, the promise and the frustration, the richest and the poorest—in brief, the political, economic, and social extremities of Mexico. Here stand monuments and museums that glorify Mexico's Indian heritage; from here have emanated the directives, agencies, and policies that have enslaved, abused, and oppressed its native peoples. Here has evolved a central government whose leader and whose institutions symbolize the legacy of Spanish authority; from here the exercise of that authority has crushed the defiant cries from the hinterland. North of the Rio Grande a political aspirant can attract broad public support by running on a platform to "make government work for the people" or generate considerable, if short-lived, enthusiasm by "running against Washington." In Mexico City the first represents naiveté and the second sheer nonsense.

In five visits to Mexico City I have never met anyone, from street-sweeper and beggar to small businessman or petty government official—I do not circulate in loftier public or private circles in Mexico—who liked anything about Mexico City. Chicago symbolizes the quintessence of American culture in its rawest form; New York, the gateway to America from the old world; and Los Angeles, the capital of America's first third-world state. Mexico City represents all of these and more. It has a market of sixty square blocks that reeks of fish and chili peppers and, it is reputed, is controlled by fifty families. It has the Mexican equivalent of Central Park in Chapúltepec, along a European-style thoroughfare, the Paseo de la Reforma, which is as lovely and is on weekends the gathering place for low-income *chilangos*.

Toward the opposite terminus of the Paseo there is yet another sprawling market, Lagunilla, where on weekends the shrewdest Mexican garage-sale characters display everything from precious stone to the junkiest of junk items. They are legendary. They can look you in the eye and know exactly how much you will pay for the item you are pointing at. On weekdays all the business of Lagunilla occurs inside, along narrow passageways featuring cheap shoes, cheap handbags, cheap clothes, cheap jewelry, cheap handicrafts. There I once encountered an Irishman who had lived in Mexico City since his twenties. He had lost his front teeth and spoke Spanish with a Gaelic twang. He had married a *mexicana* and sired two lovely daughters. He sold cheap leather goods, but I persisted, and after an hour of conversation, he reached under the counter and pulled out a black leather briefcase. "It is yours for twenty dollars," he said. "But I don't want Mexican money. It's no good. Just like everything in this city." He dreamed of going back to County Cork.

Mexico City is not a city that works. It survives. It survives because the *chilangos,* rich and poor and in between, have survival instincts nurtured over the centuries. It is a city of *los olvidados,* the forgotten ones, the title of a classic postwar film depicting the tormented lot of Mexican youth. One of the forgotten ones in the film is a likable kid who lives in a wretched Mexico City barrio with his *familia*. His father has abandoned them. He becomes a gang member, is apprehended for a petty crime, and is finally befriended by a socially conscious official. But in the end his former gang leader finds him and kills the boy. The family cannot afford a proper burial, and they cannot go to the authorities, so the grandfather straps the lifeless body on a burro and transports it to the city's monstrously sprawling dump. There he deposits the boy along with the tons of *chilango* refuse.

237

When I first saw the movie I was shocked by the severity of the social message the director (Luís Buñuel) was striving to make. He did not relay in the film anything about the forty or fifty legendary families who preside over what must be the most offensive jurisdiction of Mexico City's unofficial domain, the city dump.

The city suffocates in the smog of engine exhaust and industrial waste, the global village's worst air pollution. For half the year the air is dry and dirty, the other half it is wet and dirty. Counting the plants that ring the outer portions of the urban area, which has spilled over into Mexico state like a blob in an overfilled bowl, Mexico City has one-third of Mexican industry. It has eight million vehicles, 90 percent of which are ferrying 10 percent of the city's population. Cynical urban planners speculate that one day the busiest thoroughfares will become so clogged and the traffic will become so congested that it will simply come to a halt and the vehicles will not be able to move—ever again. What is unsettling is the fact that so many Mexicans insist on taking their cars into the city or live on one side of the city and drive to work on the other side. The buses are moderately reliable, travel to the most woebegone barrios, and are cheap. The Metro, which opened in 1969, has seven lines, and is more comfortable. At critical hours both are packed, but they run often enough to accommodate most commuters. But the 10 percent of *chilangos* who insist on bringing 90 percent of the vehicles into the city have no intention of riding public transportation.

As one aging *chilango* once told me, the city's vehicular occlusion may deprive the residents of oxygen but so many cars offer Mexico City's notoriously corrupt police an opportunity to survive. In Mexico City's officialdom the cops occupy the heights of venality. They have transformed the *mordida* into an art form. They are understaffed, the *chilangos* are told, so the police cannot be expected to curtail the city's inevitably rising crime rate. It is just as well, the old *chilango* observed, because the police form part of Mexico City's criminal class. They do not apprehend criminals because most of Mexico City's finest are busy making a living by positioning themselves in strategic places to threaten owners of illegally (and legally) parked vehicles with citations unless they offer a 5,000-peso note with a genial "May God bless your life." Attractive women often do not have even the option of a _mordida_. In the crowded downtown area they have the wrecker concession. Their patrol cars are equipped with tow-truck-style front bumpers that are suitable for pushing stalled vehicles onto side streets or to a PEMEX station. So, with all the illegally parked cars, wrong turns on one-way streets, the menace of disabled vehicles, and sexual opportunities offered by apprehending speeding _señoras_, the police simply don't have the time or the men to deal with incidental nuisances such as bank holdups, assaults, and murder.

Even before Buñuel made _Los Olvidados_, Mexican leaders saw what Mexico City was becoming, but they were as much a victim of its relentless growth as the teenage criminals of the movie. In 1940, when Mexico was still a rural country, there were almost two million people in the federal district. Even then, almost 10 percent of all Mexicans lived in the federal district, producing 30 percent of the nation's industrial output and its manufacturing. In the half century since, little of the capital's economic centrality has diminished. If anything, its share of Mexico's population has increased, and its polluted air bears witness to the continuing presence of industrial waste. For the past quarter century Mexican leaders have spoken of disseminating government agencies and institutions to other parts of the country, but always the _chilangos_ get their share and a portion of everyone else's. The capital boasts more than 40 percent of the country's educational and health institutions. In the decade after 1963, more than 60 percent of the public housing rose in the federal district.

In the mid-fifties the attention investors lavished on the capital prompted the government to discontinue the special industrial tax advantages its entrepreneurs had enjoyed. The abolition had little effect on the rural migrants who stream into the city in search of the higher wages inspired by Mexico's development scheme. In

239

1950, Mexico City's population was 3.1 million; in 1960, 5.2 million; in 1970, 8.7 million; and in 1980, 14 million. Twenty years ago, the increase was explained largely by internal migration, reckoned now at a thousand newcomers a day, but in the past decade, the city's natural increase has dramatically affected these numbers. Even as employment conditions worsened—in the mid-seventies, it was estimated, 40 percent of the working population was underemployed—and the cost of living rose faster than wages, *mexicanos* continued to pour into the city.

In 1950 most *chilangos* lived in four major *delegaciones*. After that, the district grew so rapidly that new settlers pushed into the neighboring state of Mexico or into isolated areas of the district. In the latter, they erected "popular settlements," where one day an area would be largely unsettled and then, overnight, mushroom into a squalid village of tin-roofed shanties and cardboard shacks, in which families of five, six, seven, and more would sleep on dirt floors, battle disease and rats, and somehow manage to survive. Hundreds of them would literally take over unoccupied or unused land and transform it into instant slum. The more aggressive would organize community protest groups to keep out the inevitably prying government agent. Men would scurry up electrical poles and hot-wire their squalid little *casas*. They would survive on makeshift work and odd jobs, and when they couldn't get that they would dispatch their half-naked urchins into the city to beg. In a half-dozen years they might sire three or four children with one woman, then move on to another, repeating the sexual conquest and glorying in its inevitable legacy of sequential birth, until, ultimately, they perished of dissipation or disease.

Why endure such suffering? Because Mexico City with its despair and smog and unemployment and sardinelike existence offers more than some wretched little village crammed into a deceptively tranquil little valley in the middle of Nowhere, Mexico. There is more in the federal district, more money, more schools, more doctors, more social services, cheaper transportation. In the sixties the mushrooming squatter *colonias* were growing so fast that the sheer mass of so many people crammed into them was a frightening portent. Symbol of the nightmare was Netzahualcoyotl, a rabbit-warren den of migrants to the east of the district, sprawling into Mexico state, that ultimately grew to three million, when it was appropriately styled the biggest slum in the world, a city within a city. Here the newcomers built a "city of change" on a foundation of garbage and hope. Many of them are from Oaxaca, a desperately poor Indian state, birthplace of Benito Juárez, Mexico's most revered president.

As wretched as their life has been, and as many obstacles as they have confronted, the "Netzas" persevered. The future mayor of Mexico City, Hank González, then governor of the state of Mexico, was a great defender of private property. He tried to keep them out by pushing through development schemes laying claim to the property the Netzas were squatting on. But in the end their determination to stay where they had thrown up miserable little hovels brought them a victory—of sorts. The Oaxacans created their own village within Netzahualcoyotl and called it Liberation. It was not much, but it represented so much more than what they had had back in Oaxaca they were determined to remain. The women of Liberation were often in the vanguard. They organized community protest groups. Ultimately, their dream was a piece of paper signifying ownership of their hovel. With it, they felt secure enough to splash a little paint on the outside and to decorate the modest interior, perhaps hang a small picture of the Virgin of Guadalupe or a crudely fashioned cross.

Yet, the "parachutists" kept coming, living in caves in the sand pits or worse. Minimal social services, usually beginning with the Mexico City bus line, arrived, but so did the real estate brokers, who persuaded hundreds to occupy unused land, took their meager savings as commission, and abandoned them to years of haggling over legal title with the cumbersome Mexican bureaucracy. The parachutists are country people who trust too much, are cheated, but retain their faith that theirs will be a better life. If given a little space, they will plant a garden or raise a few chickens, anything to remind them of what little security they had back in their village. Social workers call their assimilation a difficult adjustment. They try to "ruralize" the city, fail, and finally accommodate themselves to its demands, convincing themselves that a few chickens in the back make a big difference. Their children adjust more rapidly. By the third generation, they are *chilangos*.[1]

Americans looking at this urban misery often believe the poor of Mexico City are the street warriors of the revolution that will inevitably engulf the city and ultimately the entire country. To us the wretched conditions of the lower order in Mexico and the suffering of those who have little of little or *nada de nada* call for violent explosion. But the likelihood of revolution from below in Mexico is slim. The government is too omnipresent, too well organized, and too clever to permit upheaval from the forgotten ones. However grim their lot in the city of the Aztecs, the downtrodden *chilangos* have been able to wrest enough from authority to quell whatever revolutionary thirsts they may have acquired. The government shuffles the paper and gives them a secure title to their land; bureaucrats announce the opening of a school; at election time a truck bearing loudspeakers and a few nurses and doctors will dramatically appear in some long-forgotten barrio in some long-neglected *colonia*. None of these will amount to much, but it will mean enough to keep them going. It has been persuasively argued that the lot of poor *chilangos* is worse than that of their forebears in 1940, that Mexico does less for the poor of its capital than any other country in Latin America, and that the only thing of lasting value Mexico City's poor get is title to land. Yet their commitment to a Revolutionary government that does so little for them remains firm. Government simply conditions them to want less than they deserve.[2]

The city's upper and middle classes are not so easily persuaded. For them the economic benefits of a vast army of unskilled labor are small compensation for the burden of a federal bureaucracy whose leaders can dictate the political life of the district. _Chilangos_ can vote for president of the republic and national legislators and senators, but they cannot say how city monies will be spent, how urban planning will be undertaken, or even who will be their mayor. Four left-of-center parties have joined ranks with a rightist political appendage and begun a movement to make the federal district a state, Anáhuac. The momentum for what the government considers an unnecessary—and provocative—move began after the devastating earthquake of 1985. In the tragic aftermath, President de la Madrid appeared hesitant to jeopardize the credibility of federal authority by detailing the severe damage of the quake. By the time the government finally began to move, Mexico City's rich and poor had formed a momentary bond and undertaken rescue operations.

This unnatural union between haves and have-nots did not last, of course, but the federal government's slowness in responding to a compelling need for swift action convinced not a few _chilangos_ they were too dependent on the national bureaucracy. But when the statehood proposal was broached, the government was already prepared to defuse it with its alternative proposal, an offer to "democratize" the federal district by creating an assembly of sixty-six members, almost two-thirds of them from the government party (PRI) and the rest apportioned to the largest minority assemblage, National Action. But Mexico City's mayor would still be appointed by the president, and he could veto any legislation the new assembly put forward. The statehooders immediately spied in this another conspiracy. Honest elections in a self-governing federal district, one PAN leader noted, would mean victory for the minority party, something the PRI could not tolerate.

The president of the republic was more eloquent but no less political in his pronouncement: Anáhuac, he said, would lack "political viability" and undermine "national unity."[3]

On my last visit, in summer 1986, the scars of the '85 quake are still visible. Along the Alameda the hotels del Prado and

Alameda are still standing but are too weakened to permit their reopening. But farther down, the elegant Palace of Fine Arts, where the Ballet Folklórico performs to the delight of visitors from every corner of the nation, is unscathed, testimony to the endurance of Mexican architecture and culture.

In the southern reaches of the district, at the Autonomous National University, with its strikingly frescoed national library, I wander among students who scribble Marxist graffiti on cinder-block walls and listen to rock music. On this day some of them are asking for "graduation donations." Hard hit by the country's unrelenting inflation, they are trying to create a kilometer of 100-peso notes. I contribute a few centimeters to their cause and head back for the Metro. My destination is the sixty-square-block Mercado on the blue line. There I am in the same city but in a different Mexico. No vivacious and optimistic middle-class students wander these narrow passages. I pass stall after stall of *mestizos* with expressionless faces—a woman frying mounds of tortillas in spattering grease, a swarthy male cutting off bits of fried pork for taco innards, a boy creating a pyramid of defeathered chickens, a pepper-and-onion man devouring a pork sandwich and washing it down with gulps of Coca-Cola, the most lasting symbol of America in this place. It is too much, even for my Mexican-conditioned stomach. I return to Sanborn's in the Zócalo and have a club sandwich and a Tecate beer.

On my last day, I walked aimlessly along the Paseo, past the towering hotels and banks, toward Lagunilla. The buildings flatten and deteriorate; in less than a mile I pass from one Mexico into another. Farther along, there are several blocks of temporary shelters for some of the city's fifty thousand uprooted by the quake. They are small and narrow, constructed with tin roofs and tin walls, and they cling to the sidewalk. But each has a little space for hanging out clothes or planting a few flowers.

I pause at one, the lodging of an old woman who has an unsightly scar on her left cheek but retains a sparkle in her eyes. She hangs her wash on the steel fence but has no flowers. She does have two lovebirds, and today their cage stands outside.

Noticing me, she says, "They are my children. I will never sell them. Strangers pass by and ask how much I want for them. But I will not sell them, not one. They were with me before the earthquake. I lost everything else. Look at this wound on my face. But the birds and I survived. God protected us. I know that as long as they live I will live."

15

"They Lied to Us"

≡≡≡≡

In the late seventies Mexicans believed they had at last achieved a dramatic opportunity to create a more prosperous nation, and even more important, an *independent* Mexico. New oil discoveries in the tropical southeast near the Tabasco-Chiapas border and later in Campeche Sound in the Gulf of Mexico had convinced José López Portillo to channel tremendous amounts of public spending into PEMEX. In *its* petroleum wealth, exploited by *its* company, controlled by *its* government, Mexico would at long last control *its* destiny. From the beginning more prudent analyses warning of the potentially disruptive impact that heavy spending and borrowing often levy on an economy were drowned out by the chorus of nationalistic boasting about Mexico's new era.

For a few years the dream persisted. Stimulated by the projections of ever-rising oil prices, the *técnicos* in the ponderous Mexican bureaucracy under the president spoke of transforming Mexico into the "next Japan." The new Mexico, they believed, would be a truly modern industrial economy, and it would be a self-sufficient one. JLP, who had inherited a virtually bankrupt treasury, had begun his tenure with pledges to reduce the deficit and, indeed, had won a few plaudits from the international lending agencies for his endeavors. But now that Mexico had proven resources in a commodity the more industrialized countries desperately needed, prospects for exploiting Mexico's oil bonanza proved too tempting to resist. For four years the formerly suspicious bankers watched as the *técnicos* in Mexico City gloated over the impressive statistics of Mexico's economic performance—more than 7 percent growth and the creation of 900,000 jobs per year.

Then, in a sequence of economic calamities, the dream of a "new Mexico" quickly perished in a nightmare from which the country awoke to a grim reality. Once again, the somber analysts were saying, the nation had proved unable to ward off the foreign devils who had come from afar to rob Mexico of its treasure. The price of oil, which the experts had expected to continue upward, leveled and then began to slip downward under the combined pressure of reduced consumption and rising production. JLP's economic forecasters calculated Mexico's oil revenue at more than $20 billion annually in 1982. The country received $15 billion. The $5 billion shortfall took a destructive economic toll. By then Mexico had amassed a debt of $80 billion, more than half of it during JLP's *sexenio,* which took $16 billion annually just to service.

Bankruptcies increased among private businesses, whose owners, imitating the government's enthusiasm in the late seventies, had borrowed heavily against future revenues. Even before the financial collapse of 1982, the lure of higher returns for investment and persistent fears of devaluation had brought on a capital flight of more than $20 billion. To block further outflows, the government initiated a series of emergency measures: devaluation of the peso, prohibition of withdrawal of dollars from savings accounts, and, ultimately, nationalization of the banks.

I was in Mexico that year, as the accumulating dreary economic news had already demoralized a generation of *chilangos* who had listened as JLP touted Mexico's oil wealth and the blessings that would flow from it. Outside the Hotel del Prado on Avenida Juárez, less glittery than the modern high rises in the Pink Zone, I negotiated a ride to the airport with one of the cab drivers who line up in front of the major hotels. During the day, buses from the airport to the downtown hotels are fairly regular and quite inexpensive, but to snare the airport bus on the return trip is a matter of pure chance. I had to catch a late-afternoon flight, so I opted for the cab.

On the way, I began to ask the driver how *la crisis* had affected his business. Initiating a conversation with a Mexico City cabdriver can sometimes be a hazardous venture. One can never be sure that whatever topic is introduced, from soccer or Mexico City's perpetually clogged thoroughfares to some social or political scandal, will not trigger a burst of *chingar*-laden rhetoric accompanied by demonstrative gestures of the hands. My cabbie was middle-aged and, I presumed, more cautious than the hellions often drafted into the *chilango* cab corps.

"I remember all the talk," he said. "They promised us everything. The oil would make us rich, they said." He zipped past a slow-moving truck laden with melons, then shifted into another lane. I flinched as his voice assumed a more combative tone. "Would you believe I am poorer now than I was five years ago? I have to pay sixteen hundred pesos a day just to rent this cab. *Me chingarón!*"—They screwed me. "At the hotel I have to stay in line or I lose my place. And when we get out to the airport I cannot pick up another fare because another taxi company has a monopoly. Sure, I can take a chance, but if they catch me I will have to pay a five-thousand-peso fine."

He began to jumble unrelated issues and his daily economic woes into an explanation of *la crisis*. It offered no economic or even political analysis of what had happened to the prospective oil wealth Mexico's leaders had forecast, nor did it suggest what could be done about the grim situation. But in his ceaseless litany of complaints he reserved his greatest scorn for the government that had promised so much.

"They lied to us!"

For a brief moment I considered making an offhand remark to the effect that American presidents have been known to lie, and politicians who promised much and failed to deliver have been voted out. But the look of resignation on his countenance stopped me. It was then I knew and he knew that I had a choice and he didn't. As a father can fail a child, his government had failed him. Its responsibility was moral, its obligations paternal. What he did not say—perhaps because he lacked the understanding or the perspective to articulate any explanation that would make sense to a gringo—was that, ultimately, Mexico's economic crisis required thinking about what has been for almost three-quarters of a century in Mexico the "unthinkable," changing the *political system*.

Mexico's political system defies precise characterization. It is not socialist, yet the government intrudes heavily into the economy, and in critical areas such as oil, transportation, and industry it owns or controls the major companies. Political scientists have labeled it "corporatist," a more accurate definition, they say, because interest groups, social organizations, and even individual citizens express their grievances or make their claims through a labyrinthine structure—labor, peasants, and the catch-all "public" sector that encompasses public employees, small business proprietors, and even private landowners. The umbrella shielding these diverse representations of what some Mexicans call "pluralist democracy" is the official party, the Institutional Revolutionary Party, PRI.[1]

There are, of course, groups left out because they have chosen a more independent path or have no important place in the system. For all its rhetoric about including all *mexicanos* in its protective embrace, PRI does not accommodate the needs of *campesinos* who have no land or industrial workers without a union. But efforts to organize them and other discontented usually have run aground because the newcomers have so little to offer. The church, the military, and the powerful entrepreneurs are not members of PRI's political club because they are not wanted or have no reason to join. The church has been officially circumscribed since the anticlerical government campaign in the twenties, though unofficially the *políticos* have tolerated its reemerging social and educational role. (Mexicans still quip that in the United States the president cannot afford to be seen outside a church on Sundays, and in Mexico *el jefe,* the boss, cannot

249

afford to be seen inside one.) Since the days of Cárdenas, the leftist *jefe* of the thirties who reorganized the party and brought in labor and the *campesinos,* the military has lost its political clout but has faithfully maintained the authority of the state.

Trying to find an encompassing term to describe the Mexican political system, some have called it an "authoritarian democracy" or "one-party rule" with multiparty tolerance. The first is a mix of two incompatible elements, unless, of course, "democracy" is defined in the Hispanic sense of "real democracy," by which is meant not one man, one vote nor a glorification of the quadrennial clash between political candidates, but the link of the individual with the state through his "sector." And the second presumes that PRI is a political party in the western European or American sense. In reality, PRI is not a party but a creature of the Mexican state.

At first glance the Mexican governmental structure bears a strong resemblance to its American counterpart: it has executive, legislative, and judicial branches, a federal system of states, and local governments that, under the Constitution of 1917, are "free." But in reality, Mexican politicians and bureaucrats, from top to bottom, whether they are *técnicos* trained as engineers or economists who have spent most of their professional life in the bureaucracy or *políticos* who have wormed their way through the PRI maze and made it to the governorship of Veracruz or Nuevo León or Jalisco, march to a different drumbeat than their *yanqui* counterparts.

They have to. Mexico inherited a political tradition from the Spanish that centralized power at the upper reaches, and independent Mexican leaders down through the years, with varying degrees of success, have preserved authority from above. Even the Revolutionaries who tossed out the dictator Porfirio Díaz sensed that *their* inheritance of federal power should not be frittered away because of some momentary doubts about creating another *porfiriato.*

The Revolutionary generation that inherited don Porfirio's power had rebelled against him because his *system* had grown old with him, and they had sensed opportunity. In seizing control they created a new political order with new leaders who began expanding the authority of the central government and those who ruled it. To ensure the preservation of their labors (and ambitions) they structured Mexican politics along authoritarian lines. But they were alert to Díaz' errors, and since the Revolution they have reinforced their sway within the formal structure of government by making sure there is only one foolproof way to attain real political power in Mexico.

As Lorenzo Meyer, an astute historian of Mexico, has observed, the encompassing slogan of PRI is "Unity and Discipline."[2] What the inheritors of Díaz' awesome power did was not to destroy the political system the old dictator had molded over the years but to remodel it. Unlike their predecessors, the Revolutionary generation that ultimately submitted its political fervor to PRI did so in order to ensure that the sometimes bitter contests for power would not disable the *system*. Their goal was the depersonalization of power. This meant that the presidential opportunists could engage in maneuvering and even intrigue until the retiring *presidente* made his selection, then everybody had to rally behind his choice. Assured of election, the new leader, once ensconced, might speak of "new directions" or, as did Miguel de la Madrid, about "moral renovation," but his obligations to the system and its perpetuation dictated no abrupt changes.

The Mexican political system does not divide and conquer; it absorbs and dominates, usually at glacierlike momentum and with slight alteration of purpose. In a manner that would shame the most imaginative American political leader bent on domination of his party, the Mexicans have been able to co-opt virtually anybody willing to be co-opted, and, generally, to pay whatever price is necessary. All classes, rich and poor, find a niche somewhere in the system. The only elements left out are those on the extremes. But even the political extremities would be willingly taken into the family if they would agree. Thus, PRI has a place for the giddy socialist or Marxist as well as a few disciples of nineteenth-century classical economists. Even writers and artists are not immune. Ever since the 1920s those who ruled have generally set aside a comfortable place for "Mexican painters" or "Mexican philosophers" or "Mexican writers." Intellectuals find their way into the foreign service or occupy lofty positions in the federal bureaucracy. From the vast state-supported universities, heavily subsidized, the government sometimes takes both professor and graduating student into its encompassing embrace.

Institutionalization of Mexican politics, by general agreement, has brought the benefits of stability and continuity, which enabled Mexico to modernize its economy and disseminate greater social benefits than the old order. But the costs exacted have been high. Most Mexicans, even ardent defenders of the system, are uncomfortably apologetic or harshly critical of official corruption, but I have encountered few who are indifferent, especially in these harsh times for all Mexicans. But I have spoken with few who really knew how to rid the system of *corrupción* with anything less than sweeping changes, a massive displacement of persons lodged in the bureaucracy, or, if such measures proved inadequate to the job, another revolution. The first two are unattainable goals unless Mexico has the third, which is frightening to contemplate, to Mexicans and Americans, because once unleashed, a second Mexican Revolution might swallow even more lives than the Revolution of 1910. And the political *order* it would conceivably produce might be less corrupt but in every other measure be utterly reprehensible.

What is engaging about Mexican bureaucrats willing to talk openly about graft is their artful redefinition of the word "corruption." There are, for example, important distinctions to be made between "vulgar graft" (which is illegal) and "ethical graft" (which can be legal). Then there is "unethical graft" (which also can be legal). A former minister of the treasury, who served Miguel Alemán, the businessman's president and creator of Mexico's modern system of official corruption, explained the process:

"Let us say that a public official knows that a highway is to be constructed, and that he also knows the person in charge of building or directing the work. He can buy, directly or indirectly, the land that will be affected by such a highway and thus obtain an advantageous position. This is not ethically right, but legally it is not a crime. And this kind of thing is quite common, much more so than people think.

"A public official has innumerable means of acquiring advantages from his position, without there necessarily being corruption, in the sense that he need not collude to receive money as happens in the very inferior [governmental] levels. . . . [For example], fiscal inspectors do take what in Mexico is called a *mordida,* that is a bribe or a tip, in order to do or not to do a certain thing. This has several degrees. There is the *mordida* paid to have something done rapidly which one has a right to have done—that really is a tip. Then there is the *mordida* paid to have something done slowly which one does not wish done quickly—this is going much further. . . ."[3]

An American reader might find such candor shocking and, certainly, more than ample justification for reforms and a general political housecleaning. In actuality, the Mexican government could not operate without the *mordida.* The bureaucracy could not function without it. The crucial question is not its existence but the degree of toleration.

What Mexico needs, American and not a few Mexican critics have pointed out, is democracy. What it has is a centralist state that emerged from a Revolution that for many Mexicans promised much but delivered very little. The Revolutionary heirs did not sweep away the social order but rearranged it. They industrialized a largely rural economy but they created neither a socialist nor a capitalist democracy. They warred against the pre-Revolutionary political order and then fought among themselves, but they did not create—nor did they intend to create—a political democracy. A half century ago, when Mexico still reverberated with political intrigue, the Revolutionary heirs could not afford to install a democratic political regime. In modern times, with their power secure, they are unwilling to risk more than cosmetic political reforms for fear that more compelling political changes will sweep them from power.

Many Americans, trying to unravel the hopelessly confusing skein of Mexican political life, sometimes mislabel Mexicans as unrealistically ideological. In actuality there is little ideology in the traditional meaning of the word among those who describe themselves as the bearers of the Revolutionary tradition. They severely limited the power of the church and promised to redistribute the land; they committed the government to education and granted labor certain basic rights. But these were less representative of political ideology than a social and economic commitment, though it can be argued that the anticlerical phrases of the Constitution of 1917 symbolized a secular faith in state over church. No reelection, the rallying cry of earlier Revolutionaries, was firmly implanted as the requirement that no elected official could succeed himself. Mexican law may protect freedom of the press, but in practice the Mexican government can severely circumscribe the press because it controls the supply of newsprint, and when that does not restrain an especially abusive journalist, officials resort to bribery, intimidation, and, it has been alleged, assassination. Similarly, in modern times, the government's pledge of agrarian reform has suffered considerable erosion. True, in the *sexenio* of Echeverría, who made a conscious effort to direct Mexico into a position of leadership in the third world, there was a renewed interest in land redistribution. But little land was actually given out, and Echeverría's successor, José López Portillo, matter-of-factly announced that Mexico had no more land to redistribute. Besides, said JLP, the country needed to make more efficient use of its precious acreage to increase food production.

PRI has never lost an election, dishonestly or honestly conducted, at any save the municipal level since 1929. But in spite of its penetration into every isolated *municipio,* the ruling party tolerates, and in the 1977 political reforms appeared to promote, a sometimes loyal opposition. In the preceding year, with the

Communist Party outlawed and National Action unable to field a candidate, López Portillo ran largely against an empty opposition. The next year's alterations in the electoral law, which guaranteed the opposition parties a certain percentage of seats in the legislative branch, were prescribed by a secure Mexican government a bit worried that the lack of opposition would damage its image. A PRI magnate observed, "That which opposes, supports."

For a few years, in the late seventies, the nonvoter, who has become the most significant element in American elections, threatened by his abstention from the voting place in Mexico to join his indifferent *yanqui* counterpart. In part, this resignation was due to the inevitability of a PRI victory and, particularly on the municipal level, the ability of government *políticos* to manipulate social and labor organizations with promises, intimidation, and the generally reliable bribery. But it reflected as well the inability of the revivified opposition, left or right, to fashion much of a base. The PRI's logo is the flag, which appears on the ballot and is immediately recognized even by the illiterate as a symbol meriting his vote. The leftist parties, for example, have been critical of PRI "oppressiveness" but they are made up mostly of Mexico City's socialists, the Mexican equivalent of America's "martini Marxists," only too willing to trade whatever commitment they have to the "oppressed" for a little visibility in the legislature or an entrée into the inner domain of real power.

The National Action Party (PAN), born in the tumultuous church-state conflicts of the late thirties and early forties, has always been a more serious problem. When Mexicans returned to the polls in larger numbers in 1982, at a time of severe economic crisis, to elect Miguel de la Madrid, the protest vote went largely to the PAN candidate, Pablo Madero, grandnephew of Francisco Madero, the martyred successor to the old dictator, Porfirio Díaz. His link to the Revolutionary liberal democratic tradition as well as Mexico's Catholics and private business elite was symbolic. Most of the Revolutionary warriors called for social justice, land reform, and suppression of the church, which PRI has incorpo-

255

rated into its political litany. Madero, by contrast, called for "no reelection" (by which the diminutive Madero meant "no bossism"), independent legislative and judicial branches, and local autonomy, each of which the constitution promised to safeguard but its Revolutionary heirs have not protected.

Because Americans tend to gauge Mexican politics by the economic condition of the country, PAN's persistent opposition to PRI's domineering habits has inspired American political leaders to make subtle (and occasionally unsubtle) gestures indicating "our" preferences in "their" politics. The bill of indictment against Mexico's dominant party includes, among other condemnations of its generic corruption, a persuasive charge that the Mexican economy suffers from unnecessary (and debilitating) statism. PAN, by contrast, symbolizes to Americans the kind of economic and political philosophy that would, if the party was voted into power, get the Mexican government "off the backs of the people and allow the free enterprise system to work."

In the seventies, especially under the combative Echeverría, Mexico shifted leftward in its foreign policies, and the government began intruding more into the economy. The intent, said Echeverría, was to break the grip of the industrial nations, especially the United States, on Mexico and other third-world countries. Echeverría, who as head of Gobernación had dispatched the attack squad against the antigovernment protesters in 1968, vowed war against *dependencia*. The government plunged into new ventures, in industry and agriculture, and imposed tough new laws on foreign investment and technology. Inevitably, when the economy staggered under the strain, he tried to pay for the vigorous statist economy with new taxes, which the middle and upper classes resisted, and when that failed he ordered the printing presses to roll.

Trying to appease leftist demands for a more socially conscious government, Echeverría had aroused sometimes bitter recriminations from the right. But his inspiring speeches about a new era for the downtrodden merely raised expectations beyond the capability of the Mexican economy to satisfy, despite the expansion induced by Echeverría's program. In 1975, as random violence became more severe, Echeverría was blaming Mexico's lamentable condition on everything from CIA activities to the breakdown of the family. The climactic confrontation with the nation's private sector occurred when he announced that 250,000 acres in a rich agricultural region in Sonora would be given to eight thousand small farmers. In protest, the Monterrey clans called for a nationwide twenty-four-hour shutdown of businesses. In the elections of the following year, with scarcely any opposition to the government's candidate, the mood of Mexican politics was grim.

In the end, for all his efforts, Mexico remained as dependent on the U.S. economy in 1976 as it had been six years before. JLP tried to make amends with the private sector, and the status of opposition parties, especially PAN, improved considerably with the 1977 reforms, and the oil bonanza of the late seventies brought hordes of international bankers descending on Mexico with loans. When the "petrolization" of the economy took its toll from unwise spending, unwise borrowing, unwise planning, and unarguably the most disgusting graft of any Mexican government since Alemán's, the image of PAN and what it offered struck yet another responsive chord north of the Rio Grande. But, as do all Mexican leaders, JLP alertly sensed the winds of displeasure from the north and made de la Madrid the Mexican equivalent of the director of the office of management and budget. De la Madrid tightened the economic grip, but the downward spiral of Mexico's economic performance and the upward spiral of its inflation continued. Ultimately, in his last year, JLP, outwardly untroubled by the rising chorus of criticism, took the biggest gulps from the *mordida* trough but had the good sense to tap de la Madrid as his choice for the presidential sash. One month before he departed, following the dramatic announcement of nationalization of Mexico's banks, JLP committed Mexico to an international stabilization plan. With it, Mexico got the blessing of the International Monetary Fund and the American government for desperately needed loans.[4]

*   *   *

As idealists who commit themselves to government service or social work often discover, the attempts of even the most stout-hearted and competent to alter a cumbersome bureaucracy are fraught with difficulty. When de la Madrid donned the presidential sash in December 1982, he pledged "moral renovation." The *técnicos* were going to run things. This meant austerity for the Mexican economy and a campaign against corruption. PAN had won a surprising 13 percent of the vote in the election. De la Madrid was not outwardly concerned, but he recognized that some well-publicized housecleaning might improve PRI's tarnished image. The most illustrious victim of moral renovation was the former chieftain of PEMEX, Jorge Díaz Serrano, accused of enriching himself and his staff during the boom days under JLP, who went to a lavish jail cell in mid-1983. Mexico City's taxi-driver wisdom holds that he is really a "stand-in criminal" for the host of others who should have suffered a similar fate. There were, of course, lesser-known bureaucrats who felt the mild wrath of don Miguel: they lost their special guards or chauffeurs who had done private duty but were reimbursed with public funds. Actually, though their slopping at the public trough was less severe, had de la Madrid been able to foresee that the terminated employees, especially those skilled in the use of firearms, would begin robbing banks, he might have reconsidered the hazards of "moral renovation." But moral renovation failed because de la Madrid could excise only a small amount of the graft that corrodes Mexican politics. Ultimately, the *políticos,* those who *know* how the system really works, survived.

The dilemma of Mexico's ruling political elite is far too complex to be solved by more democracy. It is, for PRI's encrusted bureaucracy, a question of "credibility," for "credibility" is inseparably linked to authority and survival. The government must respond, however inadequately, to the cries from the left for a more activist state, but it cannot afford to alienate those who have (and want more) by imposing a socialist economy to pay for the social justice Americans believe Mexico desperately needs. And neither can it afford the political economy Americans increasingly identify with PAN's credos. In Mexico, those who wield political power are shackled with a system that permits only limited alterations. The middle classes may have been the beneficiaries of the Mexican economic miracle; this does not, in the minds of the PRI hierarchy, entitle them to anything resembling a two-party system.

De la Madrid was captive of the system that molded him, a reformist prisoner. In 1983, the government retrenched a bit in the political arena, and PAN captured mayoralty seats in Chihuahua and Ciudad Juárez. But in the following year, as PAN candidates escalated their assault on PRI's practice of "fingering" political choices, even de la Madrid's moral renovation did not stop the government from announcing a PRI victory in Mexicali. Already, PAN had begun to change its image from a business-oriented and pro-church party, trying to cultivate a following among discontented urbanites. At Christmastime 1985, government agents blatantly overruled a PAN victory in Piedras Negras, and infuriated protesters blocked the international bridge. This sort of public outcry, in the United States or Europe, might have prompted an investigation. But in Mexico, the *políticos* of PRI viewed it and PAN's vigorous campaign in several northern gubernatorial races in 1986 as a signal to close ranks against the menacing rightist tide. All the while, behind closed doors, de la Madrid strived to lessen the damage to Mexico's image by trying to get PRI moguls not only to democratize the party but to tolerate more opposition seats in the national congress. And he politely listened to arguments that PRI could *abandon* its middle-class constituents and survive *exclusively* on its powerful base among Mexico's working classes.

If Mexican politics can be democratized only by democratizing PRI, then it is unlikely that Mexican politics will ever be democratized, at least by any American definition of the word. It is not coincidental, I believe, that American pressures on Mexico for political reforms have come at a time when the Mexican government has been trying to deal with its most severe economic crisis since the Revolution. It can be argued that Mexico's economic prostration offers a realistic opportunity to urge upon it the political reforms many Mexicans want. And, increasingly, when observers of Mexican politics look for comparative political systems, they are paying less and less attention to the rest of Latin America and measuring Mexican politics by an American model. The government made it clear in 1986 that despite its loosening of the system it was not going to tolerate a PAN victory in any of the gubernatorial races. And when the charges of fraud inevitably were made, middle-class Mexicans symbolically staged protests, blocking traffic across several of the international bridges. Mexico City did not ignore the outbursts, but neither did a supposedly fragile government bend before the outbursts of *norteños*. PAN came away with no victory but the inspiration to go on in its campaign, convinced that there were increasing numbers of Mexicans looking at the American electoral process and wanting something like it for Mexico.

One day, perhaps. In the meantime, PAN must deal with more pressing immediate realities, the most obvious of which is that any Mexican political movement that emulates an American model and looks for American support may eventually triumph but cannot survive. For all its ponderous inefficiency and some- times blatant political dishonesty, PRI is more thoroughly Mex- ican than any of its adversaries, however threatening. The unsubtle American criticism of Mexican political corruption is not something Mexican leaders take lightly, but they know enough about American standards to realize that a resurgent Mexican economy will do wonders to reduce American pressures for political reform. As for the internal pressures, they know, too, that a little political housecleaning may work wonders in bringing disaffected protest votes back under the PRI umbrella. When their critics point north toward an American political model, they will say, in defense of the Mexican model, that it is uniquely theirs, and that the *norteamericano*'s model is ''a democracy . . . of a people who are different and profoundly proud of their electoral process'' but who suffer from a ''visible'' and ''invisible government. However much [the Americans] continue to denounce corruption, they keep on practicing it.''[5]

Across Mexico in recent years, as far south as the Indian southeast, political turbulence, precipitated by charges of fraud in elections and angry reactions of peasants displaced from the land, has been an unsettling recurrence. In the north, disgruntled middle-class Mexicans, convinced they would triumph in the 1986 elections with PAN victories, have shut down border traffic and demanded investigations. Deeper into Mexico, in incidents largely unreported by the world media because they are not widely reported by the Mexican press, indignant Mexican mobs have burned city halls and attacked government officials. These are isolated, sporadic occurrences, but they happen with such frequency that there is persistent speculation about more violent upheavals. Against the mass of the lower order and the financial clout and political appeal of the private sector, the Mexican political system, it is argued, would appear doomed.

Those who believe that underestimate its capacity to survive, to reach downward to ordinary *mexicanos,* to whom it has promised much and delivered little, and find acceptance. And they miscalculate its willingness to employ some of its considerable political muscle to teach the businessmen who have championed PAN's cause a lesson about who is really in charge.

16

MexAmerica

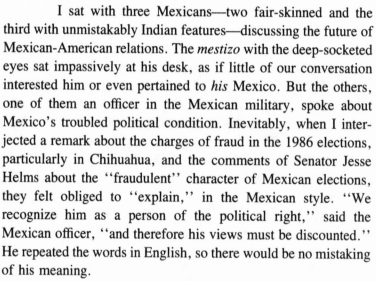

I sat with three Mexicans—two fair-skinned and the third with unmistakably Indian features—discussing the future of Mexican-American relations. The *mestizo* with the deep-socketed eyes sat impassively at his desk, as if little of our conversation interested him or even pertained to *his* Mexico. But the others, one of them an officer in the Mexican military, spoke about Mexico's troubled political condition. Inevitably, when I interjected a remark about the charges of fraud in the 1986 elections, particularly in Chihuahua, and the comments of Senator Jesse Helms about the "fraudulent" character of Mexican elections, they felt obliged to "explain," in the Mexican style. "We recognize him as a person of the political right," said the Mexican officer, "and therefore his views must be discounted." He repeated the words in English, so there would be no mistaking of his meaning.

I responded politely, "Yes, to be sure, but I have spoken with Americans of all political persuasions, and they are deeply concerned about the frauds in the most recent elections."

My repetition of the word "fraud" provoked a more defensive reaction. "There was *no* fraud. Irregularities, yes, but *no* fraud. You have to remember that Mexico is different. In Oaxaca"—one of the country's poorest states—"where the government was accused of rigging the election, many of the people are illiterate, so irregularities occur when they vote. But there was *no* fraud."

I resurrected old complaints about Mexican elections, reiterated in the charges of fraud (or "irregularities") in the Chihuahua gubernatorial race and in some chilling accounts of Mexican _official_ culpability in narcotics trafficking. Their responses were not evasive but, predictably, diversionary. "We want to cooperate," said the officer, who had dominated most of the conversation, "but our cooperation must not be at the risk of losing our sovereignty." He followed with a few sarcastic references to the heavy levels of drug consumption in the United States. "In this country," he said, "only the lower classes consume drugs, so there is not a large market for cocaine and the more expensive narcotics. The problem lies north of the border."

I explained that America _was_ waging a war against narcotics but, quite frankly, it was easier, and certainly politically more expedient, to go after producers and distributors in Latin America, especially next door in Mexico, than to circumscribe individual rights in the United States or to admit that American society was corrupt. His momentarily contemptuous glance conveyed an unspoken but telling comment about American priorities.

His companion quickly shifted the discussion back to politics. "You have to understand," he reminded me, in an avuncular tone, "that our politics cannot operate on American rules because our political system is different. PAN, the opposition party, has no base."

I cited a few statistics about the 1986 elections, not only in Chihuahua, the case most Americans knew more about, but also in other interior Mexican states. "What I don't understand, and what many Americans don't understand, is this: if the government _knows_ it can win sixty percent of the vote in a reasonably honest election, why does it feel compelled to steal another twenty percent? In the United States, sixty percent is considered a landslide." I could not think of a Spanish equivalent for "landslide," so I substituted "great victory."

The _mestizo_ at the corner desk remained silent, but the expression on his face indicated he _knew_ the answer, and so, I believe, did I. The intelligent military man tried to convey, in a rephrasing of earlier comments, the peculiarities of Mexican politics, its distinctive evolution since the Revolution. What he could not say, perhaps because he did not believe I would really understand, was that his government did not really believe it had a choice. Its leaders stole elections by huge margins because they had to. At bottom, it was a question not of honor or right but authority and legitimacy, or, to use a word more familiar to Americans, "credibility."

When we had finished, he escorted me down the stairs, through the elegant foyer, and outside to the wrought-iron gate. Bidding me a polite *buen viaje* he said, "Remember, please, that we have said nothing and you have heard nothing."

It was the last interview of my crisscrossing trip across Mex-America and left me as perplexed about the character of Mex-America as I was in the beginning, in its northernmost outpost, Chicago. There I had spoken with one of Chicago's finest about the one-man Cinco de Mayo (Fifth of May) parade, commemorating the victory of Mexicans against the invading French in 1862. It is celebrated throughout MexAmerica. In 1986, Ramón Cervantes, a Mexican American committed to Hispanic Unity, which is striving to unite Chicago's factious Spanish-speaking, chose to remember the Cinco de Mayo in a manner most of the city's jaded political observers doubtless considered "typical" of Hispanic demonstrativeness. He called local television and radio stations and announced he was organizing a parade to unite Chicago's feuding Latinos *and* to memorialize his brother, killed in a football game fifteen years earlier. Cervantes believed his parade merited a queen—any age, married or unmarried, preferably Hispanic but Polish or Italian acceptable. He donned Mexican clothes and hoisted a Mexican flag and a placard that read, in that juxtaposition of Spanish and English the Mexican American often uses, "Operación don Quixote—I Will Feed the World Now," and strutted proudly along a downtown street. His only companion was a cop on a three-wheeler.

A Chicago newspaper captioned the photo of his lonely march: "Ramón parades his cause—alone." The cop was more sarcastic: "Well, that's the way those people are. They can't get organized on anything."

Unintentionally, both rendered a common American view about the political ethos of Hispanic Americans. And behind those sometimes cynical observations about Hispanics in our society lie frustrations about incorporating not only the newcomer but the longtime Hispanic American resident into American political culture. Hispanic American political participation, though increasing in the past quarter century, has yet to achieve the levels of participation of blacks and other minorities. And behind these frustrations lie the unarticulated fears that the United States has reached a plateau in its cultural evolution. There are fears, occasionally expressed as legitimate social concerns and, all too often, as outbursts of a dormant racism, that the United States must reaffirm traditional convictions about "what kind of society we want to be" and "why English must be our official language" and adjust its laws accordingly. If we are not diligent about this manifestly necessary endeavor, it is further argued, we will become the country of choice for the third world with its attendant political, economic, and social debilities.

Our border with this unwanted world is two thousand miles long, from Brownsville, Texas, to San Ysidro, California. But its impact on our politics, our economy, and our culture reaches deep into the heartland of America.

The little old lady from Peoria worried about six Mexican "illegals" in her garden may have scanned the 1985 Census Bureau statistics that noted a Hispanic growth rate five times that of the general population. At mid-decade, seventeen million Americans identified themselves as Hispanics, 7 percent of the population. In a society with a noticeably aging population, they are younger. In a culture that has institutionalized the nuclear family, they appear more committed to its centrality in their lives. In a nation where the credo of equality of opportunity has produced, it is believed, a more just social order, they have demonstrated a willingness to sacrifice for the common good.

Of these seventeen million, ten million identify themselves as Mexican Americans or chicanos or Mexicans. Their personal ambition, their commitment to a better life, and their belief in America are no less enthusiastic than the ambition, commitment, and belief of other Hispanics or, for that matter, other peoples of ethnic America. Yet to Anglo-Americans, to Black Americans, to European-ethnic Americans, to Jewish Americans, and, increasingly, to Cuban Americans and Puerto Ricans, it is the Mexican core of Hispanic America that persistently resists acculturation. And, paradoxically, the Mexican, Americans believe, has benefited far more than other Hispanic Americans, just as Hispanic Americans, descendants of the immigrants of seventy-five years ago sometimes bitterly observe, have far greater opportunities than their forebears.

Most Americans concede that Mexico's historical relationship with the United States—the loss of half its territory in the Mexican war—and the documented accounts of mistreatment of Mexicans and Mexican Americans in this country obligate the American government (and the several states with a large Mexican American population) to correct past injustices. But most Americans believe that with social programs, voting safeguards, and educational commitments to Mexican Americans and longstanding economic opportunities for Mexican labor in this country, these obligations have been satisfied. Further, they contend, the Mexican American deserves no special consideration beyond that extended to any other minority. If any minority rates "special consideration," it is widely believed, it is Black Americans, whose ancestors came to America unwillingly, labored here unwillingly, and suffered every personal and civic injustice.

Most Hispanic Americans and even most Mexican Americans, I believe, would not dispute the cumulative grievances blacks still retain from America's racial past. And, save for the more militant chicanos, they do not expect restoration of territory that fell under

266

Anglo domination after the Mexican-American War. But they do have a claim to a just share of America's cultural identity. Thus far, they have not received it. Anglo-Americans, looking at the collective pressures of ethnic minorities, can identify more clearly and plan more coherently a political agenda for Black Americans. It has a more precisely measurable content. For Hispanic Americans, and for Mexican Americans particularly, the requirements for a similar response may be quantitatively less but qualitatively infuriatingly more complex. At bottom, I would argue, most Americans sense the gravity of Hispanic American malaise but have no ready *political* means to rectify it. They can assure that, along with other minorities, Hispanic Americans receive equal access to the ballot or that Hispanic business gets its fair share of government support or that the Hispanic impoverished have the supportive cushion of social programs.

What is feared is that these will not be enough. There is an apprehension in American political culture that Hispanics cannot be assuaged. Their collective grievance, it is believed, has no economic or political remedy. And, if they are woven into America's political fabric, it is feared they will follow no predictable or rational pattern—no clear indication of self-interest, no realistic "Hispanic agenda" that America can accommodate. More bluntly, there exists an oft-felt but rarely expressed fear that with political power Hispanic Americans will exact their revenge and will accomplish what black power was never able to do: change the character of American politics and with it the character of American culture. In this scenario, the response to the query What do they want? is: Hispanics want the Hispanicization of America.

In summer 1985, in an extensive assessment of the new immigration and the "Changing Face of America," *Time* magazine, after duly noting the rise of America's Hispanic population as "one of the most startling phenomena in American social history," reaffirmed its belief that the Spanish-speaking would be Americanized. "In all probability," *Time*'s essayists concluded after reviewing the Hispanic onslaught, "the Americanization of His-

267

panics will be far more rapid and thorough than any Hispanicization of Anglo culture.''[1] Already, their diversity and rivalries and
their insularity and common language had ceased being curiosities
to Americans. Americans alternately admired their religious and
familial commitment and their willingness to work and resented
their transformation of neighborhoods like Boyle Heights in East
Los Angeles, once Jewish, or Pilsen in Chicago, once eastern
European ethnic, or even entire cities, such as Miami, into something . . . un-American. Already, Hispanics eager to pursue the
American dream had discovered that acculturation could proceed
at a slower pace than economic advancement.

Looking at this resistance to relinquish culture, Anglos confidently predicted that the economic realities of advancing in
America would prompt the children of the Hispanic newcomer to
reject the old ways and adopt the new. The accompanying
intrusion of Spanish, from the street chatter of Little Havana to a
Spanish-language station in the Yakima Valley in the northwest
(exploited by a governor of Michoacán to talk to some of his
constituents working in the apple orchards), was often annoying
but not considered a lasting threat to English. Since then, the
battle has been joined, and from Miami to Chicago to Los
Angeles, it is the militant defenders of English who have been
waging the last defense of Anglo-America's native tongue. In the
prolonged debate over immigration reform, which appeared
dormant in that summer of national self-assessment, ominous
warnings about "uncontrolled borders" and the "third world
beating a path to our doorstep" fashioned an unlikely coalition
and produced, in fall 1986, a major revision of America's
immigration law.

What explains this resurgence of American "cultural protec-
tionism" and the accompanying backlash, directed largely
against the Spanish-speaking, from black and old-immigrant
resentments over illegals and legals who push them out of
neighborhoods and take their jobs to socially conscious Anglos
who champion immigration restrictions and the cause of English
in an English-speaking country?

It is Mexico in America. It is the unspoken fear of what is happening in Mexico and what it will mean for America. It is the unspoken fear of the obverse side of Mexican dependence on the United States: America's unacknowledged dependence on Mexico. It is the unspoken fear that our security may ultimately depend on what happens in Mexico, that Mexico is the "last domino." It is the fear that the symbiotic relationship between Mexico and the United States cannot last and must be changed but neither government can afford to do what is necessary for its alteration. It is the fear that governments may change the written rules of the relationship, but MexAmerica determines how they will be carried out.

Shortly before the 1986 Mexican gubernatorial elections, international financial analysts worried that a PAN victory by a large enough vote to deny even Mexico's political elite an opportunity to overturn it might have severe international *economic* repercussions. Given the political impact on both national and international economies, their reasoning was not illogical. If PAN scored a big triumph, de la Madrid, lauded among international bankers for his austerity program, would have to take the dominant party and the country back to its xenophobic ways. Already the international money managers were despondent over the resistance of Japan and western European economies to American pressure. But if Mexico, "the weak link" in the international economic chain, revived its historical antiforeign antipathies, then the analysis assumed more frightening projections. If Mexico turned inward, protectionist sentiment everywhere in the chain would be invigorated, and the doors to American exports and investments closed.

As things turned out, de la Madrid, despite his politically reformist ways, decided that the *credibilidad* of his Mexico's ruling party was infinitely more important than Mexico's embarrassed image as a politically corrupt nation. It was yet another indication of Mexico's persistence, even when *la crisis* dominates most discussion, in going its own way. It reaffirmed Mexicans'

269

inner conviction that the nation may be deficient in political integrity, and suffer American condemnation for it, but that Americans will tolerate political immorality in their neighbors if it will give them economic peace of mind.

A month before the Chihuahua elections, Senator Jesse Helms was still condemning Mexico's inadequacies. He repeated a charge made earlier, in the session on Mexican fraud/"irregularities": "We need to know these things because one way or another, the U.S. taxpayers will shortly be asked to prop up the Mexican economy. If the truth were known, I doubt that Mexico could meet its obligations even before the oil price fell. Mexico is in a spiral down." In 1982, he noted, "U.S. taxpayers were called in to bail out the Mexican economy . . . in a weekend deal . . . when everyone in Washington was out of town." Still irritated by criticism that he had been too harsh on Mexico, he added, "The truth, it turns out, was painful . . . for both sides. . . . Because Mexico is our next-door neighbor, we have always felt we have a special relationship. Unfortunately the word 'special' does not mean the relationship is always good. What it means is that our long, mutual border binds us together for better or for worse. What affects one of us is bound to affect the other."

Mexico could have dispatched witnesses to talk about its accomplishments, he went on, but declined. Even some American officials were reluctant to testify, preferring, said Helms, to render judgments to the media that his hearings on the "truth about Mexico" were "counterproductive." During the hearings on Mexican economic development, the absentee Mexicans got yet another unintended reaffirmation of American dependence. Senator Charles Mathias, chairman of the foreign relations subcommittee that deals with international economic policy, reminded Helms, who chaired the subcommittee on western hemispheric affairs, about American priorities. "In these hard times, I think we really have to remember that in the years since the Mexican Revolution, the Mexicans have been able to keep peace in their own society, they have been able to insure a respect for civil liberty for their own people, _and it is very important that we not shake the system."_ Mathias continued with reminders that Mexico is "only one contributer" to the problems of illegals and drugs, and its complicity in both is explained largely by its economic problems. The United States has a "strategic stake in the well-being of a valued neighbor. Mexico is a significant player in a region that is vital to the United States, and no conceivable United States interest is served by the perpetuation of Mexico's difficulties. . . . _The way to promote our national welfare and interest regarding Mexico is by direct negotiation based on respect for one another."_[2]

The word had already gone out from the State Department. A thousand miles away, in the city of the Aztecs, John Gavin's replacement as ambassador had quietly told his staff at the American embassy to emphasize the "positive" rather than the "negative" about Mexico in these troublesome days. The Harvard man in Los Pinos, Mexico's presidential residence, was pleased. He had, after all, toned down some of the more strident official criticisms that had once emanated from the Mexican government about American pressure on the Sandinistas in Nicaragua. Now he listened as a new American ambassador uttered a few unexpected compliments about a Mexican government often berated north of the Rio Grande, and a distinguished American senator had reminded a colleague who had joined the condemnatory chorus that Mexico was much more important than Nicaragua to America's security.

Senator Mathias is correct in his appeal for mutual respect as a necessary ingredient in the relationship between Mexico and the United States. Governments may create mechanisms to advance this cause, but it requires inspiration as well as rhetoric. American foreign policy has deep roots in the nation's politics and culture, and a "special relationship" with Mexico requires more fundamental changes. What is essential to this task is a redefinition of why Mexico and the United States must have a "special relationship."

It must begin with a reassessment of the value we accord

271

Mexico and Mexicans in this country. Americans do not have respect for Mexico and what it stands for as a culture because they have never respected Mexicans who came to this country, save for their labor. Over a century and a half, the evolution of this cultural denigration has wrought among Mexican Americans a tragic self-denigration, which can erupt in chicano militancy and a denial of the American in the Mexican American or emerge as shameful guilt over the Mexican in the Mexican American. A nation that can proudly recognize its ethnic and racial character can reaffirm the Mexican content of its identity as something to be admired for more than compelling economic reasons.

Our knowledge of Mexico's economic and strategic importance reassures American officials of the centrality of Mexico's place in our global calculations. But the American public is largely ignorant about Mexico, its people, its culture, its history. We are ignorant about Mexico because we are ignorant about the Mexican, in his country and in ours. We value Mexico for where it is and not what it is. We value the Mexican for what he can do and not for his Mexicanness. We do not value the Mexican in ourselves. A "special relationship" of "mutual respect" will require much more than economic measures, more than strategic considerations. It will require, as the Mexican in Puerto Vallarta said, "respect for who I am."

There is, undeniably, a continuing American frustration in dealing with Mexico and Mexicans. Marxist governments in Central America pose a more direct threat to Mexico's vulnerable southeastern oil fields and to its political stability than our own, yet Mexico persists in charting a more independent foreign policy. Mexico is *less* dependent on the American economy than Canada, yet, paradoxically, the Mexican left talks incessantly about its *dependencia*. Mexico, it can be argued, could play an important role as a newly developed industrial country and, in global politics, as a critical adjunct to the transatlantic alliance, yet Mexico defies the United States by projecting itself as a third-world leader, the champion of neutrality in the continuing cold war.

A distinguished political scientist, Peter Smith, quite rightly attributes Mexican disaffection to the uniqueness of the Mexican–U.S. relationship. The United States has more people, a bigger gross national product, a more dynamic economy, and the reassurance of its political tradition. The United States has a longer border with Canada than with Mexico, the American economy reaches much deeper into Canada than into Mexico, but the Canadian-American relationship is not rife with conflict over so many things—immigration, trade, narcotics trafficking, border pollution, the loss of American jobs to "cheap illegal labor" and the flight of those jobs into Mexico. There are disputes—some of them quite old—in the Canadian-American economic connection, but they do not seem to exacerbate Canadian-American relations nearly so severely. When I made a point of responding to the Mexicans' noticeable irritation with their country's "dependence" by pointing out Canada's vulnerability, they replied, "Yes, but the two cultures are so similar. You speak the same language and have the same political values. We Mexicans are different." As the Mexican philosopher Octavio Paz said, "North Americans consider the world something that can be perfected, while we consider it to be something that can be redeemed."[3]

Canadians, of course, often express deep resentments about the heavy-handed reach of the United States northward, especially in the economic sphere, but Canadian dependence has not lessened that nation's lofty status in American assessments of its worthiness as a nation or a culture. With Canada and Canadians, the United States government and the American people have a mutually reinforcing respect that can overcome sometimes troublesome disputes. We do not have that consistency with Mexico, nor do we seem to want it. Ironically, Mexico is an older culture with a deeper appreciation of its own past, a more acute sense of its own nationality, and a resentment of foreign intrusion into its politics that every American in the age of George Washington and Thomas Jefferson would have applauded. But we respect Canada, we do not respect Mexico.

Mexico, again, occupies a more critical place in America's

global economic and strategic calculations. Yet the measure of Mexico's worth depends almost exclusively on the *implications* of Mexican economic or political troubles for America's international interests. We must have a reassurance that Mexican oil will be available because of uncertainties about Middle Eastern oil. We must deal with the Mexican debt problem as a "strategic" issue. We must guard against "another Iran" or "another Poland" on our doorstep. We must encourage the right in Mexico because a triumph of the left would be unacceptable. Just as Americans of Woodrow Wilson's generation debated the larger impact of the Mexican Revolution, so, too, Americans of Reagan's America fret over Mexican instability. Understandably, Americans see in Mexican weakness a threat to their own stability.

Some argue for a hard-line policy that would, to cite an often-used phrase, "force Mexico to bite the bullet." Mexico has in Miguel de la Madrid the Mexican equivalent of an economic hard-liner. In his *sexenio,* de la Madrid has followed a generally consistent economic policy that largely reflects American prescriptions. Mexican acquiescence in American foreign policy, especially in Central America, would exact a psychological price that Mexico and Mexicans would long resent. A brief accommodation with America's hemispheric strategy would be a humiliating price that they would long remember. Mexico is not going to shape its foreign policy according to American directives— whatever the economic costs to the nation's well-being. Canada is no less critical of American policy in Central America, for example, but Mexico, not Canada, suffers the brunt of American condemnation.

Others would like to continue dealing with Mexico the way we always have, as a sideline matter that occasionally is shoved to center stage but not kept there. The danger here is to relegate Mexico to a lesser status on the list of international priorities until an issue—immigration, narcotics trafficking, Central America, and so on—looms so large that Mexico cannot be ignored. Even here, we approach Mexico as more of a problem than a solution.

Americans know a great deal about Mexican official complicity in the drug trade; they appreciate too little the number of Mexican officers who have perished in fighting the narcotics trade. Americans know that Mexico is heavily indebted; they know too little about Mexico's responsible behavior as a debtor nation, particularly when compared with that of other countries.

The reformers, mostly academics but not a few political leaders, primarily from the southwest, want a new "special relationship" with Mexico. The old "special relationship" simply reinforced the old notions of Mexican inferiority, Mexican weakness, and Mexican accommodation to American interests. That, clearly, even in this era of Mexican vulnerability, cannot provide a realistic foundation for the official ties between the countries in the next century or even in the immediate future. We must accept Mexican nationalism and Mexican sovereignty in form and in spirit. Nothing less will do.

And with them we have to accept a painful reality about Mexico, Mexicans, and even the Mexican in America. Mexico is defiant. Mexicans are defiant. It is the defiance of the Mexican that befuddles our assessments of Mexico, Mexicans, and Mexican Americans, about what is the "obvious" interest of Mexico in global politics and the global economy and the "obvious" role Mexico must play in both. In their defiance, Mexico and Mexicans can frustrate our political and economic calculations about their place in our scheme of things. In time of political and economic assertiveness or debilitating weakness, Mexico and Mexicans are defiant. What we perceive as political or economic logic, Mexico and Mexicans will reject. They raise the flag of defiance against the intruder, whether he comes to do ill or good. Their defiance is something more than nationalism, more than xenophobia, more than the humiliation of their experience with the outside world.

No, theirs is a defiance honed by centuries of immersion in a system they cannot change but will not permit the outsider to alter. Theirs is the defiance of centuries of bitterness about unchanged and unchangeable realities. Theirs is the defiance of a people who have been betrayed by their political and social leaders, yet who stubbornly defend the nation, have no doubts about their nationalism, and are determined to persevere.

They have brought this defiance into MexAmerica. They have made the migration across the border for a century and a half. Fences and rivers have not deterred them. As far north as Chicago, they have left their mark. They will accommodate the needs of a vigorous economy—in the southwest, illegal immigrants, principally Mexicans, have created a massive labor force without which an entire regional economy would collapse. From construction sites and refineries in Houston to the computer assembly plants in Silicon Valley to the small factories of Chicago, they labor. But they will not readily accommodate America's social and political culture. Theirs is the Hispanic's tradition of *retraimiento,* which literally means ''retreat'' but to the Mexican carries with it the determination to withstand, to defy the culture that attempts to absorb you.

And, throughout MexAmerica, from Pilsen to L.A. East to the City of the Aztecs, they have raised the challenge. They wave the banner of defiance—against friend or foe and all who will not accept them for what they are and not what we say they must be.

In the aftermath of *Time's* reassuring 1985 assessment of the nation's capacity to Americanize the immigrant, analyses about the future of MexAmerica have become more somber. Everywhere there are unsettling warnings and fears about Mexico's penetration and the Mexican route into the United States. The Japanese, several congressmen have decided, are unfairly exploiting the special provisions of the tariff law and channeling their goods through the *maquiladoras.* Along the border, there is a renewed intensity in the efforts to halt narcotics. Trucks wait for days to pass through American customs. But on the ''other side'' the *mexicanos* are speeding up their processing of trucks headed for El Norte, and the border towns are wearying from the loss of business. America is making a moral decision: it is augmenting the drug interceptor force but cutting back on the number of customs officials, so the fruits and vegetables headed for American dinner tables are spoiling and the parts assembled in Mexico are not getting to factories on the American side. Meanwhile, the INS, anticipating a mad rush of illegals into the United States before the restrictions of the new immigration law begin closing the door, is pleasantly surprised. The number of crossings decreases.

These are the immediate indicators of the subtly changing character of MexAmerica. More ominous are the statistics that lack immediacy but portend something more unsettling. One such statistic is the increasing numbers of middle-class skilled Mexicans headed northward, a momentary benefit for us but a calamity for Mexico and, ultimately, for us, for it can only mean a less democratic neighbor. And, even more ominous, there are the calculations of American and Mexican demographers that the number of Mexicans seeking jobs between 1980 and 2000 will be 20 million and the number of Americans 28 million. In the final five years of the century, the numbers of job-seekers in each country will be approximately equal, 5.3 and 5.8 million respectively. But average wage, standard of living, gross national product, and the countless other economic indicators will remain an unbridgeable chasm between the two economies. Mexico is a culture of youth; America is a culture of middle age. MexAmerica belongs to both.

Only the cultural ties of MexAmerica can create a lasting friendship and with it the respect and security that distant neighbors desperately are seeking. With this bond must come the due recognition of the Mexico in America and the place of MexAmerica in both.

Epilogue

≡

It is May 1987, a year after the beginning of my trek through MexAmerica in my search for my pal from the cotton fields of the Texas Panhandle in the summer of 1950. I found him everywhere in MexAmerica. And in my sojourn I found Mexico in America. As I discovered, the Mexicans' is an imprint of imprecise measure and uncertain legacy, but it cannot be expunged from our collective memory. It is a scar and an emblem on American culture; because it cannot be erased it can no longer be denied. There is no issue about the Hispanic content of America that does not have a Mexican connection—not labor, not immigration, not narcotics trafficking, not bilingualism. When American labor leaders bemoan the loss of jobs, they blame the Mexicans. When U.S. Official English condemns the decline of the mother tongue, its most enthusiastic proponents identify the Mexicans as principal culprits. When the attorney general of the United States expresses concern about losing control of our borders, he invariably refers to the Mexican border. When the secretary of the Treasury worries about Third World debt, Mexican indebtedness figures prominently in his calculations. In the litany of America's international economic troubles and in the prognostications of its cultural future, Mexico intrudes.

In a hospitable dining room on the campus of Oglethorpe University in Atlanta, where the mark of Mexico and Mexicans is negligible, I tried to convey to a gathering of attentive and polite academics my concerns about the issues raised in this book—about immigration, bilingualism, Mexican laborers, border culture—in short, the Hispanic character of America's future and the Mexican core of that experience. After my talk, they addressed polite questions about all these things, but the most pertinent was: "Well, considering all we have done for Mexico, what is left on the agenda?" It was a polite way of asking what Lyndon Johnson often demanded of critics of his Vietnam policy, "Well, what would *you* do?"

There was an undeniable persuasiveness to this query. America has reshaped its immigration laws, to Mexico's advantage; it has employed Mexican laborers, to Mexico's advantage. It has recognized through bilingual programs the place of the Spanish language, to the putative advantage of the 12 million Hispanic Americans of Mexican ancestry. It purchases 60 percent of Mexican exports. It has created, through the *maquiladoras* in northern Mexico, employment in Mexico for Mexicans. All this and more, it is said, the United States has done for Mexico, yet Mexico is neither compliant nor, as a former U.S. representative to the United Nations told me, "very helpful" to us in trying to resolve the common problems of two neighbors or very supportive of American policy in the hemisphere.

A domineering policy—even when the United States holds Mexico in its economic grasp—brings not acquiescence but often defiance; a conciliatory policy—even when both countries have a common interest in the resolution of an issue—often does not mitigate Mexican hostility and resentment. American officials who must negotiate the myriad issues between two neighbors must persevere; Americans troubled about the relations between distant neighbors are befuddled. The former must address problems between two governments that all too often have been transmuted into domestic concerns. Whether the issue is language or labor or border pollution, Mexico intrudes. These and related issues identified with the Mexican presence must be addressed. But we do not have to denigrate Mexico and Mexican culture in the process.

ⁿto Mexico, but in unappreciated ways
...ca. We measure the reach of Mexico
...ot value it, and unless we are willing to
... been unthinkable—to alter radically our
...kind of society we want to be—the Mexican
...remain affixed. Mexico will remain in our future.
...o is a part of America's future because Mexico and
...icans are a part of our past. The peoples of MexAmerica
have fashioned bonds that cannot be broken; the economies of
MexAmerica have forged ties that can be severed only at great
cost. We have retained much of that myth of glorious conquest
"from sea to shining sea" and the spread of the "blessings of
republican liberty." But we have discarded an inconvenient
reality from our historical memory. One-fourth of the United
States was carved out of one-half of Mexico. True, the Mexican
north was sparsely populated, the Californios were defiant of
central authority, and more Anglos than Mexicans populated
Texas, but the bitterness of the loss has not been erased from
Mexican memory, and a century of migration, legal and illegal,
has sustained what nationalistic Mexicans call the _Reconquista_.
There are familial ties no law can readily undo, migratory habits
of border residents not willingly altered. The vigorous economies
of the modern Southwest retain their Mexican connection. San
Diegans blame everything from car thefts to freeway congestion
on the human spillover from Tijuana, but when the city dispatched a trade delegation to Japan its members spoke of the two
cities as a single metropolitan trade area.

We cannot invoke the credo of economic compatibility of two
countries and simultaneously deny the human legacy the economic bonds have bequeathed. Two governments may conduct
their affairs in friendly or hostile discourse, assert their official
position on a variety of crucial or trivial issues, and spend
countless hours trying to negotiate what to each—because of
pride, nationalism, or sovereignty—is declared non-negotiable.
In the international arena, two governments may pursue different
courses, with different priorities, and even ascribe a different

meaning to the same word. But none of these things will [?] that symbiotic union that Mexico and the United States h[?] fashioned. Deep in Mexico, in the city of the Aztecs, the cultu[?] elites decry the Americanization of the *mexicano,* while the political czars look anxiously to the north to gauge the nation's economic future and *their* critics denounce Mexican dependence.

That is something that can be statistically catalogued. Mexico lost half the nation to the United States, but Mexicans did not lose their pride, their defiance, and their identity. They have brought these traits with them into America, and they express them in countless ways and in countless battles. They will accommodate America's economic agenda and its political traditions, give their sons to fight in America's wars, and proclaim their Americanism. But unlike other Hispanics who are no less committed to the nation, theirs is a special claim. The past cannot be undone but it can be rectified. America can anticipate the Hispanic imprint on its future by a neat categorization of data, but understanding what it will mean requires more than a casual look backward.

It demands recognition of the rightful place of Mexico in America. But, again, the compelling query: What do we do?

We have to begin, I believe, not so much with a radical alteration of the Mexican-American relationship as with a re-thinking and, more important, a re-evaluation of that relationship. We can begin with the Mexican-American war and its place in our mythology. There is, even among the historians, a persuasive argument that Mexican arrogance and intractability over negotiable issues brought on the conflict that culminated in the loss of half of Mexico's territory to the United States in the middle of the nineteenth century. There is, undeniably, a legitimacy to the American claim that northern Mexico was sparsely populated and that not only Anglo immigrants but a significant number of *mexicanos* welcomed incorporation into America and, as Americans of that generation said, the "spread of the blessings of republican liberty."

None of this is objectionable—not even from a scholarly viewpoint. But what approaches the disgusting in our telling of the Mexican-American war and its aftermath is that gloating of the conquest and subjugation of a "heathen race" and the ingrained sense of cultural superiority that victory brought. In this sense, the Mexican war was one of those "good wars" in the American military experience—the triumph of a proud, rambunctious republic and its armies of solid yeoman stock over a mongrel country with pretentions of dominance in North America. Had America lost, presumably, North America would have been doomed to backwardness. Economic backwardness, undeniably, but not cultural retardation. Our victory was a victory over a putatively more professional military, and we should be proud of it. Our reasons for fighting the war were debatable but, ultimately, I believe, justifiable, and even those who deny their credibility do not suggest that the Mexican territorial cession (which _was_ paid for) be returned. What is objectionable is our retained conviction that the victory was the triumph of a superior culture. A superior economy, a superior political system, a superior army—but not a superior culture.

Not only does Mexico remind us of our past, but the Mexican immigrant reminds us that the historically lauded acculturation process is not working. More than any immigrant group, it can be argued, Mexicans have benefited from our economy and our immigration laws, yet, among Hispanics, Mexicans resist acculturation and naturalization. More than any immigrant group, they will benefit from the new immigration law, yet their reluctance to come forward (in part, doubtless, out of fear) is befuddling. The proximity of a _cultural_ homeland lying next door may offer partial explanation, but, I believe, their hesitance in accommodating a government that offers what is a virtually unparalleled opportunity for citizenship may convey something more.

What they are saying, I would argue, is that American citizenship may offer the right to vote but not much more. America can offer a dynamic economy that employs them and laws that safequard their rights, but America cannot provide, even with "legalization" and eventual citizenship, that reassurance of cultural identity. Hispanics, generally, and Mexicans, especially, remind us of the shallowness of American culture, but the America that offers so much to them cannot provide in "Americanization" of the immigrant an identity that goes beyond what one *does*. An American is a citizen of the United States. Without an ethnic or religious measure or, in the case of southerners, a sense of place, the American lacks a reassurance of cultural identity. We confront in the Hispanic—and especially in the Mexican—a people who do not define themselves with such self-denigrating slogans as "You Are What You Do" or consume or, as a truck advertisement declares, "You Are What You Drive." No other society in the history of the world has searched so long for a meaningful cultural identity and failed in its quest. The lowliest Mexican fencejumper has a stronger sense of cultural identity than the American who employs him. He may not be able to read or write and have *nada de nada,* but he *knows who he is.* And he is not going to exchange his unarticulated but deeply felt sense of cultural identity for something that neither America nor Americans have been able to define.

Throughout the long and occasionally vitriolic debate over immigration reform, identifiable themes and fears surfaced. Labor organizers spoke of the loss of American jobs to "illegals" in this country and to Mexican workers in the *maquiladoras* along the border; California agribusinessmen expressed apparently convincing apprehension about getting enough Mexicans to pick their crops; public officials told about the escalating costs attributable to illegal immigration in social services, communicable diseases, and crime. More portentous was the impact of "floods of illegals" from the Third World who would alter America as dramatically as America would change them. The nation's motto, *E pluribus unum,* Out of Many, One, would read, *E pluribus plura,* Out of Many, Many. In the past, it can be argued, such diversity expressed in the second may have been the reality. A generation ago, scholars were already debunking the myth of the melting pot. But they did not deny the unifying power of those political and economic credos which the nation professed. That dream has not dissolved in a nightmare, but even those Americans with a persevering social conscience have begun to express their doubts about what kind of nation we are becoming.

Diversity, it is further argued, is leading to fragmentation. A heterogeneous population constitutes no threat to national identity as long as its participants keep their differences in language and social values out of the workplace, the schools, and government at every level. What they do in their own homes, to rephrase an American cliché, is their own business. In the past, the country was able to acculturate if not assimilate its minorities by providing economic opportunity in a dynamic capitalist system and browbeating their children in the schools about the glories of America's Anglo-Saxon heritage. They traded their votes for economic peace of mind, and when they finally got political power through sheer weight of numbers in America's large cities they wanted what their predecessors wanted—more. A political aspirant could easily count the number of votes from a given racial or ethnic bloc; once elected, he soon learned that the American voter, whatever his cultural badge of identity, pays more attention to what you do than what you promised to do. The gloom-and-doom futurists are saying that such historically unifying truths and practices of American public life are gradually dissolving in the Latinization of America. Those who ruminate on the American condition talk solemnly about a silent invasion whose numbers have transformed Los Angeles, Miami, New York, and even Washington, D.C. (once mockingly described as a "Southern city inhabited by midwesterners trying to act like easterners"), into third-world cities. "International" is a description these places covet; "third-world" is not.

As often happens in debates about "where the country is heading," assessments and evidence about the Hispanic imprint are simultaneously reassuring and unsettling. The evidence is often contradictory, so the interpretation of it can often follow a bewildering path to a conclusion that strives, in the American tradition of compromise and concession, to please everybody. We cling to our beliefs that a dynamic American economy offering equality of opportunity will ultimately break down the ethnic walls that keep Hispanics out of "mainstream America." But an Hispanic writer, Alberto Moncada, demonstrates in a series of case studies of Hispanics how the cultural shock of being judged on the basis of income, work, and consumption can be so frustrating that it produces a dual personality. As one expressed it, "My American side allows me to participate in a life of labor and competition. My Latin side lets me enjoy leisure and fantasy." The Hispanics in this study obviously appreciated the economic opportunity America offered them, but the wrenching experience of accommodating to a dynamic, competitive society led them to find cultural reassurance in their Hispanic identity.

Some kind of cultural dialectic is at work here. The anticipated cultural synthesis it ultimately begets is as yet unknown. For the moment Americans retain their conviction that legislation and public policy will make a difference and that America can determine its future and decide "what kind of nation we want to be." Congress passes a new immigration law to check the "alien tide," establishing a policy that is, compared with that of European nations, comparatively generous. The Census Bureau declares that 6 million people are in the United States illegally, but that 3.9 million of them will be eligible for amnesty. American agribusiness receives assurances that the new law will not diminish their supply of Mexican labor. The i's are dotted and the t's crossed so that no American family will be deprived of its lettuce or apples, no able-bodied American will lose a job to an illegal, and no future American attorney general will ever have to admit national debility by saying "We cannot control our borders."

From the outset there have been criticism and problems. Mayors of large cities where the illegals have clustered speak of the abandonment of hope by those who arrived after January 1, 1982, the cut-off date for getting amnesty under the new law, and the prospect of an undercount in the 1990 census, which could affect congressional representation and federal funding. The INS, charged with administering the program, shifted so many agents to the legalization centers that it left its other offices seriously undermanned. Illegals working in California's garment industry returned to Mexico. When their employers tried and failed to replace them with American workers—even after raising the hourly wage—they began making arrangements to bring in foreign laborers under the old H-2 law. Mexican rural workers, who received special consideration because southwestern agribusiness is dependent on them, are reluctant to return for fear of deportation. Almost 4 million may be eligible for what even critics admit is a "good deal," but after four months of the sign-up period of one year, exactly 612,402 had appeared, documents in hand, to claim it.

Predictably, there have been credible explanations. Social and church groups point to the alien's justifiable fear that the INS, which in the past tried to deport him, will use the law to lure him out of hiding. Aliens employed before November 6, 1986, when there was no penalty, are nonetheless reluctant to come forward lest they endanger their jobs by causing problems for their employers. The INS points to the enormity of the assignment and praises itself for a program that is "going smoothly." Others, in more ominous tones, say that the attempt to "control our borders" came too late, that America's economic links to the third world, America's military penetration of the third world, and finally America's dependence on third-world labor will ultimately frustrate efforts to transform policy into reality. A Mexican migrant from a central Mexican village who has been going back and forth across the border since the age of nine put the issue succinctly: "The law is never going to be carried out because the Americans themselves are going to break it. Only the law has changed, not the reality of the situation."

And the reality is two countries with one future, something neither government wants but neither can avoid. There is an unwanted but unavoidable Mexican connection in America's future, which ultimately impinges on such vital issues as national security or even national identity. Washington complains of

Mexican uncooperativeness on international issues, the narcotics war, immigration, border pollution, and other issues; Mexico City resists the inroads made into its sovereignty by America's political and economic reach. The cultural elites of each— Mexican as well as American—speak grimly of a Third World in their midst, encroaching upon them in the cities, a plague of human misery and desperation that neither economy can absorb, neither social service bureaucracy can accommodate, and neither can get rid of. Mexico survives by keeping the escape valve open to the north, where they will be valued for what they can do; the United States incorporates them into its economy and, when their labor is no longer needed, it sends them home.

Each government wrestles with a disposal problem. The United States wants to get control of its borders and establish some order and above all legality to its immigration; Mexico wishes to avoid worsening its unemployment situation. It is ambivalent about this question for the simple reason that to really make the immigration law work Mexico would have to agree to curtail migration from central Mexico to the rapidly expanding north Mexican cities. The United States could reassert its sovereignty only at Mexico's expense.

Unarguably, the United States has a right to control its borders, determine who shall work here, decide who will become American citizens, and even declare English as the official language. These and related issues profoundly affect Mexico and Mexicans, but Mexico does not deny our right to enact these into the law of the land. Unarguably, the American government has good reason to be irritated with Mexican delays in negotiating conflicting diplomatic issues. Mexico's political system and economy, Americans believe, have set new standards for inefficiency and corruption. A colleague who recently took the national railroad from Ojinaga across Chihuahua to the Pacific was overwhelmed by the landscape but disgruntled about service from the Mexicans. Their attitude was, he explained, "We put up with these things, why shouldn't you?" They were apologetic, my friend surmised, but will probably do little to correct their "deficiencies."

Yes, Mexico is deficient: it has a deficient economy, deficient governments at every level, and deficient service on the Chihuahua railroad. But it does not have a deficient culture. And before the American government and Americans can hope to do very much to resolve diplomatic problems or confront the reach of Mexico and Mexicans in America, we have to acknowledge— and respect—that culture and its perseverance. Mexicans retain a cultural identity that we are not going to wear down very much. We can work these people, but we can't drive the "Mexican" out of them, nor do we offer much of anything beyond employment and citizenship that will substitute. To our way of thinking, these should be enough. They were good enough for the earlier immigrants to our shores, but they will not suffice, I argue, for Hispanics, and they will certainly not do for Mexicans.

Spanish can be a cultural bond for Hispanics but English does not provide a parallel cultural utility for Americans. U.S. Official English may get English-only at the ballot box, English-only in the schools, and English-only down at city hall, but it will not fashion a deeply felt sense of national cultural identity. Whatever pedagogical justification for English-only in the schools, the campaign against the Spanish language in this country may be victorious in civic America but will not "Americanize" the Spanish-speaking in the manner we want. We cannot create an homogeneous culture making war on the Spanish language nor by denigrating those who speak it, as we have with the Puerto Ricans, who have been so pummeled with "Americanization" that they are apologetic when they speak _English_ with an accent. The champions of U.S. Official English, understandably, point to secessionist French-speaking Quebec as a portent of what can happen if Spanish is accorded a similar status in this country. Perhaps; but what is often forgotten in the Quebec analogy is that French culture has acquired its due recognition in Canada, and the French-speaking have begun to receive job opportunities beyond the low-skilled employment where they dominated in the past. French separatism has declined in the process.

In other words, the Canadians, who are no less concerned

about forging a national identity than we are, have demonstrated that it is possible to overcome the divisive currents of language if a government is willing to recognize the place of French culture in its national identity. Hispanics have not demanded these things, but they cannot accept—nor will they ever accept—a denial of the place of their language if it means a denigration of their culture. And they cannot accept—nor will they ever accept—the substitution of their own cultural identity for one that is, for them, devoid of spirituality. They will defy cultural absorption, and the "Mexican" in them will reinforce that defiance. They will persist until that unarticulated goal is achieved, and the "Mexican" in them demands recognition for who they are, not what they can do, and for their capacity to enrich America—not just make it richer.

America cannot overcome that defiance until it recognizes the place of Mexico in America. Until we do, we should remind ourselves that someone from a 2,000-year-old culture can be patient, but also very persistent.

Notes

1: Dinner at Chihuahua Charlie's

1. Wall Street Journal, May 3, 1985; John House, Frontier on the Rio Grande: A Political Geography of Development and Social Deprivation (Oxford, 1982), 4–5, 34–37.

2. For a more detailed comment on the problems caused by the El Paso/Juárez connection, see Niles Hansen, The Border Economy: Regional Development in the Southeast (Austin, Tex., 1981), 44–47.

3. Mario García, Desert Immigrants: The Mexicans of El Paso (New Haven, 1981), 230–36.

4. House, Frontier on the Rio Grande, 252–53.

5. El Paso Times, May 18, 19, 1986.

2: The Maquila Man

1. Niles Hansen, The Border Economy: Regional Development in the Southwest (Austin, Tex., 1981), 89–99; Carlos Monsivais, "The Culture of the Frontier," in Stanley Ross, Views Across the Border: The United States and Mexico (Albuquerque, N.M., 1978), 60–61; Ovid Demaris, Poso del Mundo (New York, 1971), 8–9.

2. El Paso Foreign Trade Association, Paso del Norte Trade Area, May 16, 1986.

3. Tucson Citizen, May 15, 1986; San Diego Union, August 4, 1985.

4. University of Arizona, Policy Forum on Border Economy, 100–104; 144–46.

5. Linda Fernández-Kelley, For We Are Sold (Albany, N.Y., 1984), 47–51.

6. Guillermina Valdés-Villalva, "Multinational Corporations During the Mexican Crisis," in Lay Gibson and Alfonso

Corona, The U.S. and Mexico: Borderland Development and the National Economies (Boulder, Colo., 1985), 164–73.

7. Jesús Tamayo, "Northern Border of Mexico and the Crisis of 1982," in ibid., 87–91; Alfonso Corona, "Industrial Integration of the Northern Border Region," in ibid., 101–103; LBJ School of Public Affairs, U.S. Finance and Trade Links with Less-Developed Countries (Austin, Tex., 1984), 90–96.

8. El Paso Times, May 19, 1986; Philadelphia Enquirer, March 12, 1985.

9. "Internationalization of Industry: U.S.—Mexican Linkages," in Gibson and Corona, U.S. and Mexico, 110–35.

3: Chicago Latino

1. Local Community Fact Book—Chicago (Chicago, 1984), 86; Felix M. Padilla, Latino Ethnic Consciousness: The Case of Mexican Americans and Puerto Ricans in Chicago (Notre Dame, 1985), 20–27.

2. Padilla, Latino Ethnic Consciousness, 32–59.

3. Quoted in ibid., 73.

4. Samuel K. Gore and Louis H. Masotti, After Daley: Chicago Politics in Transition (Urbana, Ill., 1982), 118–43.

5. The quotation by Byrnes' assistant is in Paul Kleppner, Chicago Divided (DeKalb, Ill. 1985), 161. See also Samuel Ortega, in Charles Wollenberg, ed., Ethnic Conflict in California History (n.p., 1975), 180–82.

6. Nuestro, January–February, 1984, 19.

7. Chicago Tribune Magazine, March 16, 1986.

8. Ruth Horowitz, Honor and the American Dream: Culture and Identity in a Chicano Community (New Brunswick, N.J., 1983), 204–13.

9. Interview, Louise Kerr, May 6, 1986. Robert Slayton has more on Back of the Yards, another Chicago ethnic community the mexicanos invaded, in Back of the Yards (Chicago, 1986).

10. Chicago Tribune, February 19, 1986; March 9, 1986; May 4, 1986.

4: "I'm Just as White as You"

1. Des Moines (Iowa) Register, January 26, 1986.
2. Interview, Catherine Rocha, May 8, 1986.
3. Nuestro, November 1984, 18–20.
4. For a convoluted description of the "problem" see Leo Grebler et al., The Mexican American People: the Nation's Second Largest Minority (New York, 1970), 318–19.
5. Interview, Carlos Cortés, May 12, 1986.
6. Manuel Machado, Jr., Listen Chicano! An Informal History of the Mexican American (Chicago, 1978), 119.
7. Pastora San Juan Cafferty and William S. McCready, Hispanics in the United States: A New Social Agenda (New Brunswick, N.J., 1985), 243–45.
8. Ricardo Parra, Victor Rios, and Armando Gutiérrez, writing in Aztlán (Summer 1976), contend that the midwest chicanos are "oppressed" even though they are less threatened than their brothers in the southwest because they have accepted as superior the Anglo-Saxon values imposed on them. They should meet Catherine Rocha.

5: Rocky Mountain High

1. Denver Post, May 8, 1986.
2. Quoted in Jack E. Holmes, Politics in New Mexico (Albuquerque, N.M., 1967), 17.
3. Richard Lamm and Gary Imhoff, The Immigration Time Bomb: the Fragmenting of America (New York, 1985), 114–23.
4. Rocky Mountain News, February 25, 1985; Denver Post, March 3, October 10, 1985. On Reies López Tijerina and Corky Gonzales see Matt Meier and Feliciano Rivera, The Chicanos (New York, 1972), 272–79.

6: The Great Valley

1. Tracey Henderson, Imperial Valley (Calipatria, Cal., 1968).
2. Ernesto Galarza, Farmworkers and Agribusiness in

California. 1947–1960 (Notre Dame, 1977), 8–15, 147–55, 264–65, 373–75.

3. Christopher Rand, Los Angeles: The Ultimate City (New York, 1967), 104–109.

4. Matt Meier and Feliciano Rivera, The Chicanos (New York, 1972), 260–69.

5. Richard Mines and Philip Martin, "Immigrant Workers and the California Citrus Industry," Industrial Relations 23 (Winter 1984), 139–49; Juan L. Gonzalez, Jr., Mexican and Mexican American Farmworkers: The California Agricultural Industry (New York, 1985), passim.

6. Eddie Adams, "Hiding in America: The Secret Misery of Illegal Aliens," Parade, January 11, 1987, 4–6. On Chávez and California agribusiness see John G. Dunne, Delano (New York, 1971).

7: L.A. East

1. Los Angeles Times, July 1, 1984.

2. Ricardo Romo, East Los Angeles: History of a Barrio (Austin, Tex., 1983), 3–7.

3. Mauricio Mazón, The Zoot-Suit Riots (Austin, Tex., 1984), 1–11.

4. Octavio Paz, The Labyrinth of Solitude (New York, 1985), 13–15.

5. Isidro Ortíz, "Chicano Urban Politics and the Politics of Reform in the Seventies," Western Political Quarterly, 37:564–77; Peter Wiley and Robert Gottlieb, Empires in the Sun: The Rise of the New American West (New York, 1982), 106–107.

6. Rodolfo Acuña, A Community Under Siege (Los Angeles, 1984).

7. Quoted in Bruce Cain, The Reapportionment Puzzle (Berkeley, Cal., 1984), 166–67.

8. Quoted in ibid., 169–70.

9. Quoted in ibid., 92.

10. Los Angeles Times, October 19, 1986.

8: *"This Is Our Country"*

1. Leo Grebler et al., The Mexican American People: The Nation's Second Largest Minority (New York, 1970), 520–21.

2. David Reimers, Still the Golden Door: The Third World Comes to America (New York, 1985), passim.

3. Joel Garreau, The Nine Nations of North America (Boston, 1981), 236–39.

4. Richard Lamm and Gary Imhoff, The Immigration Time Bomb: The Fragmenting of America (New York, 1985), 44–47; Carlos Vázquez and Manuel García, Mexican-United States Relations: Conflict and Convergence (Los Angeles, 1984), 379–91; New York Times, July 1, 1986.

5. Thomas Muller and Thomas Espenshoe, The Fourth Wave: California's Newest Immigrants (Washington, 1985), 48–49, 54–59.

6. Los Angeles Times, October 18, 1986.

9: *SuperMex in San Antonio*

1. Quoted in the laudatory biography by Kember Diehl and Jan Jarhoe, Cisneros: Portrait of a New American (San Antonio, 1985), 7.

2. Ibid., 34–38.

3. Leonard Goodall, ed., Urban Politics in the Southwest (Tempe, Az., 1967), 131–32.

4. "Black and Hispanic Power in City Politics: A Forum," PS 19 (Summer 1986); David Johnson et al., The Politics of San Antonio (Lincoln, Neb., 1983).

5. This and the preceding quotation are from Diehl and Jarhoe, Cisneros, 12–13.

6. Christian Science Monitor, August 7, 1986.

7. Dan Balz, "The Emerging Hispanic Vote and the Republican Attraction," Washington Post, July 11, 1981, 43.

8. Paul Burka, "Primary Lesson," Texas Monthly, July 1986, 104–105.

9. Nation's Cities Weekly, July 14, 1986, 3.

10: The Aging Chicano from Houston

1. Interview, Félix Ramírez, May 21, 1986. On the chicano founders see Matt Meier and Feliciano Rivera, The Chicanos: A History of Mexican Americans (New York, 1972), 244–49.
2. John Shockley, Chicano Revolt in a Texas Town (Notre Dame, 1974), 214–217.
3. Houston Post, June 29, 1986; Nuestro, June–July 1984, 24–27.
4. Armando Gutiérrez and Herbert Hirsch, "The Militant Challenge to the American Ethos: Chicanos and Mexican Americans," Social Science Quarterly 53 (1973), 830–45; Tino Villaneuva, "Sobre el termino 'chicano,' " Cuadernos Hispanoamericanos 336 (1978), 387–410.

11: Pittsburgh, Mexico

1. Menno Vellinga, Economic Development and the Dynamics of Class: Industrialization, Power, and Control in Monterrey, Mexico (Assen, Netherlands, 1979), 58–59, 71, 94–95, 100–101, 104–105.
2. Oígame, September 26, 1970.
3. Rene Villareal, "Import-Substituting Industrialization," in Reynart and Weber, Authoritarianism in Mexico, 74–75. The author estimates that in 1970 Mexico had more than 25 percent unemployment if one measured the number of underemployed (almost six million) as, in effect, the equal of three million unemployed.
4. La democracia en Mexico (Mexico City, 1965). This work has gone through sixteen editions. Manuel Mejido, Mexico Amargo (Mexico City, 1973), 245–53.
5. Miguel Wionczek, "Las problemas de la transferencia de tecnología en un marco de industrialización acelerada, el caso de México," in Max Nolff, El desarrollo industrial latinoamericano (Mexico City, 1974), 304–29.
6. Richard Weinart, "The State and Foreign Capital," in Reynart and Weber, Authoritarianism in Mexico, 124–26, argues that the state has penetrated the economy not so much to help the

elite as to protect Mexico from foreign domination—and of course to expand state power.

7. Redvers Opie, "Mexican Industrialization: Past Developments and a Near-Term Plan," in Richard Erb and Stanley Ross, eds., U.S. Relations with Mexico: Context and Content (Washington, 1981). On import substitution and Mexican industrialization see also Nacional Financiera y Comisión Económica para la América Latina, "La política industrial en el desarrollo económico de Mexico," in Nolff, Desarrollo industrial latino-americano, 642–86.

8. James Flanigan, "Mexico's Drive to Industrialize," Forbes, October 29, 1979, 44–45.

12: Hernando's Hideaway

1. Dallas Morning News, February 25, 1985; Baltimore Sun, April 10, 1985.

2. Occidente, June 22, 1986.

3. Samuel Ramos, Profile of Man and Culture in Mexico, trans. Peter Earle (Austin, Tex., 1962), 64–65.

4. Ibid., 68–69.

5. Francisco López Cámara, El desafío de la clase media (Mexico City, 1971), 16–19.

13: Over There at the Big Ranch

1. Graham Greene, Another Mexico, (New York, 1939), 38–64.

2. Harry E. Cross and James Sandos, Across the Border: Rural Development in Mexico and Recent Migration to the United States (Berkeley, 1981), 42–43; Lourdes Arizpe, "The Rural Exodus in Mexico and Mexican Migration to the U.S.," International Migration Review 15 (Winter 1981), 629–33.

3. González Casanova, La democracia en Mexico, 92.

4. Merilee Grindle, Bureaucrats, Politicians, and Peasants in Mexico (Berkeley, 1977), 86–91.

5. For a brief assessment of the SAM, see Cassio Luiselli, The Sistema Alimentario Mexicano (La Jolla, Cal., 1982); and

Rose Spalding, The Mexican Food System (La Jolla, Cal., 1984).

6. For a leftist perspective see Gustavo Esteva, The Struggle for Rural Mexico (South Hadley, Mass., 1983).

14: The Biggest City in the World

1. Alan Gilbert and Peter Ward, Housing, the State, and the Poor (Cambridge, Eng., 1985), 54–57.

2. Wayne Cornelius, Politics and the Migrant Poor in Mexico City (Stanford, 1975), 223–34.

3. Excelsior, December 29, 1986.

15: "They Lied to Us"

1. The most succinct assessment of Mexican politics is Wayne Cornelius and Ann Craig, Politics in Mexico: An Introduction and Overview (La Jolla, Cal., 1984).

2. Lorenzo Meyer, "Historical Roots of the Authoritarian State in Mexico," in Reynart and Weber, Authoritarianism in Mexico, 16.

3. Quoted in James Wilkie, The Mexican Revolution: Federal Expenditure and Social Change Since 1910 (Berkeley, 1970), 8–9.

4. George Grayson, The United States and Mexico (New York, 1984), 185–87.

5. Juan Luís González, "El submundo es parte de la 'Democracia' en E.U.," Jueves del Excelsior, July 31, 1986, 14–15.

16: MexAmerica

1. Time, July 8, 1985, 36–41.

2. U.S. Senate (99th Cong., 2nd Sess.), Economic Development in Mexico (Washington, 1986), 2–5. Italics mine.

3. Quoted in Peter Smith, "Mending Fences: Mexico and the United States," U.S. House of Representatives (99th Cong., 1st Sess.), Developments in Mexico and United States–Mexican Relations (Washington, 1985), 106.

Bibliographical Guide

▬▬▬▬▬
▬▬▬▬▬
▬▬▬▬▬

    The literature on MexAmerica is diverse, ill organized for the general reader, and, regrettably, laden with tedious studies in which real people never appear or volumes of protest in which the truly suffering are drowned out by others making a statement or trying to find that elusive thing known as "identity." There is a literature on Mexico, on the American southwest, on U.S.–Mexican relations (political and economic), on the Mexican American (and a rival literature on the chicano), on the cities of MexAmerica, and on the states of MexAmerica. There is a literature on MexAmerica in the social sciences, business, and humanities. Generally, this literature, despite the narrow focus of much of it, does an adequate job. A few volumes are truly excellent, in the scope of their coverage and the depth of their analysis and understanding. Lamentably, the field is laden with literary and analytical junk, especially in border and chicano studies. Much the same can be said for the literature in Spanish. This essay will be confined mostly to books in English.

    Some of the best general works on the Mexican American experience and the Mexican in the United States are older but still fresh in their insights. Among them are Manuel Gamio, *The Mexican Immigrant* (New York, 1969), originally published during the Depression, which deals with Mexican immigration in the twenties; two works by Carey McWilliams, *North from Mexico: The Spanish-Speaking People in the United States* (New

York, 1949) and *Ill Fares the Land* (Boston, 1942); and Octavio Paz, *The Labyrinth of Solitude* (New York, 1961). Paul Taylor's special studies on Mexican immigrant labor are worth rereading.

Of more recent books I have found the following most helpful: Ellwyn Stoddard, *Mexican Americans* (New York, 1973); Leo Grebler et al., *The Mexican American People: The Nation's Second Largest Minority* (New York, 1970), a hefty social science text; Matt Meier and Feliciano Rivera, *The Chicanos* (New York, 1972), which is briefer and moderate in its judgments; Stan Steiner, *La Raza: The Mexican Americans* (New York, 1970), a "good read" in which real people appear; and Rodolfo Acuña, *Occupied America: The Chicano's Struggle for Liberation* (New York, 1972), which can be read as either indictment or diatribe.

For the aficionado of "what's what among Hispanic Americans," a good beginning is the Hispanic Policy Development Project's *The Hispanic Almanac* (New York, 1984). A more statistical companion volume is the National Association of Latin Elected Officials handbook that identifies Hispanics in public office from the grassroots to Washington. In the past few years, immigration reform has wrought a general interest in Hispanic Americans, and the social scientists have responded. Joan Moore and Harry Pachon, *Hispanics in the U.S.* (Englewood Cliffs, N.J., 1985), is largely aimed at the college audience. Pastora San Juan Cafferty and William C. McCready, *Hispanics in the United States: A New Social Agenda* (New Brunswick, N.J., 1985), will please the academic reader but bore the general reader. For those interested mostly in the impact of Hispanic labor, two studies, George Borjas and Marta Tienda, eds., *Hispanics in the U.S. Economy* (New York, 1985), and Vernon Briggs, *The Chicano Worker* (Austin, Tex., 1977), analyze the Hispanic impact on the labor market.

On immigration and especially its economic impact, the literature is overwhelming other issues by its sheer quantity and controversial nature. I began with Richard Lamm and Gary Imhoff, *The Immigration Time Bomb: the Fragmenting of America* (New

York, 1985), which makes a "statement" about the ultimately destructive impact of illegal immigration and the Spanish language on "America." David Reimers, *Still the Golden Door: The Third World Comes to America* (New York, 1985), is more moderate, more scholarly, and ultimately more convincing. Alejandro Portes and Robert Bach, *Latin Journey: Cuban and Mexican Immigrants in the United States* (Berkeley, 1985), and Silvia Pedraza-Bailey, *Political and Economic Migrants in America: Cubans and Mexicans* (Austin, Tex., 1985), show how the U.S. government made a "political statement" in its immigration policy.

California provides an illustrative case study of how immigration can affect the economic character of a state. Sasha Lewis, Sidney Weintraub, and Ernesto Galarza have produced, from three perspectives, studies of the impact of immigrant labor. But the general reader should begin with Thomas Muller and Thomas Espenshade, *The Fourth Wave: California's Newest Immigrants* (Washington, 1985), a brief but surprisingly informative study by the Urban Institute; then follow with Walter Fogel and Philip Martin, *Immigration: California's Economic Stake* (Berkeley, 1982); and then Wayne Cornelius, *Mexican Immigrants and Southern California: A Summary of Current Knowledge* (San Diego, 1982), a succinct and pithy summing-up of a controversial subject by the most knowledgeable person in the United States on Mexican immigration into this country.

On border economy, culture, and politics, the most readable literature can go from depressing to grim. I started with Ovid Demaris, *Poso del Mundo* (Boston, 1970), and followed with James Mills, *The Underground Empire* (Garden City, N.Y., 1986), in which Mexico and Mexicans play a sordid role in the drug trade. Both works jar even the most insensitive reader, and detail most of the sordid features of border life. But they do not accurately and sensitively assess border culture. For that, a handy compendium is Stanley Ross, ed., *Views Across the Border: The United States and Mexico* (Albuquerque, N.M., 1978), which covers all aspects of the U.S.–Mexican relationship from both sides of the border. From there the reader can follow different

301

routes. Cecil Robinson, *Mexico and the Hispanic Southwest in American Literature* (Tucson, Az., 1977), evaluates (with occasional insights) the still unappreciated Hispanic connection in American literature. Most of the chicano leaders—César Chávez, Reies López Tijerina, and "Corky" Gonzales—wrote autobiographies or were the subject of biographies, but often the more revealing studies are those not of the person but the cause he championed. In this category, John Dunne, *Delano* (New York, 1967), is especially noteworthy in capturing the mystical quality of Chávez and the nuances of the grape strike. Ernesto Galarza, *Barrio Boy* (Notre Dame, 1971), is a gem but not widely known among general readers.

Economic matters dominate border life, and the analysts have responded. For the border industrialization program and the *maquiladoras,* see Donald Baerrensen, *The Border Industrialization Program* (Lexington, Mass., 1971); Niles Hansen, *The Border Economy* (Austin, Tex., 1981); and Mitchell Seligson and Edward Williams, *Maquiladoras and Migration* (Austin, Tex., 1982). On broader economic issues, the reader should consult Sidney Weintraub, *Free Trade Between Mexico and the United States* (Washington, 1984). But if the determined reader cannot plow through these, a surprisingly informative substitute for all is a geographer's perspective, *Frontier on the Rio Grande* (Oxford, 1982), by John House, an Englishman who demonstrates once more that the English, who should know little about the U.S.–Mexican border, can be a fount of wisdom and insight. On the political impact the border economy and related issues have on U.S.–Mexican relations, George Grayson, *The United States and Mexico* (New York, 1984), provides a reasoned assessment uncluttered with social scientese.

Finally, the general reader plunging into the literary conundrum Mexico has willed to those who try to "understand" Mexico and the Mexicans should begin with the admonition "Don't try to *understand* Mexico and the Mexicans." Among general works, the most readable account is Alan Riding, *Distant Neighbors: A Portrait of the Mexicans* (New York, 1984). Those who want a fast-paced narrative history should read T.R. Fehrenbach, _Fire and Blood: A History of Mexico_ (New York, 1973). Frank Brandenburg tried to provide a dual-sided image of modern Mexico in _The Making of Modern Mexico_ (New York, 1964) and encountered the official wrath of the government for daring to portray some of the "negative" aspects of the country. Among texts, the best-known and, I believe, the best is Michael Meyer and William Sherman, _The Course of Mexican History_ (New York, 1983). The Colegio de México two-volume _Historia general de Mexico_ (Mexico City, 1976) has appeared in a brief English-language edition.

Any one of these directs the general reader into Mexican history, politics, culture, economy, literature, art, and archaeology. For Revolution cultists there is a bountiful offering. A photographic history of the Revolution that makes a powerful statement is Anita Brenner, _The Wind that Swept Mexico_ (Austin, Tex., 1971). John Womack captures the Revolution's symbolism in _Zapata and the Mexican Revolution_ (New York, 1969). For those who insist on trying to penetrate the Mexican character there are Octavio Paz, _The Labyrinth of Solitude_ (New York, 1961), and Samuel Ramos, _Profile of Man and Culture in Mexico_ (Austin, Tex., 1962). Graham Greene demonstrated that it is possible to dislike Mexico and understand it in _Another Mexico_ (New York, 1939), reissued in 1947 as _The Lawless Roads_. On Mexican politics, Peter Smith, _Labyrinths of Power: Political Recruitment in Twentieth Century Mexico_ (Princeton, 1979), is analytical and perceptive. On Mexican society, Pablo González Casanova, _Democracy in Mexico_ (English ed., New York, 1967), though a quarter century old, retains its clarity and persuasiveness, two attributes sociologists rarely achieve in their work. Anthropologists still rely on Oscar Lewis, _The Children of Sánchez_ (New York, 1961). For the Mexican economy, which suffocates from political intrusion, there are dozens of English-language studies. The general reader will discover a good introduction is Jorge Domínguez, ed., _Mexico's Political Economy: Challenges at Home and Abroad_ (Boulder, Colo., 1982).

Index

310